DEADLY SILENCE

On October 7th, Diane Andersen received Mayo's report confirming Crafts's extramarital affair. When Helle Crafts came to Andersen's office shortly thereafter, she seemed hurt, though not hysterical, and determined to divorce. She also seemed to have something else on her mind.

The divorce writ was compiled and ready to be served by November 12th. To spare her husband embarrassment in front of the children, Helle arranged for the sheriff to come to the house on the afternoon of November 14th when the children would be away.

Afterwards, divorce clients usually pestered Andersen with calls. But Helle Crafts didn't. By Thanksgiving, the lawyer wondered why she hadn't heard from her client. She tried to contact Helle, but without success.

Diane Andersen remembered Helle's words: "If something happens to me, don't assume it was an accident."

She picked up the phone and dialed Keith Mayo, private detective.

THE WOOD-CHIPPER MURDER

ARTHUR HERZOG

Authors Choice Press

San Jose New York Lincoln Shanghai

Authors Choice Press
an imprint of iUniverse.com, Inc.

For information address:
iUniverse.com, Inc.
5220 S 16th, Ste. 200
Lincoln, NE 68512
www.iuniverse.com

Originally published by Henry Holt and Company

Credit for Graphic: Chris Rush

ISBN: 0-595-18354-9

Printed in the United States of America

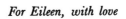

For Eileen, with love

Contents

Acknowledgments

All the material in this book except for my own observations is derived from official records and reports, many interviews, and the two trials of Richard Crafts. For information that came from the first trial of Richard Crafts I've had to rely on my own notes, since the transcript had not been completed when I finished writing. I will not attempt to list the large number of individuals who cooperated with me, but I would like to single out a few who were especially helpful: Helle's friends Rita Buonanno, Jette Rompe, Trudy Horvath, Lee Ficheroulle, Lena Johanssen-Long, Sue Lausten, and Betty Bell; Lieutenant James Hiltz, commander of the Western District Major Crime Squad of the Connecticut state police, and his men; Patrick O'Neil, journalist, whose reporting also helped in the writing of the final chapter; and finally, the Newtown detectives and their chief, Michael DeJoseph, even though I strongly disagree with some of his conclusions.

Arthur Herzog
Salisbury, Connecticut
February, 1990

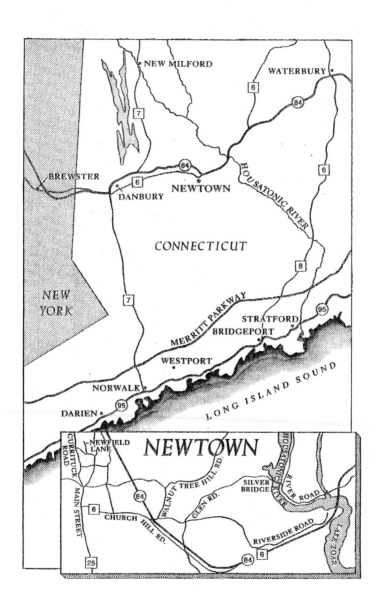

Prologue

At 11:15 A.M., local time, Tuesday, November 18, 1986, Rita Buonanno, Helle Crafts, and Trudy Horvath crowded aboard a Pan Am airport bus in Frankfurt, Germany. It was the day after Rita's thirty-seventh birthday, and Rita carried the flowers Trudy had given her the night before. Helle's presents had been a teddy bear and a cake, which Helle had persuaded the Pan Am caterer to bring to the plane moments before it left New York.

The return flight was late to depart, but the three flight attendants were accustomed to delays. On board the 747 Trudy went upstairs and the other two stayed below in the tourist section; Helle would work the drinks cart and Rita the food service, their usual airborne roles. The women, who were good friends and neighbors, had bid successfully for the Frankfurt run and expected to work together for the balance of the month.

Several hours into the flight, while the movie played, the women relaxed over a meal, and Rita overheard Helle talking with another flight attendant. Each had a failing marriage and was distressed by a cheating husband and the unsettling prospect of impending divorce. Rita knew how hard Helle had worked to keep her marriage alive; she

11

knew, too, of Helle's bitterness over her husband's behavior. Helle worried about her children and how divorce would affect them.

Rita was aware that Helle had discussed her marriage with others, as if seeking reassurance that the step to divorce was the right one, weighing it against consequences she seemed in some unspecified sense to fear. But even with Rita, Helle never revealed exactly what she was frightened of.

Because of head winds, the return trip took nine hours. The plane landed an hour late.

After they whisked through the crew members' customs exit at Kennedy, Trudy stopped to phone her husband and asked him to hold dinner. Rita didn't usually bother to call over such a minor delay, but possibly shamed a little by Trudy's dutifulness, she, too, phoned home. Helle did not telephone.

At about five, the three women set out for Newtown, Connecticut, in Trudy's Datsun station wagon. It had been Rita's turn to drive, but her car was in the shop. Both women remembered that Helle had volunteered to handle next week's turn in her new Toyota Tercel if Rita's car hadn't been fixed by then. As usual the women found much to talk about, especially the forthcoming holidays, but neither Trudy nor Rita recalled any discussion of Helle's marital problems during the drive.

On the outward flight to Germany, however, Helle had complained angrily about her husband's pretense that he was a dutiful father, especially galling, as Rita remembered, since Helle had said she practically forced him to attend their daughter's fifth birthday party. Trudy Horvath hadn't met Richard Crafts, an Eastern Airlines pilot, but from Helle's comments he sounded difficult and unreliable. Trudy had concluded that Richard was by no means enough for Helle. Attractive herself, tall and ash blond, Trudy regarded Helle as someone special. She couldn't understand why Helle stayed in her marriage. Smart, pretty, and caring, Helle at thirty-nine could find a more suitable mate.

12

And Rita agreed. As she thought about Helle later, Rita could still see her straightforward smile, the dimple in her chin, the manner she had of clasping her hands in front of her, as if in prayer.

Now, on the way home, Helle appeared calmer. Although her marital situation had worsened and depressed her ever more frequently, Rita noted, she was never one to stay down. Perhaps to escape the past, Helle talked of the future, seeming to savor it. The following day she was to meet with her children's teachers. She had placed a deposit for a family ski vacation in Vermont in January, and in December she would be making the long Rio de Janeiro run to earn days off for it. Turning in her seat, Rita observed a glisten of tears in Helle's eyes as she proudly confided that her three children — Andrew, ten, Thomas, eight, and Kristina, five — had voted to help pay for the ski trip with the Christmas money her mother had sent them from Denmark. Rita understood the reason the contribution was necessary: Richard, as usual, failed to pitch in. He was tightfisted with his family, and Helle was always short of funds.

Helle spoke with enthusiasm about her special recipes for Thanksgiving, only nine days off. She had ordered two turkeys, she said with amusement, because almost everybody, including her in-laws and their children, preferred drumsticks. Thanksgiving talk led to Christmas and the presents the three women had bought in Frankfurt, loaded in shopping bags in the wagon's rear.

Helle reminded herself out loud that the uniforms she was having altered ought to be picked up.

It was 6:45 when they reached Rita's house in Newtown. Outside Rita saw her husband, Frank, and Johnny, their young son, putting lawn furniture under cover. A snowstorm was predicted, Frank said. Trudy became a little anxious, as though snow might fall at once.

Rita took her bags from the car and with them *The Red Fox*, a novel belonging to Helle, for bedtime reading. Later, thinking the story of assumed identity might have given Helle ideas, Rita would search the book for clues to her whereabouts.

Trudy would remember the next few minutes and relate them to the police. She drove Helle to her house surrounded by other houses on a cul-de-sac. Looking at the assorted vehicles in the driveway, Helle said, matter-of-factly, "Richard's home." Helle told Trudy the Craftses' live-in nanny was working that night at McDonald's, but she'd be home later on. The children were there.

Helle loaded her heavy flight bags, her garment bag, and the presents into a collapsible cart, and started up the driveway. Trudy hurriedly backed out into the street without waiting for her to enter the house. She then headed for Southbury, a fifteen- or twenty-minute drive. It was 7:00 P.M. and the last time Trudy saw Helle Crafts.

Part 1

A Disappearance

1

Helle's Friends

Blowing in from the Midwest, the unseasonably early storm was big and unexpected. At Connecticut State University's Weather Center in Danbury meteorologist Mel Goldstein had first predicted only rain, but as the temperature fell steadily during November 18 he changed the forecast to snow showers. By 9:30 that night, returning to his office, Goldstein knew that a severe storm was about to strike, with heavy winds and lightning. In Newtown about five inches of snow had fallen—more in some parts of town—when the storm tapered off at 5:00 A.M. on November 19. The snow was wet and heavy and caused considerable damage to tree limbs and power lines when it froze.

That evening, Rita and Frank Buonanno, whose house was without electricity, went to the grocery store. From the road they noticed lights on at the Crafts house. Rita had tried the Craftses' number several times that day, getting no answer, and when she got home, she called again. Richard Crafts answered.

"She's not here," he said, sounding amiable.

"When will she be back?"

"I really don't know."

"Well, have her call me, will you, Richard? Make sure

17

you tell her I called."

"Okay. You have power at your house?"

"No," Rita said bitterly. She lived in the neglected boondocks.

"Well, if you care to use the shower here, feel free."

"Thanks. We might just take you up on that."

Rita couldn't understand why Helle failed to phone that evening, and in the morning, she tried again. This time Marie Thomas, the young nanny, answered the phone. "Helle's not here, Rita."

"Where is she?

"Must be flying."

"Oh." Rita hung up. She lit a cigarette and walked from the kitchen counter into the living room. Helle had come back from Frankfurt on Tuesday afternoon. Regulations required a forty-eight-hour stand-down between flights; but this was only Thursday *morning*. And if Helle was flying, why hadn't she called to let her know? Rita got Marie on the line again.

"Are you certain Helle is flying?"

"She must be flying because her flight bags aren't here," Marie said.

The concern that had been lying in the back of Rita's mind stirred to life.

From time to time Rita suffered, and knew she suffered, from needless anxiety, so now she tried to examine her recollections with absolute objectivity. Before the trip to Frankfurt, Helle had told her — Rita remembered the words exactly — "If anything happens to me, don't think it was an accident." At the time she had thought Helle did not intend to be taken seriously, but now she wondered whether she hadn't misinterpreted her tone. Biting her lip, Rita blurted to Marie, "I'm supposed to do something if she's missing."

"She's not missing," Marie insisted.

At three that afternoon Crafts called Rita to announce that Helle had phoned from London. She'd left early the previous morning — the morning of the snowstorm - and was on her way to Denmark to visit her mother, who was

18

seriously sick in the hospital. That surprised Rita, as much as anything else, because Helle had spoken with her mother, Lis Nielsen, from Frankfurt four days earlier and had said nothing to Rita about her mother being sick. Crafts said Helle would be returning around Tuesday and had told him to give Rita a check made out to Helle for three hundred dollars; she would understand what the money was for. Rita knew: She and Helle had started a lace curtain business and a COD order from Germany waited at the post office. She told him to keep the money until Helle returned.

Rita asked Crafts if he had called Pan Am to request an emergency leave for Helle. If she missed three consecutive flights and was, in the airline's word, "uncontactable," she could be fired, which Rita knew was the last thing divorce-bound, overtime-hungry Helle wanted. Crafts mumbled that maybe Rita would take care of the leave. She said she would if she could and asked for Lis Nielsen's phone number. When Rita's father had been ill, Helle called every day to ask how he was, and she wanted to return the gesture. Crafts gave her the number.

On Friday morning at ten, Helle and Rita were both scheduled for a routine training class. Reporting to Mary Lou Ruddy, a supervisor of Pan Am flight attendants, that she couldn't attend because her house was without power for the third straight day and her son had a fever, Rita added that Helle required emergency leave. When Ruddy called her back to say that Richard Crafts had to request the leave, Rita passed the information on to Marie, who said she would relay the message to him.

The next day, Saturday, November 22, arriving at 4:30 P.M. for the Frankfurt flight, for which Helle was also scheduled, Rita saw her friend's Tercel in the Pan Am parking lot, but Helle failed to report for the trip. It seemed strange to Rita that a woman who had a perfect flying record and commendations from the airline would suddenly become unreliable and in danger of losing her job, but she supposed that Helle had assumed her husband would have put her on leave.

While at Kennedy Airport, Rita told a supervisor, Angela Meaney, that Helle was in Denmark, so Angela contrived to get Helle a forty-eight-hour leave, reporting that Helle had requested it. (Angela had gone out of her way, against regulations, to help Helle.)

Ever more concerned about the leave question, Rita flew to Europe. She placed several calls from Switzerland to Newtown in an attempt to warn Crafts that he or Helle had to call Pan Am by the following Monday at 5:00 P.M. On Sunday, November 23, Rita phoned the number in Denmark that Crafts had given her. It appeared not to be Mrs. Nielsen's, but Rita couldn't be sure because neither she nor the German flight attendant who helped her make the call could speak Danish.

Rita returned to New York on Monday afternoon, only to discover from Pan Am that Crafts still had not acted. With mounting frustration, she phoned the Crafts house, finding at home only Thomas, the second son, who couldn't help. On the drive to Newtown she called Crafts from a phone booth; he claimed Pan Am lines were busy. If all else failed, she reminded him sharply, he could send a telegram. From home, Rita again pestered him to make the call and asked with gnawing suspicion, "Have you heard from her?"

Crafts replied that no one answered at the number in Denmark.

"I tried, too," she said, "but it seemed to be wrong. Give me the number again." He repeated the same number and mentioned that Helle's cousin in California, Poul Gamsgaard, would probably have the correct number. "I really want to talk with her," Rita persisted. "Would you call him?"

Crafts said hesitantly that he would call Gamsgaard, but he was extremely busy with parent-teacher conferences.

Crafts had always been chary about imparting information, so though she was aware that his story sounded odd, Rita tried to convince herself that he was simply displaying his characteristic reserve. But as Tuesday came, a knot of

20

anxiety formed in Rita's stomach. Waking in the middle of the night possessed by the dreadful idea, Rita told her husband in the morning, "This isn't right. It isn't at all like Helle just to take off. I . . . oh, damn . . . have to say it, I'm frightened. I have a feeling that Richard has done something to her."

The year before, Crafts had generously given Frank a plow and a free load of firewood—Crafts in his old clothes and unkempt hair looked more like a woodsman than a pilot. Frank, who had been grateful, thought Crafts a bit strange—when Frank had showed him an antique gun, Crafts had refused to touch it; yet Frank knew Crafts himself collected guns.

Rita shared her fear with Trudy Horvath, who, while disturbed by Helle's extended absence and failure to communicate with them, also told her she was crazy to think about homicide.

Helle's statement—warning, premonition, whatever it had been—began to flash in Rita's mind like a neon sign. Helle's face floated before her eyes as if demanding something, as if laying an enormous responsibility on her tense shoulders. Would they never be tourists together again, as when they had visited the Taj Mahal? Would they never take the children on little outings? Was Helle really gone for good?

Rita went so far as to consider bringing formal charges against Crafts but didn't dare. Suppose her friend turned up? And perhaps, after all, Helle had sent or left her a message. Unknown to Crafts, Helle and Rita shared a safe-deposit box in which Helle stored jewelry and papers. Forlornly, Rita inspected the box: no word. Then she checked the post office address they used for their curtain business, praying that Helle had written she'd run off with a lover, unlikely as it seemed; but that hope proved empty, too.

On Tuesday, November 25, using a language assistance operator, Rita called the number in Denmark a second time. The voice at the other end confirmed the number was not Mrs. Nielsen's.

Marie Thomas, the Craftses' nanny, had been stopping in at the Buonannos' on the pretext of buying eggs—the Buonannos raised chickens in the backyard. Marie bought more eggs than the Crafts house could possibly need, but eggs were only an excuse to unburden herself. Because the girl was frightened of her own suspicions, the Buonannos came to realize, she dolloped out information. On November 22 Marie told Frank that Crafts had bought a dump truck to use in building a house on a piece of property he and Helle owned on Currituck Road in Newtown, close to their house. Rita had heard of no such plan from Helle.

On November 25 Marie nervously produced really startling news. She told the Buonannos that she had seen, on November 22, a dark-stained patch the size of a grapefruit on the master bedroom rug. A few days later Crafts had taken up the rug and also the one in his daughter's room, and subsequently had removed the rug from the boys' room.

Marie also reported that on November 20 Crafts had been examining a list of phone numbers posted by Helle on the back of a kitchen cabinet and her address book, as if not certain his wife was in Denmark (or, Rita wondered, had that been an act of some kind?); both the list and the book vanished after Marie left the room. Also missing was Marie's own address book containing phone numbers of Helle's friends in case of emergency. The girl was convinced Crafts had taken it.

By Wednesday, Frank too was beginning to entertain the idea of murder. One reason that the Buonannos had moved to Newtown from Miami was to escape crime, but here they were in an atmosphere, real or imagined, of danger. If Crafts had murdered Helle, might he not retaliate against Rita for her relentless questions? They kept their eyes on windows facing the road, and Frank suggested Rita should stop her phone calls, but she spoke again that day with Crafts.

No, he hadn't talked with Helle, he calmly reported, and

he'd been too busy to contact Poul Gamsgaard. "Richard, why aren't you doing something?" Rita cried. She asked him for Gamsgaard's number and that of Crafts's sister whose name Rita didn't know but who was Helle's friend. Crafts said he had no time to give Rita the numbers. He had dentist appointments for the kids and, for Thanksgiving, it "looks like I'll have to cook some turkeys."

Rita encountered him that afternoon at the office of her son's dentist—Johnny was being fitted for braces and so was Andrew Crafts. Richard Crafts appeared startled and, behaving as though Rita were following him, went to the electronic game in the rear of the office and then to the treatment room where both boys were, as if to make sure Johnny was present. He left without a word to Rita.

The Buonanno family went to Massachusetts for Thanksgiving, November 27, returning the same day. On the drive back, Frank, a mechanic at a Volvo dealer, suggested they confide in a Newtown cop, a neighbor of theirs. No such thing, Rita said sternly. Crafts had been a member of the Newtown force before he joined the Southbury police—a Newtown cop might tell him. Still, Thanksgiving was pretty much the deadline for Rita—if Helle hadn't appeared by then Rita would really have to accept the worst. Thanksgiving came and went without tidings from Helle on Rita's answering machine.

On Friday, Rita flew, arriving early to see if Pan Am had Mrs. Nielsen's correct number, but the office was closed for the Thanksgiving holidays. Helle's car was still in the lot. She ran into Lena Johannsen-Long, another Pan Am stewardess, who had just returned from a flight. The two had met briefly at the Craftses'. Rita said, "Have you heard from Helle?" Lena said no.

Trudy Horvath was with them, and they went for coffee in the employee cafeteria. Rita related Marie's shocking information but kept Helle's warning to herself. She needn't have held back. Lena, blond, thin, good-looking, burst out: " 'If something happens to me, don't think it was an accident.' That's what Helle told my husband and me." This was

23

the first time any of Helle's friends realized that she'd made the statement to other people.

"Rescue me," she seemed to have been saying, but nobody had understood from what.

Now, sitting in the cafeteria with Rita and Trudy, Lena began to tremble. Murder had to be viewed as a serious possibility.

In the post office box she and Helle shared, Rita had found a receipt for a retainer Helle had paid to Dianne Andersen, her tough and expensive divorce lawyer. Asking Lena to contact Andersen, Rita and Trudy took off for Zurich.

On the flight Rita and Trudy Horvath put together lists of "Dids" and "Didn'ts." Did Richard murder Helle or didn't he?

Did

1. wrong Danish phone number
2. Helle's not calling home
3. not calling Pan Am
4. rugs
5. missing phone list
6. Helle leaving in a snowstorm
7. he is the only person to speak to her
8. bad marriage
9. her statements to people
10. supposed to be home in 4-5 days
11. he has not tried to phone her
12. will not reveal any phone number
    (Garnsgaard, his sister Karen)

Didn't

1. money
2. car at airport
3. having heard nothing that night (Marie)
4. suitcase missing
5. doesn't claim to have spoken with her
   (since she called the first time)
6. *appears* concerned

24

In the briefing room Lena had heard Helle unsuccessfully paged for the Zurich flight, and Rita had told her this was the second straight trip Helle had missed. Like Rita, Lena now took Helle's hint of possible trouble to come as a personal responsibility.

So did her husband, David Long, a certified financial planner who had formerly worked for Pan Am. Long asked a contact at the airline to examine the passenger manifests of European flights that could have taken Helle at least partway to Denmark; her name wasn't listed on any of them.

Lena phoned Crafts, who, she would remember, "never had two words to say to me." He was sorry she'd had to fly over Thanksgiving. Lena told him she'd heard Helle's name paged but she hadn't appeared.

"She hasn't missed a flight in seventeen years, has she?" was his reply. He reaffirmed his wife's presence in Denmark and said, "She's due to come back on Sunday."

"I'll call her," Lena said.

"You do that."

Lena hung up and dialed Lee Ficheroulle, another of Helle's flight attendant friends, in case she knew where Helle was.

Lee said, "Why, she's in Copenhagen."

"How do you know that?"

"Richard told me. He's talked with her."

On November 24 Lee had spoken to Crafts on the telephone. He had said that Helle had left on the day of the snowstorm and had called him from Copenhagen. He didn't know when she would return.

Lena said, "I have a feeling something's happened. Something bad." The two women agreed that the circumstances were suspicious and Lee said she'd call Crafts again.

She said to him, "Is she still away? You said she'd be back."

"Well, her mother's sick, like I told you," he replied. "The old lady's having a tough time. She's soft in the head." But he said he had become a little worried. He would phone a Danish cousin of Helle's—Ulli or Olli, he wasn't sure of the name. He'd be calling the next day around noon (when, Lee subsequently learned, he was scheduled for a flight).

Crafts gave Lee Lis Nielsen's supposed phone number, but like Rita, she found it was of no use. She reported that to Lena.

Lena, a Swede, could communicate in Danish if she spoke slowly. On Saturday she rose early and called the number Crafts was distributing to Helle's friends. She was able to ascertain that the number was definitely not Mrs. Nielsen's. Lena then called greater Copenhagen information, from which she got the correct number, with a different area code and one digit of the number different from Crafts's version.

When she spoke to Mrs. Nielsen she chose her words carefully so as not to upset her. "I'm a good friend of Helle's," she said. "I'm going to visit my parents in Sweden and I understand Helle's staying with you. Maybe I could stop by and see her."

"No, no, she's not here," Mrs. Nielsen said. "She's with her children. Do you know how they are?"

"All right, I guess." Lena wasn't agitated about the children. "How are you feeling?"

"Fine. Why?"

"I must have misunderstood," Lena said tactfully. "When do you expect to see Helle again?"

"Not until April, when she has a vacation."

Crafts had expressed doubt about his mother-in-law's mental health. Lena and Lee now established that Helle's vacation was indeed coming up in April. There was nothing wrong with Mrs. Nielsen's mind.

At nine o'clock on Saturday morning, without waiting for Crafts to call Helle, as he had said he would, Lee called to confront him with Helle's absence from Denmark. From him, silence.

When Lee asked him, "Have you any idea where Helle might be?" Crafts claimed Lis Nielsen must have lied. She'd lied, he said, when Helle's father was sick—though he failed to specify how. Either that or Lena had misunderstood her; Lis's English was poor. Lee reminded him that Lena was Swedish and Swedes and Danes could understand one another. Well, he countered, maybe his wife was with her friend Vivi in Paris. He didn't know Vivi's last name or phone number and suggested that the next time Lee's husband was in Paris he might try to look Vivi up.

Lee found Crafts's response bizarre and grew even more suspicious. When she couldn't penetrate his curtain of casualness she hammered away at the issue of emergency leave. Lee had called Pan Am herself and had managed to persuade someone to protect Helle's job until Monday. She urged Crafts to press the airline. He was the only one who could save her job, which she'd need, Lee pointed out, especially if Eastern pilots had to take another pay cut on top of the one imposed earlier in the year.

It had occurred to Lee that Crafts might have injured Helle and might be unwilling to admit it, so to prolong the conversation she went on, "Have you and Helle fought so badly that she left?"

"Well, I admit we haven't been getting along, but we didn't row, no. In fact, the relationship's improved."

Lee said, testing him, "Has Helle gone away to think?"

"I hope so. I really do."

Lee and Lena, each now hardly stirring from the telephone, both spoke with Jette Rompe in turn. Jette, a tall blond who'd known Helle since 1969, found Helle's leaving her children for nine days without contacting them and her failure to notify Pan Am completely unlike her. Shocked, Jette, who had the correct number, called Lis Nielsen to verify Helle's absence from Denmark. She spoke to Marie Thomas three times that day and finally got Crafts.

Speaking more volubly than usual, Crafts told her that on the morning of the snowstorm he had taken his children and Marie to the home of his sister and brother-in-law in Westport and had expected his wife to join them. He said that Helle had left with a large Haliburton metal suitcase,

27

which Jette knew she possessed, her flight bags, and a fur coat. Jette did a double take: Helle stored her red fox, too short and out of style, at a Newtown cleaner.

Crafts told Jette he didn't know the location of the Pan Am employee parking lot—ignorance Jette thought almost impossible, since the Eastern lot lies across the road from it—and claimed he'd neglected to call Helle's friends because she had taken her phone numbers with her.

Jette believed Crafts was lying, but she needed a little while to consider and reconsider what had been said—and not said. She spoke with Lee about the inconsistencies in Crafts's version of events.

On Saturday night Lee called Helle's cousin Poul Gamsgaard in California, whose number Crafts had given her. Could Gamsgaard shed light on Helle's disappearance? He could not, but he, too, found her abandonment of the children strange and was convinced that Helle would never have taken a trip without telling her mother. He'd call Denmark the next day to learn if anyone had heard from Helle. No one had, he reported back to Lee on Sunday. Gamsgaard knew of stresses in the marriage and commented adversely on Crafts's personality. He asked to be kept informed and offered to provide any assistance that might be required.

Lee called Karen Rodgers, Crafts's sister in Westport, but Karen knew only that Helle was in Denmark. Her brother had told her so.

On that same Sunday, November 30, Jette spoke with Crafts again, urging him to go to the police or contact the FBI. He brushed her off, saying she'd been watching too much "Miami Vice." If he reported Helle missing, she'd be annoyed when she returned; she carried plenty of identification, and if anything had happened to her, he would have been notified.

Unease spread among Helle's friends.

From Sunday, when Rita got back from Zurich, the Buonanno home became a command post.

Helle's friend Sue Lausten reported that on November

28

19—it seemed a century ago—Crafts had told her Helle was in Denmark. On November 19 Crafts had told Rita he didn't know when Helle would be back; only on the twentieth had he told her that Helle had phoned to explain she was on her way to Denmark. That Sunday Rita called Crafts on this point, but he smoothly switched tracks. He'd learned (he failed to explain how) that Helle might be at a Club Med in the Canary Islands with her pal Helen Dixon, or maybe Betty Bell, a friend of Helle's who lived in Florida, would know her whereabouts. Rita called Betty Bell, who had nothing to contribute.

Rita's large black eyes filled with tears.

2

First Step

On September 4, 1986, Keith Mayo, a private investigator, talked with a Danbury divorce lawyer, Dianne McDougall Andersen. Jobs weren't always plentiful for the struggling Mayo, and Andersen seemed to be offering him one. "I have a client whose husband is probably playing around. She found a number on a telephone bill. I'll ask you to handle a surveillance if her suspicions are right. Could you check on the number?"

Mayo's fee for identifying telephone numbers was $100. He had a secret resource: Dave. Mayo had never met Dave and couldn't have told you his last name. Dave was a computer pirate. For $40 he would identify any phone number in the country, and for an additional fee he would supply telephone bills.

Dave had the information for him in fifteen minutes, and Mayo dialed the lawyer. "One Nancy Dodd. Lives in Middletown, New Jersey. I have the address."

"Be back to you," Andersen said pleasantly. She added, "My client is a little scared."

Dianne Andersen was in her early fifties, tall, gray-haired, lean, handsome. Helle Crafts had come to her office in Danbury on the recommendation of another female airline employee; Andersen had long experience with airline personnel.

To obtain an appointment with Andersen might require a six- to eight-week wait. She saw some 250 clients a year, though many wanted only a consultation or second opinion, and at any one time she had twenty-five to thirty divorce cases under way. Male Danbury lawyers saw their female counterparts as emotional, but Andersen was brisk and businesslike. She thrived on intimidating her opponents in court.

Her procedure for the first visit was usually an interview of an hour or hour and a quarter. What Andersen learned from Helle was fairly standard.

Richard Crafts was forty-nine. He was a pilot for Eastern Airlines. The couple had been married since 1975, the only marriage for both. Home life was tense. Helle blamed the situation on her husband's involvement with other women and bad communications. Unable to talk, they avoided each other; he was not around much, and she did not know where he went.

Phone bills had aroused her suspicions. Helle normally paid them. She was checking the nanny's long-distance calls when her husband had snatched the bill away and said, "I'll take care of it." After that, phone bills no longer arrived at the house. Calling the telephone company, Helle learned the bills were now being sent to a post office in Hawleyville, a section of Newtown. She managed to gain access to the box because she had one there too, for the curtain business with Rita Buonanno. In it she found the family's phone bills and listed on them were many calls to a New Jersey number, which, when Helle called it, was answered by a taped message from "Nancy." Nancy had to be one of her husband's girlfriends.

Helle had no clear idea of her husband's flight schedule, but adding up the check marks he placed on a calendar when he flew, she deduced he was exceeding the Eastern contract limit of eighty-four hours a month, or pretending to do so. Since Helle herself was frequently away from home, she couldn't easily monitor his activities and wondered how long the affair had been under way. She searched for old phone bills, but they had vanished. She planned to order duplicates.

In August 1984, after losing considerable weight, Crafts had been operated on for cancer of the colon, losing a foot and a half of intestine, lymph nodes, and a section of liver. He'd been out of work, but in December 1985 his pilot's license was reinstated, and he'd been flying almost a normal schedule ever since. He'd stopped receiving chemotherapy in July 1986, and his health appeared satisfactory, despite the steep medical odds against him. Helle told Andersen about Crafts's cancer and remarked sorrowfully, as though she'd been taken advantage of, that they'd been closer when she was nursing him. However, before his illness, the marriage had been rocky, and she referred obscurely to an event, nine years earlier, when he had abused her. He drank one or two six-packs of beer a day, his wife said, and paid scant attention to the children.

Dianne Andersen believed adultery would be the most effective charge if Mrs. Crafts went to court.

Finances were the next subject. Though Helle wasn't quite clear on the figures, as a first officer, or copilot, on an L-1011, Richard Crafts's base pay was $82,000 a year, after a 20 percent pay cut Eastern pilots had taken in 1986. He had put in a bid for promotion to captain, with a salary increase to $90,000. He also made $5,000 as a part-time police officer in Southbury, Connecticut.

Helle Crafts's base pay was $28,000, though she picked up $4,000 more in overtime. Each had a pension fund—his, about which she was vague, was much larger than hers—and both had an IRA of about $10,000. They had little in savings accounts.

The lawyer punched a calculator and produced sums. Mrs. Crafts could expect between $25,000 and $35,000 in combined alimony and child support, which would roughly equalize their incomes. They owned the Newtown house they lived in, which Mrs. Crafts complained was in terrible condition because of Crafts's neglect and habit of never finishing projects. The place was worth only $150,000 in its present state, she said. (Actually, it was worth more.)

Dianne Andersen remarked that considering Richard Crafts's income, the couple had scant tangible assets, and Mrs. Crafts replied, skirting the possibility that her husband spent money on his girlfriend or girlfriends, that he lavished equipment on himself—a backhoe, for example, and fancy guns, of which he had a large number in the basement. Some were loaded; she worried about the children accidentally shooting themselves and wouldn't let them go down there without a grown-up.

Andersen believed in self-help. "I explained to her," she dictated in a memo to Helle's file, "that we could probably get an ex parte order with regard to confiscating the guns and getting them out of the house. . . . I made a suggestion that she simply take the guns and get them out of there and put them in a safe place and explain to him what she had done. She said that she thought that this would lead to a bad confrontation, and she really wasn't willing to do that at the present time and would take her chances."

Helle murmured that she was afraid not only of the guns, and her next words would linger in the lawyer's memory: "If something happens to me, don't believe it was accidental."

There was no reason for Andersen to have reacted in any special way to her client's predicament. The abuse had happened long before and Helle had glided over it. As for her warning, Andersen had heard such statements many times: 10 percent of her clients uttered them in one form or another.

Andersen's fee was $200 an hour; an uncomplicated divorce would require fifteen hours, or $3,000, assuming there was no fight over custody of the children—and the lawyer didn't anticipate any. Despite her flying schedule and the assistance of a nanny, Helle was the primary source of home and health care. Still, though Helle would give her husband all the visitations he wanted, a custody battle couldn't be ruled out.

Andersen requested a retainer of $2,500, which Helle paid with a check drawn on the Connecticut National Bank. The couple had separate bank accounts as well as a joint one.

Helle was to gather financial information about pension and retirement benefits for both parties, and "see what develops with regard to the girlfriend."

For Andersen all this was routine. Papers, alimony, child support, divorce. The lawyer found Helle poised, collected, personable, determined. She began the file memo: "Mrs. Crafts will make a good witness on her own behalf."

Andersen called Mayo at his office four or five days later. The client, first name pronounced "Hell-a," wanted to hire him. "I told her you'd want a retainer."

Mayo, thirty-four, was about six feet tall with dark hair and a dark mustache, both showing traces of gray, and just slightly overweight. In six years of business, he had conducted 350 to 400 marital surveillances for clients, about half of them men and half women. Not all were nice people. At the beginning he'd been stuck with bills occasionally, and for an unpleasant chore at that—endless hours of waiting in a car for something that might happen and might not. Adulterers' plans changed often.

Helle called that afternoon from a pay phone. They met at noon the next day in Andersen's conference room. Sue Schneider, Mayo's young assistant, came with him.

Mayo took note of Helle's long, graceful neck and bright blue Scandinavian eyes. She was tall, slim, and attractive. That the woman seemed apprehensive wasn't surprising. Her interview in Dianne Andersen's office might have seemed abstract to her, but now she was about to put a private eye on her husband.

Fault does not have to be proved to obtain a divorce in Connecticut, but the no-fault statute provides for the courts to consider not only finances but also the causes of domestic strife, such as the three A's—adultery, alcoholism, and abuse. Mayo was to take photographs that could be used as a weapon to force the husband to settle out of court.

Helle said slowly, deliberately, "I've given this plenty of thought. I don't like the idea of having you take pictures, but I guess I must, for the children." The pictures would allow her to avoid or win a custody fight. She had a habit of pushing her long blond hair, parted to one side and curled under, from her cheek. Mayo realized he found her sexy. "I'd prefer holding the marriage together but as it is . . ." She added with controlled anger, "Nancy Dodd is a flight attendant for Eastern. I met her at a party a long time ago. I hardly remember what she looks like."

Mrs. Crafts seemed honest and straightforward—sex with her husband, she said without a hint of embarrassment, had been a problem ever since his cancer operation. She was patient during the discussion and had come well prepared with photocopies of gasoline and food bills her husband had insisted on saving. To Mayo, he sounded like a compulsive record keeper. A good many of the receipts pointed to his frequent presence in New Jersey.

Mayo inevitably asked, "What does he drive?"

"I came here in it. I'll show it to you. An LTD Crown Victoria like the state police use. It's an '85. He's a part-time cop, you know, and he carries a gun. He makes his own ammunition."

Mayo and Schneider exchanged glances. The longer Helle spoke about him, the kookier Crafts sounded. Helle added "cold" and "detached" to the list of his characteristics. Mayo wondered why she stayed in the same house as Crafts, but he was paid for photographs, not psychotherapy.

"When might he and Dodd be together? When you're flying?"

"I'm . . . not sure."

"Is he adding phony days to his trips?"

"He must be. He's done it before," she said with reluctance, as though wishing the truth were otherwise. "I have a contact at Eastern. I'll learn Richard's real schedule. Then we'll have the times he's lying about."

"Let me know."

Dianne Andersen had already told her client, Mayo assumed, that he wouldn't let an investigation drag on without prospect of success. Now he explained that his fee was $35 an hour for one operative, $50 for two, plus expenses. If tailing was necessary, he'd need two cars and two radios. To get proof a judge would accept, sometimes a surveillance had to be conducted more than once. Depending on its length, the investigation would cost between $500 and $2,500, not more. Mayo requested a $500 retainer.

Under no circumstances should Richard Crafts learn of his employment, Mayo said. In fact, he always advised his marital clients to be extra friendly with their spouses to avoid suspicion. He handed Helle his office and home phone numbers written on the back of somebody else's business card in case her husband went through her purse.

Helle paid Mayo with a $500 money order, explaining that it came from her savings account at the Pan Am credit union.

Mayo continued his business—divorce stakeouts, job applicant investigations for companies, accident, theft, criminal defense, and negligence cases. One evening a week or so later the phone rang in his home, where he preferred receiving calls so as not to tie up the office line. He recognized the voice.

"Richard says he's due back from Florida September twenty-second, but he actually returns on the twenty-first."

September 21 was a Sunday. That day Mayo picked up Sue Schneider in his Jeep Cherokee and they set off. Sue was twenty-two, tall, dark-haired, with a heart-shaped face. She packed an S&W .38 special in her bag and had a license for it, of course. Mayo had the same weapon plus others.

Since speaking with Helle, Mayo had hired Metro

Investigations, which for $40 had gleaned from the New Jersey motor vehicle computer what kind of car Nancy Dodd drove, the plate number, and her height, weight, and birth date. Dodd was in her early forties, slightly older than Helle Crafts.

At 9:52 P.M., when the private eyes arrived outside Dodd's split-level development condo in Middletown, they saw her red Honda, with the plate letters spelling JOB, and nearby Crafts's silver Crown Victoria with a spotlight, backed in for a quick exit, cop-style.

The investigators were trying to establish that Richard Crafts spent the night with Nancy Dodd. At 11:20 the house lights went out. Schneider and Mayo sat in the Jeep and aired their differences.

To Sue, Mayo was impatient, overbearing, quick to take offense. In his view, she was simply too young. More or less on a quarterly basis he fired her and always rehired her at once. (They parted permanently the following year.)

They agreed to disagree less, stared glumly into the dark development, and at 3:00 A.M. departed, Mayo having to be in court early on another surveillance case. But the quarry was bedded down, and next time they would photograph him.

The Connecticut telephone system is a crazy quilt. Sometimes calls made to nearby towns count as long-distance calls and the numbers appear on the bills. So to avoid detection by her husband, Helle continued to use a phone booth. Mayo told her he had discovered Crafts's car outside Nancy Dodd's house. The second surveillance was set for the following week, when, according to Helle, her husband had listed himself for another bogus return date. Mayo asked for an additional $500, which Sue Schneider collected, meeting Helle at a Newtown gas station. To Sue, Helle seemed resigned about the surveillance.

SURVEILLANCE LOG

That morning Mayo had fired Schneider again. She was
working as a waitress when later in the day he called to ask
her to come along on the surveillance — two operatives were
better than one in case of an emergency. They arrived in
Middletown at 11:30 P.M. since, according to Helle, her
husband was scheduled to land at Kennedy Airport at midnight, but the Crown Victoria was already there. The house
lights were out, preventing quick photographs through a
window. The investigators napped in the Cherokee. They
woke at six, had coffee down the street, and resumed the
vigil, armed with photographs of Crafts supplied by his
wife. At 8.05 the front door opened, and a woman in a
white robe emerged to pick up the newspaper. She left the
front door open, and the detectives could see into her
kitchen At 8:25 they saw a man rise from the kitchen table,
move around, and sit down again. "That's him!" cried Schneider.

At 9:30 Richard Crafts and Nancy Dodd emerged, and
as he reached for his camera Mayo remembered that Crafts
carried a gun, which he probably kept in his car. Suppose
Crafts spotted them, each equipped with an expensive Bo-
lax Chinon, Sue on one side of the Cherokee, Mayo behind
the spare tire at the rear, both snapping away like Japanese
tourists? Would Crafts, who had a police shield, shoot also?
But Mayo had learned that lovers were too preoccupied
with themselves to be observant. Nancy Dodd, a small,
pretty woman in white pants and a pink shirt, once stared
directly at Mayo, but she had her arms around Crafts and
was rubbing his neck and kissing him. For about five minutes the pair was exposed to the merciless memory of film.
They left in their separate vehicles.

Mayo followed to get a photograph of the Crown Victoria

38

under a Middletown road sign. The surveillance had been a success, and in divorce court Richard Crafts would be dead meat.

Mayo had the film developed quickly and the following morning, October 2, met with Helle at the Blue Colony diner in Newtown at eight-thirty.

When she climbed from her car and into his, Mayo was struck by the change in her appearance. The woman looked tired, strained, sad.

"Want to go inside?"

"I don't care for anyone to see me like this." She wore a jogging outfit and sneakers, but Mayo didn't believe she referred to clothes.

Helle wouldn't look at him, not once. She was holding back tears, and Mayo hated when women cried.

"Listen, you don't have to examine the photos," Mayo said. He didn't want her more upset than she already was. But she held out her hand and he gave her the pictures. She studied them carefully and without a word started to sob. Mayo offered his handkerchief two or three times before she finally accepted it. Helle cried so hard that he feared she'd wet the photos, and he took them back. She blew her nose into his handkerchief. It was a dark day, raining torrents by then, and Mayo wondered what he would say if anyone came over to them, but you couldn't see through the windshield.

Helle appeared to struggle with herself. She still loved Richard, she said. When Mayo asked her if she intended to pursue a divorce, she replied, "I don't know. If only he'd give her up." She talked about wanting to go with her husband for family counseling.

At the same time, it seemed to Mayo that Helle was frightened. She said Richard Crafts slept with a loaded gun in the dresser.

Helle began to cry again, and Mayo gave her the handkerchief once more. She left with it. He watched her get

39

into her station wagon in the downpour, and that was to be the last time he saw her

The fee Helle Crafts had already paid was adequate, and Mayo didn't charge her more. She faded from his mind.

He had a final talk with her on the telephone early in October, when she asked if he knew of a gun appraiser — she planned to include her husband's arsenal among his assets - but Mayo said no.

Dianne Andersen received Mayo's report and the photos on October 7. When Helle Crafts returned to Andersen's office, she seemed hurt, though not hysterical, and determined to divorce. Andersen had intended to go into the family finances in detail, but instead the meeting was short, because Helle had only partly filled out the financial form Andersen had given her. Helle had something else on her mind.

On October 2 Richard Crafts's cancer doctor had given him his semiannual physical examination. Helle had decided not to serve Richard with the divorce papers until she knew the results, and if he were close to death, she wouldn't burden him further. "But she wasn't reluctant to proceed," Andersen says.

And Helle had brought Polaroid photos that told a story of their own: in the basement, racks of guns, and two gun safes that contained them; a revolver nesting in an open drawer along with handkerchiefs and socks; boxes of ammunition, human target silhouettes in the backyard; an unfinished cement foundation with deep cracks in it; smoke smudges from a leaky stovepipe; a broken railing on a sun deck. Richard Crafts seemed to care more for his weapons than for his house.

On October 14 Helle called Andersen and told her to go ahead with the divorce. Richard Crafts phoned Andersen that same day, but she didn't return the call. She deduced, from what her secretary reported, that he wanted to know if the grounds would be adultery. By November 12, the divorce writ was ready to be served, but Crafts claimed the sheriff who was to serve the papers had failed to show. (The sheriff, James Sullivan, called Crafts, who said he'd call him back but failed to do so.)

Crafts claimed he was prepared to accept service, and to spare her husband embarrassment in front of the children, Helle arranged to have Sullivan come to the house between noon and 2:00 P.M. on Friday, November 14, when Marie Thomas would be taking the children swimming. But instead, Richard Crafts slipped out the back door with the children. A third appointment was set for Saturday, but on that day Crafts flew.

Most divorce clients pestered Andersen with phone calls, especially at the start, but Helle Crafts didn't. Around Thanksgiving, the lawyer wondered why she hadn't heard from her. She asked her secretary to contact Helle, and Arlene tried, without success.

3

December 1

Shortly before nine on December 1 three calls came in to
Andersen, two of them at the same time.

Jette Rompe, Rita Buonanno, and David Long had all
tried to reach Andersen during the weekend, but her home
phone number is unlisted. They introduced themselves as
friends of Helle Crafts and they were all highly agitated.
None of her friends, they told Andersen, had seen or heard
from Helle since November 18. For a responsible mother to
absent herself from her children was most unusual. That
she hadn't appeared for the Thanksgiving dinner she'd
planned was unthinkable. Her husband had been presenting contradictory accounts—at least one of which had
proved false—as to her whereabouts.

Dianne Andersen inspected Helle Crafts's file and remembered her saying, "If something happens to me, don't
assume it was an accident." The lawyer dialed Mayo.

Mayo, who hadn't been to his office in New Milford since
the day before Thanksgiving, had hoped for a quiet day to
catch up on paperwork. As usual, he had brought the New
York *Daily News* for the horoscope. When he arrived, Sue

Schneider was in already, and they read the column together. Nothing astrologically astonishing was scheduled.

The phone rang just after nine. The collected but strained voice of Dianne Andersen concisely explained the facts as she understood them.

"Call you back in ten minutes," Mayo said. What if the Middletown surveillance had led to tragic consequences?

The preceding year, Mayo had rented a one-room office attached to a building occupied by the New Milford law firm of Baker, Moots and Pellegrini. Roland Moots was his friend and mentor.

Now, Mayo made straight for Lon Moots's office.

"Remember a surveillance I did in the fall? An airline pilot?" Mayo began excitedly.

Moots vaguely recalled the surveillance. "I guess so."

"Well, she, the wife, a stewardess, has been missing for about two weeks without a word. The husband's stories about where she is don't seem to add up. Maybe Helle's been bumped off. Dianne Andersen thinks it's a possibility."

Though Moots wouldn't handle homicide cases, he had experience in criminal law. And he was surprised—murders don't just drop in from the blue on a Monday morning in New Milford. He knew Mayo tended to dramatize, but tough Dianne Andersen was also a friend of his, and he respected her judgment. "What are you going to do?"

"Investigate," Mayo said with a sigh, his mind reverting to the rent. He doubted he'd be reimbursed for the time put in on Helle's disappearance, if she really had vanished. But he had ingrained doubt, perhaps from his own experience, about the effectiveness of local police. "The cops will take weeks to act, if they act at all. Might be what the guy counts on."

Moots absorbed that. "Where does she live?"

"Newtown."

"Have the Newtown police been notified?"

"No. At least I don't believe so."

Moots bridged his fingers judiciously. "I'm concerned with the propriety of looking into this without informing the

43

police. Have a missing-persons report filed before you investigate." Moots was worried that Mayo might put himself out on a legal limb with an unfounded accusation and be sawn off.

Ten minutes had now gone by. Back on the telephone, Mayo repeated to Andersen what Moots had said, and she agreed. He arranged to meet her at Danbury superior court at a little after ten.

Keith Mayo had taken a two-year course in criminal justice at the University of New Haven and had served on the New Fairfield police force or, rather, constabulary. (The Connecticut state police, though in fewer places than formerly, officiates over small towns, with a state trooper in charge of the local police if there are any. The system can lead to friction if the state police assume jurisdiction over bigger cases the hometown cops want to investigate themselves.) Subsequently Mayo had joined the New Milford police force. He caused a commotion by accusing the head of the local police commission of leaking to his favorite cops questions from a written examination for promotion to sergeant. When a new examination was given, Mayo finished eighth out of thirteen takers. Deciding he'd never be promoted, he quit.

After a stint as a security man with Carrier Corporation, Mayo, encouraged by Moots, struck out on his own as a private investigator, New Milford's first and only. Moots, who has employed Mayo two hundred times, says of him, "Keith is a fine detective, though he can be difficult."

Mayo knew Captain Norbert Lillis, chief of detectives for the New Milford police. He called him, explaining the circumstances, and asking whom he should talk to at the Newtown PD. Hillis suggested Detective Harry Noroian or his boss, Lieutenant Mike DeJoseph. Mayo reached the Newtown dispatcher and said he'd like to speak to DeJoseph.

"Not available."

"How about Harry Noroian?"

"At a seminar."

"Maybe I should speak to you."

"You'd better talk to the chief." Mayo was put on hold.

When he came on the phone, Chief Louis Marchese was abrupt but not unfriendly. Mayo identified himself and Marchese said, "Well?"

Mayo knew Crafts had been a volunteer Newtown policeman; cops, he figured, tended to stick together. He stated his case plainly and succinctly and asked to talk to a detective as soon as possible.

The chief ran his bailiwick with an iron hand. He disliked both outside pressure and private investigators. "I can have someone at four-thirty," he said firmly. To him, Mayo sounded intrusive.

"Not earlier?" Mayo persisted.

"Not earlier."

"Well, I can't wait until four-thirty."

Andersen and Helle's friends had voiced concern about the Craftses' nanny, Marie Thomas. If Crafts was a killer, might he try to silence the girl? Mayo wanted her under police protection.

At seventy-two, Lou Marchese was the oldest practicing police chief in Connecticut. Every year, like others of its size, his small station house received at least a hundred reports of missing persons, almost all of whom reappeared within a day. The statistics were with the chief; Helle Crafts would show up too, even though she had been gone since mid-November and even though she was a mother. Marchese said combatively, as was his wont, "Mike DeJoseph comes on at four-thirty. I want him on this."

"Can't you get DeJoseph in before that?"

"Nothing I can do. Take it or leave it."

Mayo battled traffic on Route 7, arriving in Danbury at about 10:30. The courthouse—a justice factory—had six courtrooms on two floors. He found Andersen upstairs, smoking a cigarette. "You won't believe this, but the chief won't act until late this afternoon."

"Let's go downstairs." Downstairs on the first floor were the state prosecutors, who normally handled only what police brought to them.

Assistant prosecutor Robert Brunetti had once worked for a New Milford law firm that had employed Mayo. Brunetti was newly appointed; some believed he'd accepted the post for job security and because he didn't like to solicit business. When the local lawyers passed the numerous idle moments in the courthouse corridors in analyzing the six Third District prosecutors, they awarded Brunetti high marks for approachability and fair-mindedness, which was more than they gave some of the rest. In his late thirties, about six feet tall and slightly chubby, Brunetti could produce a boyish grin.

Mondays, and especially the Monday after Thanksgiving, were hectic in the courthouse, but the assistant state's attorney received Andersen and Mayo in his small office.

That Dianne Andersen didn't so much as dabble in criminal law underscored, for Brunetti, that something was out of the ordinary. She explained what she knew about her client's absence. Mayo added that Crafts was presently affiliated with the Southbury police, and Andersen worried about the safety of Marie Thomas, potentially a witness against Crafts.

Brunetti walked down the hall to Walter Flanagan, the state's attorney, and relayed a little of what had been said to him. Flanagan's gray eyebrows rose. Brunetti, well acquainted with the Newtown force and its four-man detective squad, found nothing strange about Marchese's refusal to meet with Mayo before late afternoon, but he wanted to oblige Andersen and, besides, if by chance something happened to Marie Thomas, Brunetti didn't care to be held responsible. He asked one of the inspectors in his office to phone Marchese, who said, "I scheduled that guy for four-thirty, when DeJoseph comes in. He handles missing persons."

"I can't get the chief to move any faster," Brunetti told An-

46

dersen and Mayo. "Tell you what. If you're so bothered about the nanny, pick her up and put her on ice for a while. And tell the Crafts woman's friends to report their worries to Newtown."

Getting some names and numbers from Andersen, Mayo called Sue Schneider and asked her to phone Rita Buonanno and Trudy Horvath, the last of Helle's friends to see her alive. Buonanno had told Andersen that Marie Thomas worked part-time at a Newtown consignment store, Put 'n' Take (a job she held in addition to her other part-time job, at McDonald's). Bringing with him Bill Cavanaugh, a friend of his who had previously worked with him on cases and who was also an auxiliary policeman, Mayo drove to the store.

Marie Thomas had not yet arrived. Mayo showed his private detective license to the owner, Fred Watley, and inquired about the girl.

"Supposed to be here but she isn't. I don't know why."

More adrenaline pumped into Mayo's bloodstream. Had something happened to the nanny as well as to Helle Crafts? "This is important. Has she been late before and not called in?"

"Almost fired her for it." So probably Thomas wasn't dead.

Watley asked what the men were after, but Mayo wouldn't tell him, and they retreated from the store owner's wrath to wait for Marie. A silver VW Rabbit drove into the parking lot, and a heavy-set blond of nineteen or twenty got out. Mayo assumed this was Marie Thomas, showed her his private detective license, and said he wanted to speak with her about Helle Crafts. She started to sniffle. Watley, thinking Mayo was harassing her, refused to let her talk to him without the police being present, so Mayo phoned Brunetti, who asked the Newtown police to send a representative.

Newtown patrolman Henry Stormer, told to drive to Put 'n' Take to meet with a Mr. Mayo, arrived at about 12:15, to be told by Watley that he wouldn't let Marie leave the store with Mayo unless the state's attorney approved, so Stormer phoned Brunetti, who gave his approval. With Watley still muttering, Stormer escorted the girl to his police car. Mayo followed them to the Newtown station house, while Cavanaugh returned to Danbury. In an anteroom in the station house, a nervous Marie Thomas told Mayo her story.

Helle, always precise about her schedule, which was posted on a bulletin board in the kitchen, had noted that she would return to Kennedy from her trip to Frankfurt at 3:45 P.M. on Tuesday, November 18 (the plane was late). Marie had been living with the Craftses since June, watching the children and keeping house, and working at two part-time jobs, the one at Put 'n' Take and another at a Danbury McDonald's, where she worked from 6:00 P.M. until midnight or later. Crafts had given her the day off on the eighteenth; when she came home briefly at the end of the afternoon, Helle hadn't yet arrived, and she drove to work in Helle's Toyota Tercel, as she often did.

Because of road conditions brought by the storm and a chat with her boyfriend at a gas station, Marie Thomas didn't return home until 2:00 A.M. She noticed that Crafts's Toyota pickup wasn't there.

She entered the house through the garage, which opened into the basement, turned off the porch light, looked for messages in the kitchen, and may have peeked at the children in their two rooms across the narrow hall from the master bedroom, the door to which was shut. All seemed well, and at 2:30 Marie fell asleep in her bedroom (which had its own bathroom) over the garage.

At 6:00 A.M. Crafts knocked on her door—Marie established the time by her battery-powered clock. He wore a robe and slippers. He said, "Come on, get dressed. The power's out because of the blizzard, and the house is going to turn real cold. I'll take you and the kids to my sister's."

Crafts's hair was wet and matted, as if he had just showered, and he looked tired. He was in a hurry, which Marie felt was out of character. She wondered why he didn't just light a fire in the fireplace or use the kerosene heaters. (She might also have wondered why Crafts failed to utilize the gasoline-powered Honda generator in the basement; he later claimed a valve was stuck.)

The children were quickly dressed and fed, and the group left the house not through the garage, which would have been easier, but through the front door, which the family rarely used, out onto a drift-filled cement slab, and down an icy little hill onto snow-covered flagstones. (Some years before, in that same place, Crafts had slipped and broken his leg.) Marie remembered treading on a set of footprints, but had no idea whose they were. (The police would surmise that the footprints belonged to Crafts, attempting to imitate his wife's.) Helle's Tercel, which Marie had parked a few hours before at the garage door, was gone; it could not have been driven to the street while the pickup occupied its present position, because the Ford Crown Victoria, parked beside the truck, would have blocked its way. (The Ford lacked four-wheel drive.)

Once outside, five-year-old Kristina whined that she had left her mittens in the house and wanted to go back for them, at which point Crafts almost threw her into the back of the pickup. Kristina cried, but Crafts didn't fetch the gloves himself. Marie found that out of character also: in the past weeks, he had displayed a new solicitousness toward the children.

There was little snow on the pickup's windshield and as she climbed in, Marie saw from the lever that the four-wheel drive was engaged, though Crafts usually didn't use it. He must have been driving during the night.

She asked Crafts where Helle was, and he answered, "She left before us. She'll meet us at my sister's."

Crafts's sister Karen and her husband, David Rodgers, lived on Clapboard Hill Road in Westport. Because of the snowy roads the trip took longer than usual and must have seemed especially long to the children inadequately dressed.

Helle wasn't at the Rodgers house. Marie again asked Crafts where she was, and he said he didn't know. He sounded irritated, and Marie didn't press the question.

Karen departed for the store she owned in Darien, and Crafts fixed pancakes for the six children—three Craftses and three Rodgerses. At about nine o'clock, he left for his own house.

When Crafts phoned Westport at around noon, he said the electricity was still off; when he called again, at 3:30, he reported the power had just been restored. He told Marie (he said the same to Karen) that the Ford Crown Victoria was stuck sideways in his driveway.

Crafts returned to the Rodgers house at 7:00 P.M. in the Crown Victoria. Driving home again from Westport, he fell into a doze and let the car drift to the wrong side of the road toward a culvert; Marie woke him with a yell.

On Thursday morning after she had spoken with Rita Marie found a note from Crafts: "Helle called." He didn't come home until late that night, but on Friday morning he told her that Helle was visiting her sick mother in Denmark and would return the following Monday.

Marie had been talking to Mayo for a half an hour when Patrolman Stormer appeared and escorted her to another room, informing Mayo that Detective Noroian would soon arrive.

Very serious questions had been raised, and Mayo tried to sort them out. Why had Crafts expected his wife to arrive in Westport when she was bound for Europe? The only possible explanation was that she had left the house without telling him where she was going, but had Helle then called her mother from a pay phone and headed straight for the airport? In that unlikely event, why hadn't she called the Rodgerses' house to explain her change of plan?

And how had Crafts occupied the ten hours during which he had been gone from the Rodgerses'? Had he been disposing of evidence? What had he been up to the night before that had made him so tired?

Forty-five minutes later Detective Noroian made his appearance. In his late forties, olive-skinned, with a gray-white mustache and pepper-and-salt hair, friendly Harry wasn't so friendly with Mayo. He let him know he was early, not being expected until 4:30. Mayo formed the indelible impression that Noroian, who was about to depart for a ten-day vacation, didn't want to be bothered with the Crafts case.

"It was obvious from the outset," Mayo has said, "that Detective Noroian felt the complaint was baseless. He told me that disappearances occur every day of the week. 'She has a burr up her ass and she'll come home when she's ready.' He made reference to Helle being a stray dog and said when she got tired she would return home. More than once Noroian became disgusted and stated to me, 'What do you want us to do?' After much insistence on my part, the police finally took a statement from Marie Thomas."

Marie was questioned for two and a half hours by Patrolman Stormer, about whom Mayo complained that a rookie had no business on the case. Mayo remembers Noroian as unwilling to listen to all of the statements and refusing to look at his surveillance reports on Richard Crafts.

At Noroian's display of nonchalance, Mayo's temper rose.

Noroian's remembrance differs. He claims to have accepted Mayo's surveillance photos, has flatly denied making any reference to a stray dog, and says that Mayo kept demanding dramatically, "Did he kill her? What do you think? What do you think?" to which he remembers replying in exasperation, "I don't know." Noroian had almost never encountered anyone quite so certain that a person had been murdered, he has said.

As ordered by Mayo, Sue Schneider had called Rita

Buonanno, and Rita had come to Mayo's office. After hearing a little of what she had to say, Schneider drove her to the Newtown PD, where Noroian made them wait in the anteroom while Marie completed her statement. While Rita delivered her story to Stormer, which required an hour and a half, Mayo and Schneider took Marie to retrieve the VW and followed her home. Crafts wasn't there. Marie handed Mayo a set of keys for Helle's car, which Rita had told him was in the Pan Am employee parking lot.

Then he fetched Rita and drove her home. They talked about the Newtown cops. Rita had been surprised to learn that Noroian, the man in charge of her friend's disappearance, was about to go on vacation. Mayo was irate because he believed the Newtown Police Department ought to have demonstrated greater concern.

Helle's friends were constantly on the phone. Trudy Horvath had delivered a handwritten statement to the Newtown police that noted that Helle appeared to be in a good mood when dropped off at her house and had said, "Richard's home." Trudy believed this remark showed that Helle wasn't planning anything unusual, such as a disappearance, but the police fastened on the fact that Helle had failed to express fear.

Mayo got home at 8:30, drained. He made three phone calls to the Southbury resident state trooper, Michael Smarz, and finally reached him. "Look," he said, "I think you ought to know you have a murder suspect on your staff." Not surprisingly, Smarz was quiet.

Mayo phoned a friend. "Am I crazy?" he began.

4

December 2-December 7

Helle's death—if she was dead—at the hands of Richard Crafts—if he had killed her—was for her friends a shattering idea, and in their homes and on the phone with one another they talked of little else. That Helle had been in their estimation such an exemplary individual added to the shock of having someone in their own circle murdered. Living well in attractive communities in America's highest-income state, they had felt themselves to be insulated from violent crime. A headline, a TV shot of a stretcher being wheeled to a silent ambulance were as close as they had previously come to it. Murderers and their victims were peculiar, not men and women they knew.

Helle's friends would never have described her as peculiar (except for her endurance of a peculiar marriage), but Crafts was indeed strange, even stranger now that they viewed him in the context of Helle's disappearance: secretive, aloof, silent, a loner who puttered in his basement all the time, doing and thinking only God knew what. They had abandoned the attempt to understand him, saying with a shrug, "That's Richard," as if he occupied some unfathomable pocket of the universe. But kill?

Looking for a motive confused them even further; they

couldn't discern a wraith of one. Helle wasn't an heiress like Sonny von Büulow. Financially, Richard had nothing serious to gain. They couldn't believe Helle had lovers, so a *crime passionnel* seemed out of the question, especially for so cold a man.

Nor did Helle's demand for a divorce seem probable cause for murder. When she had talked with Richard about serving the writ, he had said, "Anything you want, dear." Yet he had avoided service.

On Tuesday, December 2, also unable to perceive a motive, Mayo backed off a little, certain that the normal pattern of Helle's life had been sharply interrupted, less certain whether murder was in question. But his reluctance didn't last long. He couldn't explain away a devoted mother's continued absence and her husband's evasive statements, the words of a man with something to hide.

Mayo phoned Dianne Andersen with the festering complaint that he had voiced the day before. The Newtown police would treat Helle Crafts as an ordinary missing person; they wouldn't launch a full-scale inquiry; Richard Crafts would have time to erase his tracks, if he hadn't already done so, police interest would lapse; Crafts would get away with murder. "We must push them," he said.

The attorney seemed slightly reluctant, as if she, too, had had second thoughts. She said, "Okay, but let's wait a day or so."

Mayo drifted full-time into a case that would not bring in any cash, though it might well turn out to be profitable in terms of publicity. Like most of us, he well knew that press and TV exposure could bring in business, to which he was far from averse. Suppose he solved the mystery of Helle's disappearance or her murder? He was determined to try.

Several times on December 2 Mayo called Brunetti, finally reaching him. His question was whether Crafts had reported his wife missing. Brunetti had been in touch with the Newtown police: no, Crafts hadn't. Mayo inquired if Newtown planned to talk with the man, and Brunetti said yes. (In fact, Newtown already had.)

To ascertain whether Helle's car was still in the parking lot, Mayo called Pan American. Mary Lou Ruddy of In-flight Services, whom Rita had found helpful, was kind enough to look. The Toyota Tercel was still there. Ruddy also checked on whether Helle had used a Pan Am courtesy pass to fly to Europe; no record existed. Maybe Helle had flown by Scandinavian Airways; Ruddy would investigate.

Mayo logged some twenty calls on the Crafts matter on Tuesday, but the only result was continued uncertainty. He tried and failed to obtain a list of Pan Am employees who might have seen Helle in the parking lot on the morning Crafts claimed his wife had left; that statement, after all, couldn't be disproved.

Mayo also remembered a bit of information imparted by Marie Thomas: Crafts didn't like to drive Helle's car. If that were true and if Crafts's fingerprints were to be found in the Tercel, maybe he had driven it to the lot, perhaps during the unaccounted-for hours on November 19 between trips to Westport. He might even have moved his wife's body in the vehicle, leaving bloodstains or other forensic evidence. But Pan Am informed Mayo that to conduct a search he'd need the consent of its legal department or of Richard Crafts. Mayo was shocked that the Newtown police hadn't already seized the automobile.

When Sue Schneider's sister, Ursula, a Pan Am flight attendant unacquainted with Helle Crafts, called from Kennedy Airport, Mayo asked her to photograph the car and look into Helle's message box. She found a few items. There was a note from a friend, dated November 2, saying "Good luck with the lace curtain business. The other 'business' takes time but in the end you'll be better off. Happy Thanksgiving." (The "other 'business'" must have been a reference to the divorce.) Sara Cushing Page had left a check for $9.95 for Shaklee vitamins Helle had sold to her. A notice informed Helle that her uniforms had been altered and should be picked up.

In the afternoon, Mayo phoned Randy DiBella, a New Milford lawyer for whom he and Bob Brunetti had both worked, and who thought highly of his investigative abilities. "I have to talk to you," Mayo said with an urgency that was fast becoming habitual. "Something's eating at me. I'm not sure if I'm chasing ghosts, but I have this feeling the Crafts woman, the one I'm trying to find, got snuffed by her husband."

DiBella had a hunch that Mayo only wanted to let off steam, but he advised him to go through official channels. "I'm worried," he said. "Make allegations against Crafts and you could have a defamation problem."

Tragedies were uncommon in Newtown, and unpleasantness unacceptable — in the past the Newtown *Bee*, famous nationally for its antiques section, had avoided reporting traffic accidents because they were unappealing. The bedroom community hadn't had its sleep disturbed by a homicide in nine years and seven before that, but in November 1986, right before Helle Crafts vanished, three had occurred.

Patrick O'Neil was a bright young reporter for the Danbury *News-Times*, stationed and living in Newtown. He hung around the police station, where the cops, who liked his quick takes, gave him latitude to look around. On December 1, following up on one of the murders, he observed a man in a camel's-hair coat and an entry in the stationhouse log: "Keith Mayo arrived." He also saw two attractive women (Sue Schneider and Rita Buonanno), who he was told were airline stews.

The next day, Patrolman Stormer let O'Neil listen to some taped records he was making from his interviews with Marie Thomas and Rita Buonanno, but when Chief Marchese came in, Stormer quickly stopped. That evening O'Neil said to Ray Connor, Newtown's counsel, "Looks like we have another murder on our hands."

On Wednesday Jim Smith, the *News-Times* city editor,

phoned O'Neil and asked him to come to Danbury. Mayo had called Ed Frede, the editor of the paper, and said conspiratorially, "I don't know if I can trust you with this, but . . ." Frede had employed Mayo on an accident case and believed he was worth listening to. He agreed not to divulge Mayo's sources indiscriminately but insisted on knowing who they were. Frede wrote the name of the missing woman on a slip of paper—"Hella" he spelled it—and gave it to Smith, who passed it on to O'Neil.

On the brief drive to Newtown, in his windowless VW Thing, O'Neil's mind went to the only missing-persons cases still open on the Newtown police books—Elizabeth Heath, vanished for two years, and Edwin Dubbs, disappeared for five. Dubbs was fresher in O'Neil's mind, because the previous June he'd written a story about the absent Wall Street stockbroker. The Newtown police were still working on the case, but the trail was cold. Had Dubbs been murdered? Where did all the corpses go?

O'Neil was known for his rumpled clothes, long red-blond hair, and fresh grin. Then twenty-eight, he had been with the Danbury *News-Times* for five years and had recently won a journalism award. "On the infrequent occasions Patrick chooses to honor the downtown office with a visit," says Frede, "the first thing I do is to see whether he has socks on." (O'Neil wears them only in the dead of winter.) "I've never thought of firing Pat," remarks Jim Smith, "but of strangling him, yes. Pat's good at developing stories. He's a jewel of a reporter because people trust him."

O'Neil went to work almost the moment he returned from Danbury. He was diligent and knew his way around the town hall. Filling notebooks with facts, he noted that the Craftses owned a property on Currituck Road, about 600 yards from their home at 5 Newfield Lane. That might have been a perfect place to hide a body.

Though Crafts and his three children and Marie Thomas were still living at Newfield Lane, the place was almost eerily quiet during the day when O'Neil drove by to get a line on the man Mayo accused of murder. The driveway was a clutter of vehicles — red-and-white 1986 Ford dump truck, Ford Crown Victoria, Volkswagen Rabbit, disabled International truck, old Audi without plates — like a redneck's house, O'Neil thought. He understood Crafts was a pilot and correctly assumed that he was flying for Eastern as though nothing untoward had happened.

Also on December 3, Mayo — "supercharged," in Brunetti's view — appeared in Brunetti's office without an appointment, still wishing to know if Crafts had been interviewed by Newtown. Brunetti told him to return after lunch.

The afternoon produced a surprise for Mayo. Noroian had spoken with Crafts the previous morning. If he hadn't reported his wife missing, Crafts said, it was because, for the sake of Helle's reputation and his own, he didn't wish to "air his dirty linen in public." She'd run off with a boyfriend, an Oriental from Westchester County, New York. Noroian said Crafts was a straight shooter; no reason not to believe him.

At this Mayo said sarcastically, "Oh, I'm happy. They caught Crafts in a lie. He tells the nanny the wife's in Denmark but not about the Oriental guy. Did Noroian get the guy's name? Has he proof?"

Brunetti lifted the phone again; this time he spoke with Lieutenant DeJoseph.

He reported to Mayo, "DeJoseph hasn't read the statement. It probably hasn't been typed."

"Well, they have the sitter's statement and Rita Buonanno's too."

For the third time Brunetti called Newtown. He asked for the statements on the Crafts case so that he could review them; they never arrived. Brunetti gave Mayo another piece of news: Richard Crafts had agreed to take a lie detector test.

Lie detector test or no, Helle remained absent and

58

Crafts's various statements had led her friends to conclude that foul play was involved. Brunetti had told Mayo the Newtown cops wanted nothing to do with him. Why? And why was the department pursuing the investigation with so little diligence? Why, in a certainly puzzling case, with lots of angles, hadn't Newtown brought in the resources of the state police?

He placed numerous phone calls to state policemen with whom he was acquainted, to detectives in various jurisdictions around Newtown, to a prosecutor from a different district. The verdict was unanimous: Lou Marchese could be difficult. Like a stubborn old sheriff in a Western movie, Marchese was a law unto himself. His department had been taught not to share, especially with the state police, whom Marchese hated. In the matter of Richard Crafts, the consensus went, Newtown would proceed on its own, if it acted at all.

That Crafts would take a polygraph had shaken Mayo. He had considerable faith in the procedure. Was Crafts willing because he *hadn't* committed murder? Was Helle Crafts alive? When Mayo got down to it, he knew almost nothing about the woman. Perhaps she had proclivities that had eluded her friends—a desire to escape married life, a yearning for Nepal. Might she suffer from amnesia? As Randy DiBella had suggested, he could be laying himself open to a defamation suit.

His fears increased the following day, Thursday, when incessant calls to Brunetti eventually produced the news that Crafts had passed the state police polygraph test. And Brunetti added that, on joining the Southbury police force in February, Crafts had passed a lie detector test designed to show he hadn't committed a crime, didn't use narcotics habitually, wasn't a homosexual, and so on down the line of police no-nos.

Brunetti warned Mayo, "Newtown won't spend time on this."

Crafts seemed off the hook, and Mayo had to reexamine his position. He wasn't an amateur sleuth with a private income, a Sherlock Holmes or a Nero Wolfe. He depended on payments from clients, and in bookkeeping terms every hour he spent on Helle Crafts to the neglect of other work cost him $35, his hourly fee. Sue Schneider was a volunteer on the case, too. He was tempted to drop the investigation, but if he did so, Helle Crafts might exist only in records of missing persons.

Mayo phoned Jan Rieber, a security expert he'd met while at Carrier. Rieber's clients were multinational companies and major law firms. When plea bargains were in question and the FBI insisted on polygraph examinations, Rieber would evaluate the results, which might vary from examiner to examiner. He distrusted polygraph tests, because, though infrequently, mistakes were made.

Mayo put the problem to Rieber. He knew from Brunetti that Crafts had been with the CIA's Air America in Asia. Rieber thought Crafts might have been trained to fool a lie detector, in case he was captured, by causing himself pain when answering the questions designed to establish his normal level of response. He could press his foot on a tack inserted in his shoe, bite his tongue, or dig a fingernail into his hand, and the pain would raise peaks on the graph. When asked the key question, "Did you kill your wife?" he would refrain from hurting himself, and the peaks on the graph would be of the same size as those made by his answers to the innocent questions. That was how a polygraph could be lied to successfully and how the state police might have been duped. Rieber said, "Crafts sounds like the kind of guy who could pass—cool, collected, a flier. . . ."

On Friday, December 5, Mayo spoke with Dianne Andersen. He was tired of being alone and unpaid. A meeting was fixed for Monday morning. Andersen, Mayo, and several of Helle's friends were to be present.

5

December 8-December 10

Nobody at the two-hour meeting in Dianne Andersen's conference room knew everyone else, so one purpose of the meeting was to get acquainted. Present besides Andersen and Mayo were Jette Rompe, Rita Buonanno, and Lee Ficheroulle. Lena Johannsen-Long was flying that day, but her husband, David, attended, as did Pierre Ficheroulle. Helle's friends struck Mayo as well dressed and yuppyesque with a trans-Atlantic flavor.

If the police had been strongly in the picture the group wouldn't have gotten together at all, but as it was they felt that Helle's disappearance wouldn't be solved unless they persisted. The atmosphere was somber.

Mayo repeated his assertion that the Newtown police would not act, especially since Crafts had passed the polygraph. He outlined the three different versions of Helle's whereabouts Crafts had presented. Rita, Jette, and Lee told their stories, which added up to Helle's having been scared, though not necessarily for her life, and Crafts's having shown remarkably little interest in tracking down his wife, as though he wasn't expecting her to return.

Andersen observed that though she supported Mayo for the job, the group need not engage him. They both left the room for a few minutes to let Helle's friends confer. The friends favored Mayo, though most of them believed the investigation should be kept in the family to avoid possible litigation by Crafts. They offered to help raise the money and underwrite Mayo themselves as a last resort. Andersen contributed the $1,000 she had left from Helle's retainer. Rita suggested that the jewelry in Helle's safe-deposit box could be sold, if necessary. She had been informed that the Newtown police regarded Helle's female friends as gossipy housewives with nothing better to do with their time than stir up trouble, a slander that infuriated these hardworking women.

Attention then focused on Helle's car, which was one tangible thing, at least, amid the shadowy circumstances of her disappearance. David Long seemed especially irked that the Tercel should have been allowed to remain in the Kennedy parking lot. And how, they all wondered, had it gotten there? If Helle hadn't driven the car on the morning of November 19, Crafts must have.

Mayo remained curious about the Oriental lover Crafts had mentioned to the Newtown police, but Helle's circle hadn't heard of him. They did know about a United Airlines pilot named John Parrott, who lived somewhere on the West Coast. Helle had had an affair with him before she married and had written him the previous year in care of the Rompes' address, but Don Rompe had refused to be a mail drop and Helle, not wanting her husband to learn of the correspondence, had planned to give Parrott the address of the post office box she shared with Rita.

So Mayo emerged from the meeting with his assignments. Find Parrott -- top priority, since conceivably Helle had sneaked off for a visit. Videotape Marie Thomas. Look at two cartons of papers Helle had left with the Longs.

The group dispersed. Mayo thought that if Helle Crafts had merely walked away from her marriage, he'd be on very shaky ground

* * *

That afternoon, Mayo remembered a pilot who had formerly lived in New Milford and worked for Pan Am, and now worked out on the West Coast for United. He phoned the man and virtually begged him to locate John Parrott. The friend complied: Parrott lived in Seattle.

On Tuesday, December 9, Mayo spoke to Parrott, who made a strangely worded denial:

"Well, you must have the wrong John Parrott, although I guess I could call you back, but I must be the wrong one."

Mayo regarded the receiver solemnly, pretty sure he had the right John Parrott, who for some reason didn't care to admit he knew Helle Crafts.

At Mayo's request Mary Lou Ruddy of Pan Am checked Helle's account at the credit union, Mayo's concern being that if Helle had simply taken a trip on or about November 19, she might have required funds, but the only recent withdrawals were two of $500 each, obviously used for Mayo's own fees.

The Tercel remained a preoccupation. Bob Brunetti had been unable to provide assurance that the Newtown police would inspect the vehicle. Mayo considered driving the car away, using the keys Marie Thomas had given him, to have it examined by forensic experts, but he feared arrest for theft and, besides, he was wary of disturbing evidence. But even for a cursory look, Ruddy had told him, he'd have to talk to William Worrell, director of Inflight Services. Sounding (to Mayo) perturbed, almost injured, at being approached, Worrell had said only a letter from a prosecutor or the police would give Mayo access to Pan Am property.

Late that afternoon David Long called to remind him about the papers Helle had left at his house; she had intended to duplicate them on the Longs' copier. Mayo inspected canceled checks, records of credit card numbers, and a number of receipts and warranties going back a long time, including one for a chain saw, which meant nothing to him. Overcoming Long's objections—the legality of turning over Helle's papers worried Long—Mayo took the boxes home and crouched over the documents. He was trying to find a deviation in Helle's life—a secret hideaway or hang-out none of her friends knew she frequented, or a clandestine lover, even a history of having been institutionalized.

Mayo scrutinized the papers until midnight, but Helle's routine seemed maddeningly uniform.

Although Mayo said that the intensity with which he pursued the case stemmed from identification with the Crafts children, who were the same ages as his own, he felt like a cop again. He liked to believe that he himself might be the one detail Crafts hadn't counted on.

Patrick O'Neil was also plugging away. He picked up odd details that didn't quite fit the usual picture of suburban life. On the Crafts residential property was a foundation, started years before and unfinished, that evidently had been intended to carry a garage for a backhoe, an eyesore that had been the subject of criticism by neighbors; one had filed a formal complaint. Crafts had moved the machine to the Currituck Road land, but the complaining neighbor's cat had returned home shot in the face.

O'Neil tried to assess the mood at the Newtown PD. Clearly, the possibility that the mild-mannered man who had been one of their own could have perpetrated a murder was a hard idea to accept, especially after he'd passed the lie detector test; and Chief Marchese wasn't pressing his subordinates. Detective DeJoseph, as late as Friday, December 5, appeared to have written off Crafts as a suspect, yet on Monday the investigation continued. O'Neil's impression was that the Newtown cops changed their minds almost daily about Crafts's innocence. "How," they asked, "can we apply for a search warrant on the house? Where's the body?"

On December 10, O'Neil called Crafts, introduced himself, and said, "I'd like to talk with you about a missing-person report on your wife. Is she really missing?"

"Not to my knowledge," came the laconic response.

"But what about the report?"

"I don't think this conversation needs to progress any further. I thank you for your interest. Have a good afternoon."

"He was always precise about the time of day," O'Neil remembers.

In his office that morning, Mayo had had another interview with Marie Thomas, using a rented videotape camera.

Marie had answered an advertisement placed by the Craftses in the Idaho *Statesman*. (Easterners recruited in the West because lower wages were asked there.) She had been hired at $500 a month to take care of the children and clean house.

Marie added details to her previous short statement to Mayo. On the morning of the drive to Westport after the blizzard, Crafts had seemed nervous. He was tight with money, and Helle complained about paying bills out of her own pocket. Some days after Helle had vanished he told Marie he didn't care about his wife anymore—she was out of his life.

Marie told Mayo, as she had Rita Buonanno and the Newtown police, about the dark patch she had seen on the master bedroom rug. Crafts said to her he had spilled kerosene on it—she had smelled kerosene—and a day or two later he had removed the rug from the house. A man had come to measure the room for a new one. The rug, which was Helle's favorite of all the rugs in the house, had been professionally cleaned only in October. (Weeks would go by before anyone considered that kerosene, a cleaning agent, does not stain and its odor does not last.)

That was the first Mayo had heard about a kerosene-splotched rug.

He asked Marie whether she knew Helle's closet.

"I looked in her closet. I see two uniform shirts aren't there, or her toiletries in the bathroom. She usually takes two, maybe three flight bags on a trip, Pan American flight bags, blue and gold handles. Yesterday I saw them in the hall closet."

65

Previously, Marie had told Rita Buonanno that Helle's flight bags were gone; now she had found them. However, unknown to Marie Thomas and to Mayo, Pan Am had recently issued new flight bags to its airborne personnel. The bags Marie saw in the hall closet were the new ones. Helle's old flight bags were indeed missing.

"The kids asked me where their mother is, and Kristina is getting cranky. I'm afraid to question the kids because they'll tell their father. He says I can go home for Christmas. I'm going to change jobs, because I don't feel comfortable in the house with a man . . ." A man without a wife.

Asked whether she knew anything about an Oriental boyfriend, Marie replied, "There aren't any boyfriends, and no Oriental was in the house. The only time Helle wanted nobody around was when she was talking to her lawyer."

The moment Marie departed, Mayo called Brunetti; this was their first conversation in six days. "Bob, the Crafts woman doesn't travel without her flight bags, and they're there at the house. And her favorite rug's been removed from their bedroom. It had a dark spot on it. Blood, maybe?"

Brunetti passed the information along to the state's attorney, Walter Flanagan, who had begun to follow the case intently.

At home that evening, Mayo impulsively jumped up from the dinner table and dialed Bob Tvardzik, a Newtown detective who was substituting for the vacationing Noroian. Rita had said she believed Tvardzik would cooperate with Mayo. Mayo impolitically sounded off about Noroian, but offered the information he already possessed — including the two cartons of papers from the Longs — and volunteered to find evidence. Tvardzik viewed Mayo as a potential legal problem, so he replied, "You're private and I'm public. I have to follow the letter of the law and you don't have any rules to follow." Tvardzik said no.

A meeting had been hastily called for that night so that Helle's friends could watch the tape Mayo had made of his interview with Marie Thomas. They planned to compare her statements with those of Crafts and decide whether the girl, who to Mayo looked more and more like a key witness, seemed credible. He was asked to bring the tape to Sue Lausten's house. Helle had discussed her Thanksgiving menu with Sue, who offered suggestions — sweet pork sausage, cornbread, a salad with cranberries, mandarin oranges and walnuts in raspberry Jell-O — and Lausten refused to believe she would simply disappear after planning her feast. Sue's husband, Lewis, was present and so were the Longs, the Rompes, and Lee Ficheroulle. When Mayo arrived at eight, he had the impression they'd dined together, though in fact they hadn't, and he felt, defensively, like a hired hand.

After the tape a solemn discussion commenced and a startling notion was introduced. Did they really want Crafts convicted of murder? Would that be good for the children? If Helle was dead and Crafts were jailed, the children wouldn't have parents, so maybe it would be better to cancel the investigation.

Mayo said, "Want me to stop? It'll have to be now, because if I come up with anything, I'm not about to hide it. I'll go straight to the prosecutor." And, he neglected to add, to the news media, as he told Dianne Andersen he would if all else failed.

Jette Rompe declared they wouldn't let that son of a bitch Crafts get away with it.

Mayo wouldn't have quit in any case. But, a suspicious soul, he was no longer certain that Helle's friends were happy with him. His intuition was correct. Starting that evening, they found him overbearing, insensitive in constantly talking up a homicide they were still gingerly trying to accept, and pushy about being paid. His sudden outbursts of temper were offensive. Rita, for one, vowed to have no further dealings with Mayo, and when Jette was designated spokesperson for the group, it was because nobody else would willingly talk with him.

After the meeting Mayo called Poul Gamsgaard, Helle's cousin, who wished to contribute to the cause. Gamsgaard praised his efforts, Mayo said, and registered disgust with Crafts, who hadn't reported Helle missing even to members of her family. Mayo told him, "We're losing time. Crafts must believe he's in the clear."

While interviewing Marie Thomas, Mayo had received a call from a friend of Parrott's who explained that Parrott hadn't cared to identify himself because he was married. Late that night—Mayo had put in a sixteen-hour day—he spoke with Parrott, who stated that many years ago he had been in love with Helle Crafts but had not seen her since a year or so previously, when he had run into her at an airport. She had written him one letter, to which he had replied via a flight-attendant friend of Helle's, and he had not seen or heard from her since.

"We believe she has been killed," Mayo said.

Parrott said, "Jesus Christ. Unbelievable."

6

The Rug

Mayo acted and sounded to others as though Richard Crafts's guilt in the murder of his wife could be taken for granted and as if convincing proof would arrive any day, but he asked himself if his suspicions, which as far as he knew, law-enforcement authorities refused to take seriously, were a product of group hysteria.

When he wondered too much whether Richard Crafts might be innocent, however, he reminded himself of Marie's revelations about the flight bags and the rug. He was sure the rug had been stained not with kerosene but with Helle's blood, and he was determined to get to the bottom of the case, no matter how many people he offended.

Increasing Mayo's resentment against the Newtown cops was a mention from Pat O'Neil that they regarded him as a money-grubber out to fleece his clients through unsubstantiated accusations of homicide.

He phoned Dianne Andersen to complain about the police and inform her of Marie Thomas's latest contribution of clues. Sounding a little breathless, the lawyer agreed to meet him at Bob Brunetti's office the next morning.

Four hours of Thursday evening Mayo spent in his car on a surveillance. He ran the engine to keep warm and tried to rid his mind of Helle Crafts. He got home at two-thirty in the morning but was at superior court at nine to meet Dianne Andersen, who did not keep the appointment. Mayo half convinced himself that she wanted to put some distance between them because in his agitated state he was becoming increasingly difficult to deal with.

Though busy, Brunetti received him. Mayo complained once more that Helle's Tercel had been in the Pan Am parking lot for almost three weeks without attracting police attention. "I'll give them another call and see what they're up to," Brunetti promised.

Mayo attempted to prolong the conversation, Brunetti being his only channel to the state's attorney. "Anything new?" he asked.

Unwittingly, Brunetti proceeded to ignite a fuse. He'd heard that the Southbury police had a key to the town's garbage transfer station, which contained a dumpster. He also knew that Richard Crafts had been caught in a lie about his wife and had been confronted with it at the IBM construction site in Southbury. Brunetti confused the two incidents, for the story he told Mayo was that Crafts had been seen acting peculiarly at the Southbury garbage transfer station.

Mayo said excitedly, "He could have dropped the rug there, the rug the sitter mentioned to me, the rug with the stain!"

Brunetti, caught in a tangle he wished to avoid, repeated, "Newtown's not going to do anything because of the expense, and anyway they don't believe Helle Crafts has been murdered." He added thoughtfully, "I don't know where Newtown garbage goes."

"Maybe New Milford." The thought depressed Mayo, because his local dump was so large. "What if I track down the rug? Yes, I'm going to do it if it's at all feasible."

Mayo and his assistant went straight to the New Milford landfill, as it is termed, and talked with a manager who said that New Milford did not take Southbury garbage. Like an increasing number of American towns, Southbury, population 18,000, lacked sufficient space for refuse and had to ship it elsewhere. Mayo inquired of the Southbury first selectman's office where the trash went. The Yaworski landfill in Canterbury, he was informed. Canterbury? Where the hell was that? Mayo had traipsed over the entire little state of Connecticut, ninety by seventy-five miles, and never heard of the place. He established that Canterbury was tucked in eastern central Connecticut, just west of the Rhode Island border.

He asked to speak with Yaworski, the landfill owner, to be told, "Jerry's at lunch." Mayo eyed his watch: close to two o'clock. Maybe garbage guys lunched late. He left his number.

Yaworski promptly returned the call from a restaurant. Mayo presented his private detective license number, as always. "Look," he said, using one of his two usual conversational openings ("Hey" being the other), "there may have been a murder. I'm searching for evidence."

A friendly man, Yaworski was not unacquainted with the idea that a landfill was an obvious place to dispose of evidence, including, *in extremis*, a corpse. A while ago, someone had been murdered near Canterbury and the clothes deposited at the Yaworski landfill. But whether it was feasible to hunt for a rug from Southbury that had been there for weeks, he didn't know. Bob Stringer, one of his operators, would.

Stringer surprised Mayo by calling almost at once. Mayo explained what he was after. "My God," said Stringer in a low voice, "you're looking for a body. I seen a bra. I stepped from the cab to the fender and I picked it up. I showed it to Ron Hatt, who works with me. I knew it was from Southbury — we get two, maybe three, twenty-ton loads a week from there. The bra had dried blood on it, but I threw it back."

A bra with dried blood on it and Stringer had *thrown it back!* Had he figured a woman had cut herself shaving? That bloody bra might be the first tangible evidence of murder. Was it forever lost in a heap of filth?

Stringer drawled, "You're in a little bit of luck. Because of the weather. Rained a lot, so we haven't worked the spot where Southbury garbage is, sort of swampy. Finding the bra's, well, possible." But, communicated the tone, improbable.

71

Yaworski came on the line. Mayo said, "I want to drive up there tonight."

Almost diagonally across the state, Canterbury was two and a half to three hours away. Yaworski said, "Makes no sense. It'll be dark. Come first thing in the morning."

Mayo called Brunetti, Andersen, and O'Neil, who said he'd try to make the trip. The night passed slowly; Mayo couldn't sleep. Fatigue and excitement almost convinced him that Brunetti was telling the Newtown PD about everything he did and that the Newtown PD was telling Richard Crafts his every move. Might Crafts not strike again? Were the Mayo children in danger? Perhaps he shouldn't have let Brunetti know about the bra.

Snow feathered down on Saturday morning, December 13, when Mayo left the house at 4:00 A.M. to be in Canterbury by seven. Only one lane was open in places, but four-wheel drive got him through. He was alone. To his vast irritation O'Neil hadn't appeared. Mayo wanted his search publicized.

Yaworski, dapper, with a mustache, and Stringer, who had a short gray beard, were waiting for him. Huge Mack trucks hulked about in anticipation of fetching loads from all over the state. In Yaworski's view, Mayo had taken on a Herculean task in trying to find a rug, much less a bloody bra, in that mountain of mess. Mayo's naïveté was incurable; he wished to commence the following day. There was no snow at the landfill. But Yaworski objected. The landfill was closed on Sundays, and, in addition, the people down the road would get suspicious about what was being unearthed.

Besides, the dig would require larger equipment than Yaworski had. He led Mayo to the nearby construction office of Frank Strmiska, who was able to free up an Akerman backhoe for Monday. When Mayo complained about being short of funds, Strmiska let him have the machine, with his son Jeff as operator, for $800 a day instead of his normal $200 an hour. Mayo was sure he dealt with a bunch of angels.

The treasury consisted of $1,000 from Dianne Andersen,

$2,000 from Poul Gamsgaard, and $1,000 from Jette Rompe, who wanted her contribution kept secret so as not to appear to have more money than the rest of Helle's friends.

In New Milford Mayo phoned Gamsgaard, and after some haggling—Mayo balked at all attempts to pin him down on costs—Gamsgaard agreed to put in $1,000 more. Mayo was covered through Monday on previous and present expenses and fees, and still believed the job could be done in a single session.

On Saturdays Mayo usually coached little kids in basketball, but as he reached into the refrigerator for something to eat, an idea rushed out. When Crafts removed the rug, could he have left a snippet on the bedroom floor? Mayo snatched up the phone and dialed Sue Lausten.

She phoned back later to report that she had a sample of the rug—removed, with Marie's connivance, from under a strip of metal in the bedroom doorway—and Helle's bra size: 34B. Mayo could collect the piece of rug tomorrow.

Forgetting basketball, Mayo phoned a friend of his, Jim "Bear" Sholwater, state highway worker, for a favor. "I have to round up some guys and pick through a dump."

The bear would rather have hibernated. "Got to think about this. I don't really want to be involved." Mayo barely listened. "Maybe some guys at the firehouse?"

Both were volunteer firemen at Water Witch Hose Company No. 2, where a handful of guys hung out on weekends, pitching horseshoes. En route, Mayo saw a construction crew at work and unsuccessfully tried to recruit them. He had no better luck at the firehouse.

Despite Mayo's efforts, the diggers consisted of Sholwater, to be paid $100 a day, a young Englishman Mayo had found at the home of a local politician, for $75 a day, and Sergeant John Roma of the New Milford police, with whom Mayo had worked when a member of the force. As a cop, Roma wasn't supposed to participate in free-lance sleuthing, and a reprimand or suspension would be the price of being discovered, but having been taken off the detective squad and assigned to patrol, he missed investigations and felt nostalgic about the days when he and Mayo had been a team. Roma was to be paid $100 a day. They were apprehensive not about locating the rug but about what might be wrapped in it: a body.

Mayo, Sue Schneider, and the others arrived in Canterbury at 8:00 A.M. on Monday, December 15. Steam rose from the thirty acre landfill like an exhalation from hell. Stuffed with garbage, the organic part of which was decomposing, the pile was warmer than the air. The target area, where tons of garbage had been deposited on and around November 21, was about seventy feet by thirty and fourteen feet deep. Every working evening, as decreed by law, the new loads were covered with dirt. Every morning Bob Stringer and Ron Hatt piled into Payloaders—Caterpillar tractors with massive spiked wheels—to "feather" the trash around in preparation for still more loads to be laid on in accordance with the arcane architecture of landfills.

Somewhere in the heap—so bright with strips of plastic that Stringer got headaches—might lie a bloody bra, a telltale rug, and, conceivably, a corpse, not that Mayo really believed Crafts would have been rash enough to dispose of his wife's remains in so obvious a fashion.

With his Payloader rake Stringer pushed away a layer of dirt and created a plateau on the hill thirty feet above the ground. ("This is my business. I *know* garbage," he assured them.) In it he dug a trench—a "cell" to the trade—from which the foul smell of methane gushed. The territory to be searched would be roughly defined by a layer of black ash at the bottom (also required by law) and by the trash's origin from localities other than Southbury, as determined by such clues as labels and addresses on envelopes and magazine wrappers.

Jeff Strmiska started work with the backhoe. The Akerman, a Swedish machine, had a reach of about twenty-five feet, and so precise was its grasp that Jeff could pick up a quarter dollar in the huge scoop. But it had a blind side, and Sholwater, who had experience with heavy machinery and devised the method they followed, watched carefully to be sure the New Milford crew wasn't injured. Working in a semicir-

74

cle, Strmiska would dig out a hole, raise the arm, and drop a column of debris. With pitchforks and shovels the garbage pickers would crawl over it like rats. In minutes, they had ransacked a two-ton pile. They performed this task again and again, while Sue Schneider provided coffee and peppermint schnapps she fetched from a liquor store.

The previous week, Mayo had explained the circumstances shrouding the fate of Helle Crafts to Orlando Mo, who had once been on the New Milford police force and was now, as a state policeman, resident trooper in Salisbury, in the northwest corner of the state. Mo believed that Mayo was on the right track but said he couldn't help, because state police acted only if they were requested by the local jurisdiction that had the case, were ordered in by a state's attorney, or had developed independent evidence in neutral territory, such as state highways.

Inactivity in what he perceived as an imminent murder investigation made Mo, a thin thirty-two-year-old, wearing the inevitable police mustache, restless. He shared Mayo's view that the Newtown police would permit the Crafts case to die and, like Mayo, he wanted to bring the state police into the case.

For Mo, the man who mattered was Lieutenant James Hiltz, commander of the Western District Major Crime Squad, but Mo felt he had to work through the normal chain of command. When he was advised to call Hiltz by Sergeant Brian Logan, supervisor of the resident troopers in the area, Mo had obtained the permission he sought.

On Friday, December 12, Mo had called Waterbury, Western District Major Crime Squad headquarters. Hiltz listened intently to his recitation of Mayo's facts. It was Hiltz's first knowledge of the case. The lieutenant proceeded to stick his neck out. He suggested Mo call the Eastern District Major Crime Squad, in whose jurisdiction Canterbury lay.

Sergeant Martin Ohradan, veteran cop and Hiltz's second in command, came on the line. He too betrayed curiosity and

75

promised, "We'll send someone if evidence is found." Mo told Ohradan to expect a call from Mayo.

On Monday Mo drove across the state to Canterbury. He wore a brown jumpsuit with "State Police" inscribed on the back; and concealing his official identity with a coat, he joined the diggers. By Monday evening they were all cold, tired, and discouraged. There were defections. The Brit wouldn't return if his life depended on it. Sholwater could have wangled another leave day but believed the odds for success were worse than hitting the daily double. Roma heard Mayo mutter, "Give me a miracle."

At 5:00 A.M. on Tuesday, December 16, Mayo and Roma set forth once more. For Roma, the camaraderie was like the old days, when they had gone out on cases, though maybe it was only an attempt to comfort themselves because there were so few of them and a heap of garbage to exhume. In the interest of time, bras would be forgotten. The focus would be on the rug.

At midmorning, after another long drive, Mo reappeared. As he had the day before, he took the precaution of putting his light bar in the trunk of his car. For this enterprise he could have received a suspension. Instead he got a "That-a-boy," as troopers call a letter of commendation, for his early interest in the case; but that was later, when the state police were pounding themselves on the back.

Mo had already gone when Stringer found a section of blue rug, and then another, both wet. (Stringer and Hatt were still on the job at five, though normally they quit at three.) Mayo was uncertain if the rug from the dump matched that from the Crafts bedroom. The pieces had the same twist and backing, yet when the fibers were pulled apart, differences in shade could be seen. However, exposure to the landfill easily could have resulted in discoloration.

Just after Mayo departed to call Hiltz, Stringer and Hatt found an entire rug, but the material didn't appear to be the correct shade and they dropped it back in the hole. The next morning, Wednesday, they peered at it again, wondering if it might be the right rug after all, despite the greenish-black tinge of its exterior. They hauled it out once more, carried it to the service road, and gingerly unfolded it, fearful of what might be inside. The interior was blue and on it was a dark, brownish stain.

The two men waited eagerly. Neither Mayo nor Roma was present. Roma had the night shift and was in no condition to return to the dig, and Mayo had an appointment with Hiltz in Waterbury at 8:00 A.M.

Ed Frede had been reluctant to proceed with the Crafts story in the *News-Times* because of the adverse effect on the children, but both he and O'Neil feared being scooped. Mayo was in the field on his dig and would undoubtedly call the news media if successful. Most important, Jim Smith had reached the conclusion, from what O'Neil had told him about Newtown's intensified investigation, that Crafts might be arrested, and he gave his reporter the go-ahead.

On Tuesday night, December 16, O'Neil called Crafts again. "I'm sorry to bother you, but I'm writing a story that your wife is missing. I want to give you a chance to talk. I wonder if anything's changed. I'd like to ask you a few things. Is your wife thirty-nine?" said O'Neil, who knew the answer but hoped to lure Crafts into a conversation.

Crafts sounded relaxed. "I'm sorry, but it's probably best I make no comment at all. You need the right spelling of her name—H-E-L-L-E. But I have no comment. You ought to go back to your original sources. Good evening."

O'Neil's story, appearing on December 17, the day Mayo met with Hiltz, was headlined, POLICE SEEK MISSING NEWTOWN WOMAN. Lieutenant DeJoseph was quoted as saying, "We are investigating all the possibilities." Chief Marchese told another reporter, "Until something that is direct evidence is turned up, we will continue to carry the case as a missing person. However, we are investigating all the possibilities."

The job of the three Connecticut major crime squads is investigation of serious crimes of violence, such as homicide, rape, arson, and bank robbery, and their specialty is crime-scene investigations. Hiltz had thirty officers under him, most spread out in various barracks. They wore street clothes, drove unmarked cars, and were considered an elite.

With Hiltz now was Sergeant Robert Connor, a longtime state cop. They listened gravely to Mayo's two-hour recitation of events thus far and compared the pieces of damp rug from the landfill with the pieces from the Craftses' bedroom – Mayo had cut the bedroom sample in half. That all were part of the same rug was not ruled out, but Hiltz said, "I can't just charge into this. We have to be invited, and Newtown will never ask." Mayo wasn't entirely discouraged. He had a hunch Hiltz was itching to enter the case and to gore Marchese.

Having changed from suit to work clothes in Frank Sirmiska's trailer, Mayo arrived at the landfill to discover Stringer and Hatt hanging over a rug. Mayo looked and threw up his hands with joy, feeling "as though I had hit a home run in the seventh game of the World Series." The rug appeared identical to the samples from the bedroom.

Mayo phoned the Eastern District Major Crime Squad and was told that trooper Michael Foley would arrive in an hour. Failing to reach Hiltz and Brunetti with the wonderful news, Mayo then left to serve as Foley's guide to the landfill.

Foley produced a test kit and poked the fabric with swabs; emerging brownish, the swabs went into vials. Uncommunicative, he radioed from his cruiser for a truck. Mayo, beside himself, pestered him until the trooper finally said, "I've been to a lot of murder scenes and in my opinion it's blood."

Mayo called Hiltz. "I got the rug!" he shouted. "I got the rug. No doubt about it. We've got that son of a bitch!"

The rug left — bound, Mayo assumed, for the state police forensic laboratory at Meriden. After extensive talk on the radio, Foley said that neither the state police nor Newtown would pay for further excavation. Mayo was out of money. Thus ended the dig with perhaps a quarter of the Southbury lode unexplored.

Mayo phoned his wife, Karen, who told him that the first story on Helle Crafts's disappearance had been featured that morning in the Danbury *News-Times* and that a reporter from a different paper had already called. Convinced that the reporter had learned about the rug hunt from the police, Mayo panicked. If the reporter knew, so must Crafts, with his ties to the Newtown department. He ordered Karen (who ignored him) to pull the kids out of school in case Crafts tried to retaliate against them, and he raced back to New Milford.

Mayo was vexed about the rug. Three or four urgent calls to the Eastern District had revealed that it was sitting in the state police barracks at Montville and would remain there overnight until its jurisdiction had been established. Probably it was destined for Newtown. Mayo groaned. He called Brunetti, who may have regretted giving him his home phone number, to rage over what he believed to be prosecutorial passivity toward Chief Marchese, and then Dianne Andersen, who said she'd try to light a fire at the courthouse in the morning.

She phoned Mayo at about ten o'clock Thursday morning. Walter Flanagan had assured her that Louis Marchese was about to be ordered to cooperate. "You've finally done it," Andersen congratulated him, but instead of joy, Mayo felt nausea, uncertain Flanagan would obtain results. He went to his office to await news, but nobody called.

At two, unable to tolerate the suspense, he reached Hiltz and was astounded to learn that the Western District Major Crime Squad hadn't yet been assigned to the case.

Shocked, he dialed Andersen, got her out of court, and told her, "The state police are *not* in. Somebody's lying to you."

After a conference with Flanagan in the chambers of Judge William Lavery, Andersen phoned Mayo and said, "I can't tell you right now what's going on, but they want the sitter to come to the courthouse tomorrow to talk with Flanagan."

Mayo found Marie at David and Lena Long's. "Send her home to get some clothes," he ordered Lena. Lena was hard to convince. She thought returning to the Crafts house too dangerous for Marie. "You'd better goddamn do what I tell you to do," shouted Mayo. Lena hung up on him.

In ten minutes David Long called. "I understand you cursed at my wife. How dare you talk to her like that?" Mayo replied that Lena had deserved his curses. "Never call this house again!" said Long and slammed down the phone.

Marie Thomas was shipped somewhere else for that night and then on to Sue Lausten, who was also angry with Mayo for his treatment of Lena. Flanagan had suggested that either Sue Lausten or Mayo should bring Marie to the courthouse. Reluctantly, Sue finally agreed that Mayo could take her. Marie was quite happy to go along. She seemed not to understand what was happening.

In the criminal justice system paradox can be king. Some days later trooper Foley reappeared at the Yaworski landfill, to be accosted by mild Bob Stringer, now thoroughly irritated that he hadn't been told the result of his rug labors. He said to Foley, "What's going on?"

Foley replied, "Let's put it this way. The rug isn't right, but you guys got us into the case."

Stringer beamed.

Part II

The Crafts

7

Them

Richard Bunel Crafts (Bunel was his mother's maiden name) was born in New York City on December 20, 1937. He had two younger sisters, Suzanne and Karen. Their father, John Andrew Crafts, called Andy, forty-three years older than his son and thirteen years older than his wife, Lucretia, had been a college football player and a pilot during World War I. That he'd been married before was kept secret — Karen learned as an adult and only by accident. He was a stern disciplinarian and rather aloof, and he had a fierce temper, especially when he had had too much to drink. Richard Crafts was closer to his mother.

The elder Crafts was a successful certified public accountant with his own firm on Park Avenue in New York City, a firm that he eventually sold to a major accounting company. By then the family had moved to Darien, Connecticut, building a large house in an expensive section of town and joining the exclusive Wee Burn country club — their membership number was sixty-five. In the 1950s Lucretia opened a children's clothing store in Darien called Fashions for the Young, which Karen bought from her mother and continues to run.

Crafts could not have been described as underprivileged. He

attended a private primary school. His teachers' notes do not report him as having been a problem. Though he got in some scrapes, they were minor. A daydreamer, he liked to roam around in the fields, and when a house went up in a field across the street, he shot out windows with a BB gun. Darien high school suspended him for having firecrackers on the premises, and he was caught siphoning gas from a neighbor's car. A local kid described him as mean and said he threw ice balls and books at the others.

A high-school classmate recalled him as having a slight build and as being only an average athlete. "He didn't stand out. He wasn't a scholar or anything unusual. He was a quiet, outdoorsy sort of guy." Of all the youthful faces on the yearbook's pages, only Crafts's is unsmiling under its crew cut, perhaps because he felt self-conscious about his slightly protruding teeth, which, in about 1966, he had capped.

A habit he retained as a grown-up, he collected odds and ends. His family learned not to send him to the dump because he'd return with more than he left there. Another trait Crafts brought into manhood was secretiveness: not even his mother could make him divulge his companions or activities.

Always a C or C-plus student, Crafts graduated from high school in 1955 and matriculated for a semester at the University of Connecticut at Storrs. He had intended to major in agriculture, but the academic grind proved too much for him and in August 1956, he enlisted in the Marine corps as a private with a five-year commitment. Lucretia later said his "joining the military was the only thing I ever got mad at him for"; and Andy had a temper tantrum at the dinner table, while the rest of the family sat silently. He'd wished his son to be a professional man like himself, but Crafts wanted to become a flier—which his father had been in his own youth.

Crafts was in his element at boot camp on Parris Island. He made private first class before anyone in his unit and was head of a drill team that traveled around the country. Then he was accepted at the U.S. Naval Air Training Station at Pensacola, Florida, where he learned to fly fixed-wing aircraft and helicopters. He became a helicopter pilot, which indicates that he was in the bottom half of his class, since jet fighters were considered more glamorous and the higher-ranking students flew them. In December 1958, he received his wings and commission as a second lieutenant.

Crafts was assigned to a small town in North Carolina. A fellow Marine recalls that he was always after women, but "for satisfaction only. He wasn't selective. The women could be unattractive, stupid, he didn't seem to care. Nor did he have to try too hard—women always came to him."

After a year, transferred to the Far East, Crafts was stationed in Korea and Okinawa with his squadron. Off hours he drag-raced motorcycles on abandoned airstrips. He made three carrier tours across the Pacific.

Crafts showed interest in police work, and when promoted to first lieutenant, he assisted both the prosecution and the defense in courts-martial. He is remembered to have said about breaking the law, "Oh, I'd never do anything wrong." Malcolm Bird, who served with Crafts and married his sister Suzanne, has said of him, "He fit in easily. What he loved most was to fly."

In 1960, while still a Marine, Crafts volunteered for an assignment that took him to Taipei and northern Thailand. His employer was Air America, a wholly owned subsidiary of the Pacific Corporation of Delaware, an arm of the CIA. Air America had assets of $50 million, more than 5,000 personnel, 167 aircraft, and, under an affiliate, Air Asia, massive maintenance facilities on Taiwan. Officially a private charter company, Air America was part of the CIA's secret war in Laos and Vietnam, a war that came to a temporary halt in 1961, after the Geneva accords.

Crafts returned to his Marine unit. He had planned to remain a Marine, but feeling cheated out of the promise of a base assignment, he took a discharge and in May 1962 rejoined Air America (officially, he flew missions for the U.S. Agency for International Development). He was part of an elite group of pilots whose job was to evacuate and ferry personnel, haul farm machinery, search for downed aircraft, transport food supplies, and provide the Laotian army with an air force. The work could be difficult and dangerous. "Soft rice" flights carried food and nonmilitary equipment, "hard rice" flights weapons and ammunition, some-

85

times dropped by parachute in ground fire zones. Crafts helped train Laotian and Thai pilots, accompanying them on combat missions. He flew the Sikorsky S-58 as he had in the Marines and also fixed-wing aircraft, including the hard-to-operate Helio Courier, a STOL (short-takeoff-or-landing) plane. Crashes were frequent because of the mountainous altitudes pilots had to fly at, and Crafts had several accidents. In 1962, while flying, he was hit in the leg by flak.

One of his then companions, James MacFarlane, has described Crafts as a "tremendous pilot and a tremendous individual. He wasn't violent and didn't get into bar fights. He was neither extroverted nor introverted. He wasn't timid and enjoyed himself on Laotian beaches and on R-and-R stints in Bangkok and Saigon." (Like others among Crafts's former associates, Mac-Farlane found inconceivable the idea that Crafts murdered his wife.) But Crafts had a temper. He once went after Malcolm Bird, his future brother-in-law, with a two-by-four and, missing, put a hole in a wall.

"The Air America guys adjusted quite well to civilian life," says Professor Andrew Leary, a University of Georgia historian who interviewed Crafts for a book about Air America pilots, *Perilous Missions*. "They weren't eighteen-year-olds exposed to combat in Vietnam. Almost all were sound, although Richard was very quiet."

Crafts quit Air America in July 1966. In July and August, he flew as a firefighter in Utah and Idaho, quitting because the work was too hazardous. His next job was flying tourists around Manhattan in a helicopter, which led to work as an aerial photographer. Eastern hired him on January 8, 1968; with 5,342 flying hours he was highly qualified.

He flew Electras on the New York-Washington-Boston air shuttle. That Crafts remained a flight engineer was not a sign of inferiority. Under a formula taking in the number of passenger miles flown and the weight of the aircraft, the pay of a flight engineer aboard wide-bodied L-1011s, for instance, was higher than that of a copilot on smaller planes. In preferring cash to status, Crafts was unusual; most airline pilots want to be captains above all else.

Crafts sometimes wore boots and had frayed cuffs. His hair was a little long, though within regulations. On his wrist he wore a gold bracelet bearing his name; the bracelet, which he had bought in Asia, had links that could be detached one by one to pay for food if he were shot down (he complained he lost $500 a year in rubbed-off gold dust). As a venturesome bachelor, he claimed he went all the way to Japan to buy a watch—as an airline pilot he traveled free or at a discount—and to Germany for several Mercedes cars, which he brought back to the United States, after using them in Europe to reduce customs fees, to sell at a profit.

He was affable if not especially communicative, though he liked telling Southeast Asia stories. Two that he found funny shed some light on Crafts and his milieu. Transporting "bad guys," Air America crews would leave the cargo hatch open and watch their frightened prisoners slide helplessly around when the plane was put into a spin. They would take up monkeys, tie little parachutes onto them, and throw them out of the plane; the monkeys did fine until they plucked at the shrouds.

Crafts didn't like animals, but his behavior could be contradictory. He talked of finding a chick in an Eastern cargo area at Kennedy and carrying it to Puerto Rico and back to Newtown, where a neighbor's cat killed it.

If Crafts was eccentric, associates didn't notice. He received a commendation from Eastern in 1971 and at least one letter from a passenger applauding his conduct on a flight. He had excellent manners when he chose. "I liked Rich being part of the crew," says an Eastern pilot who flew with Crafts a hundred times. "He was pleasant, efficient, and captain material. He had consummate patience. If I made a mistake, he'd cover for me. He was extremely deliberative. If you said it was a nice day, he'd examine the sky. He never talked about his wife. I thought it was a marriage of convenience. We all knew about his New Jersey stewardess, and there were other women."

In 1969, while in Florida for recertification for the DC-8, he met Helle Nielsen.

Helle Lorck Nielsen was born on July 5, 1947. She grew up in Charlottenlund, a small town north of Copenhagen. Her mother, Elisabeth Fredericksen Lorck Nielsen, who believed women should work, was a secretary in a school. Her father, Ib Nielsen, who owned a gas station, had been active in the underground during the Nazi occupation in World War II. When Helle was seven, her parents were divorced, the cause being Ib's mistress. They were reunited a few years later but remarried only when Helle was in her twenties in order to smooth the way for Lis to inherit if Ib should die. They doted on their only child. Because he had been in the Home Guard, Ib had a gun, and Helle learned of its danger. Her father gave her riding lessons. Her mother bought her the most expensive shoes; good shoes, Lis believed, made good feet.

Helle was, and remained, extremely close to Lis.

Starting school at six and attending for ten years, like most Danes, Helle was a good student, popular with classmates and teachers alike. She studied in England, living as an au pair girl, worked as an au pair in France as well, and attended interpreter-translator school in Copenhagen. She spoke Danish, English, and French, understood some German, Norwegian, and Swedish. In 1967 Helle worked as a stewardess for the now defunct Capital Airways, which leased planes and crews to Air Congo, flying the African run out of Brussels and Frankfurt. When Pan Am advertised in Copenhagen for flight attendants, she was one of eight Danish girls selected from 200 who applied there. The group was trained in Miami, and because of her previous experience, Helle Nielsen was the star of her class.

With her high forehead, prominent cheekbones, firm chin, and her slim and upright figure—she always watched her weight—Helle attracted male attention whether swimming in a bikini or walking down Fifth Avenue in a fur cap she had bought in Moscow.

The thrill of her working life was encountering new cultures, meeting people who were different, reading newspapers in foreign cities. For Helle the excitement of being a sojourner in strange lands never seemed to pall, and a vacation might see her going off on her own to Club Med in Tahiti.

She was cheerful, rarely dejected, independent, and reserved. "Maybe it's a Scandinavian trait," said Hanne Schneider, a Dane who was in Helle's flight-attendant class, "but Helle wouldn't easily open up. For instance, she didn't tell you intimate things about men she saw. She was far too cautious to have been promiscuous, but she had a few lovers."

In Florida, the group in training lived at Lennie's Hideaway, near the Miami airport, where cockpit crews came to pick up women by the pool, and where, on May 24, 1969, she met Richard Crafts, who was good-looking and had a romantic-sounding past. Her attraction to him was instantaneous and mystified her friends, who believed she could get almost any man she wanted. "He was like a lumberjack," says Hanne Schneider. "His hair was down on his forehead. It was odd. Helle was so particular about everything—food, clothes—and Richard was, well, scruffy."

Pan Am's flight attendants were based in New York for easy access to international flights, and at first Helle's group stayed in a Manhattan hotel, five and six to a room. They didn't want to live in Manhattan—"too crowded and scary," said one—so Helle and four other women rented a floor-through apartment in Queens, which Helle persuaded Crafts to help her find. It had only three bedrooms, but since somebody was invariably on a trip, the place didn't seem crowded. Little by little their number dwindled. Down to three, they decided to separate. One reason may have been that Crafts was involved romantically not only with Helle but also with another of the women.

For Crafts, who told the police he was engaged to someone else at that time, Helle was "one of my first extracurricular activities." He had an apartment in Queens, and spoke of accidentally winding up in the same elevator with both women. He was anything but faithful, but Helle was crazy about him and he provoked her curiosity. With one of her roommates she would drive to Eastern terminals at New York airports and wait for hours to see which woman he left with. "Helle just wanted to see him and have him see her," her friend says, and one of his former girlfriends says with a laugh, "Oh, all of us would hang around the airport to see who Richard was taking out."

With his unaccounted-for comings and goings, imperturbable façade, and offhand manner, Crafts was attractive to many women. One flight attendant who went out with him for seven years while well aware that he had other girlfriends, including Helle, has described him as "having a feline grace, a good build, and nice hair. He was handsome and a considerate lover. He was cocky but not a braggart. He told Asia war stories. He was a little odd, I suppose, but for me probably the basic attraction was his unattainableness."

Though ordinarily in complete control of himself, there were times when Crafts would lose his self-possession. He would rise from Helle's dinner table, wander into the living room, and cry, and at night he sometimes woke screaming. Helle believed his emotional condition was related to his Indochina experiences. But he was also perfectly capable of putting on an act.

In 1970, Crafts has said, he and Helle were "on the verge of serious romance," but in 1972 he was transferred to Miami and Helle maintained her own social life in New York. In 1973, returning to New York, he moved in with her, then rented his own apartment. Alternately he rejected and charmed her. Also in 1973, Helle traveled with her parents to Bangkok as a tourist. To her delight Crafts, flying in unexpectedly from New York, tracked them down to the cheap hotel they had found, got them much better lodgings through his Thai contacts, and wined and dined them. Her parents were impressed.

But the relationship was always stormy and characterized by fights. Once Helle chased Crafts down the street in her bathrobe. He blew hot and cold and would stop seeing her for months at a time. When a friend asked her why she let him treat her in such a fashion, Helle said she loved him and knew he'd come back. She suffered but she waited.

For a long time Helle believed she was unable to conceive; even without birth control she did not become pregnant, and she'd been with Crafts, however intermittently, since 1969. They had an arrangement: they would marry if she got pregnant. The first time she conceived Crafts beat her up and she obtained an abortion. The second time he left her for weeks and then returned but still balked at marriage. Helle scheduled an abortion, but Crafts then decided that he wanted the child and would marry Helle after all. He told his sister Karen, and Karen, who adored Helle, wholeheartedly approved.

Crafts proposed and Helle set the date for a few days thence. She already had a bridal outfit and was afraid he would change his mind again if given time. The wedding took place in the New Hampshire home of Helle's friend Floortje, a Dutch woman married to an Eastern pilot named David Smith. Helle had visited the place and enjoyed horseback riding with the Smiths.

When they were married, on November 29, 1975, Crafts was almost thirty-nine, Helle twenty-eight and four months pregnant. Present were Lucretia Crafts, Karen and her husband, David Rodgers, Jette Olesen and her fiancé, Don Rompe. Helle missed her parents, but they worked and could not come at such short notice.

The bride and groom were handsome to look at, but negative notes could be heard. The Smiths believed Helle had used the pregnancy to make Crafts marry her, and he was now back to demonstrating reluctance. He voiced doubt that the baby was his — though none of Helle's friends had the slightest doubt that he was the baby's father — and was heard to remark that he worried about marriage, because for him it had to be perfect; divorce, he said, was something he would not willingly undergo.

Both compromised, Helle in marrying a man she was well aware could be hard on her, Crafts in marrying at all. But he viewed her as a breeder. He'd settle her in a country house, have more children, and continue to live as before. Other women were always a major irritant to Helle — she believed he had one-night stands ("targets of chance," in the military parlance) — but Crafts displayed indifference to her concern.

His attitude toward sex was markedly casual. On the verge of arrest he told the police, "In the airline business, there are numerous opportunities presented to you, and I'm away from home [many] nights every month. And you run out of books to read. And sometimes when there is no movie close by — I cut down on my drinking — so there's not much else to do. I do not consider myself — if I could think of a word — I'm not sexually overactive . . . but if the opportunity presents itself I would not turn it down."

In 1976 the Craftses bought a house in Newtown.

8

The Couple in Newtown

Founded in 1705, sixty square miles with a population of about 20,000, Newtown had once been New Town, like other New Towns in New England, but unlike Hartford, for instance, also a New Town once, it had altered its name only slightly. The area is hilly and rural, and people drive from Bridgeport, seventeen miles away, to picnic on the banks of Lake Zoar, a section of the Housatonic River, eleven miles long, nestled between Stevenson and Shepaug dams. At the upper reaches of Lake Zoar the fo·rensic drama of the Crafts case was to unfold.

If the town has a benevolent ghost it is Mary Elizabeth Hawley, born in 1857. She was the daughter of Marcus Hawley, who made a fortune from hardware, farm implements, rail, ship, and water work investments, and strong-willed Sarah Booth, whose ancestral Newtown home, where the Brontëan figure grew up, is now Hawley Manor, a small hotel. Mary was a plain girl, with poor marital prospects, until she met and wedded Reverend John Addison Crockett. They honeymooned in Europe, but the Hawleys followed, brought their daughter home, and dissolved the marriage; Mary resumed her maiden name. She lived in seclusion, like a prisoner, until her father and mother died, the latter at the age of ninety.

"Mary was sixty-three then," wrote Betty Smith in *Fairfield County* magazine, "and seemed to take a new lease on life. She appeared in new clothes and furs, put a tile bathroom and other improvements in the old house, and bought a Pierce Arrow to replace the family carriage horse. In 1921 Miss Hawley presented the town with the Hawley school [which the Crafts children attended]. She gave the obelisk Soldiers and Sailors monument to commemorate the World War I dead and a Memorial Vault in the cemetery. She had the Edmond Town Hall named after one of their ancestors, built in 1930, and gave an endowment for its maintenance."

Newtown lore was largely lost on strangers who flooded the town. "I used to know everybody at the post office," says R. Scudder Smith, editor-publisher of the Newtown *Bee* and the third generation of his family to run the paper since it was founded in 1877. "Now I'm lucky if I know one out of ten."

Between 1960 and 1975 Newtown's population doubled, but the absence of a passenger railroad—it had gone out of business in the 1940s—held down the price of real estate. According to a rule of thumb used by realtors, prices rise $1,000 a mile from Newtown to the Gold Coast, by which they mean the shore of Long Island Sound from Greenwich to Westport. Taxes were low in Newtown and the location convenient, not much more than an hour away from New York by car.

Newtown lacked the glitter of New York City but it was also spared the urban woes. Its population consisted largely of the families of corporate executives, of retirees, factory workers, a few farmers. Social life centered on volunteer activities—Newtown has more than a hundred community organizations—and the people, in the view of

Sue Lausten, a civic leader, are "quite isolated in their houses. They don't pay much attention to neighbors, or see them at all." Life was as uneventful there as the Newtown *Bee* made it sound.

Number 5 Newfield Lane, the development house on 2.6 acres of land bought by the Crafts in 1976 in both names, cost $73,000. Their mortgage was $50,000. It is an unassuming, L-shaped wood structure with gray shingle siding and white window trim and has eight rooms in all: three bedrooms plus one over the two-car interior garage, a living room, a family room, a dining room, and a kitchen. The Crafts later bought a 3.6-acre piece of land off nearby Currituck Road for $36,000. The mortgage for that was $13,000.

The house, about a mile from the shopping district, is pleasant but hardly extravagant. Because of Crafts's stinginess it was heated by a wood stove in the basement until the price of oil fell; Helle was often down building a fire. She furnished the place in good taste but inexpensively. Crafts refused to bring furniture from his New York apartment, which he kept as a crash pad.

An early arrival soon after the Crafts moved in was Lil Orlowsky, who visited newcomers to explain what the town had to offer in stores and services. One out of ten families she went to see were those of airline pilots. Most people she encountered faded from her memory, but more than a dozen years later her recollection of Helle Crafts remained fresh.

"The phone wasn't listed, which surprised me. Here almost everybody's in the book, except the police, who don't want to be called at home. [The phone wasn't listed at Crafts's insistence — probably to keep his women from calling.] So I dropped in unannounced. Richard Crafts was flying. Helle was businesslike and wanted to get it over with but she seemed to appreciate learning about the community. She had a small baby [Andrew], but was still

94

working and had quickly found help. She maintained a certain aloofness. She struck me as a nervous person. She mentioned that she felt remote, isolated, and edgy about living in our town. I guess she considered it the country — you know, no streetlights."

Though worlds unto themselves, the neighbors noticed the Crafts. Ann Moran talked with Helle, but in the ten years she lived across the street from Richard Crafts she had never spoken to him. Joe Tessitore knew him only to wave to, though Crafts had helped dig out his car in a snowstorm. Mona Rasekh in the mirror-image house next door also knew Helle better than Crafts, though she'd see him outside working on his endlessly unfinished projects.

Betty Bell, who lived next door before she moved to Florida, knew Helle best of all the neighbors. Both women were reserved, which Betty puts down to their European origin (she is Scottish). Yet they became intimate friends, seeing each other almost every day when Helle was at home, and arranging outings for the children. Betty talks of Helle as an "absolute love, intelligent, artistic."

Betty liked Helle for her sense of humor and for her devotion to her children. Helle made Halloween costumes for her children instead of buying them, though it took her hours. Only a moderate skier herself, she taught the children to ski and swim. "Helle was a very patient, understanding mother and the children adored her," Betty remembers. "If she was traveling, and I took care of them, she'd call every day and talk with each of them."

Christmas was Helle's season. In Betty's basement the two women fabricated Christmas wreaths out of pine cones. Helle made Advent calendars for the children, and put lighted candles on the tree. Since Crafts refused to play Santa Claus she'd get somebody else to dress as Santa and pass out gifts.

Betty liked Crafts, though she wasn't as close to him as

she was to Helle. He was never rude to her. He'd fix dinner for her and her two children when Helle was away. Once, mistaking a dog for Betty's, he took it into his house and gave it a bath. He snowplowed her driveway unasked. (He wanted to make a pass at Betty, he told someone.)

Thick as they were, Helle kept things from Betty, revealing them later or reluctantly. Her mother had been sick. She'd earlier caught Richard in a lie about his flight schedule, concluded he'd been with another woman, and put up with it. Once, Betty noticed that Helle's face was discolored around one eye.

"What happened?"

"Oh, I ran into a cabinet," Helle said awkwardly. She wore sunglasses the next day. She finally admitted that Crafts had hit her, and not for the first time.

But she did tell Betty that Richard was a good lover.

Acquaintances were impressed by Helle, though not always in the same way. One found her "a charming, outgoing lady. She stood out. She had a European style, was polite, etiquette-conscious, well mannered, and she was a wonderful mother." Another thought her "attractive though not glamorous, the opposite of the stewardess stereotype, quiet, down-to-earth, a homebody. She was a great cook. She taught me how to bake bread. She was a nut on nutrition."

Many stories are told of Helle's kindness and spontaneous generosity—bringing dinner to her friend Gunilla Horrocks when Gunilla returned home from the hospital after having a baby; when Betty Bell moved next door, leaving a basket of fruit and flowers outside to welcome her, though they hadn't met yet.

Helle was a genuinely nice person, and that she had so many loyal friends was testimony enough to her character. But even they failed to realize fully how adrift she was psychologically and, despite her children, how alone.

96

With her friend Sue Lausten, Helle attended Trinity Church; the rector there, Father Frank Dunn, saw Richard Crafts only once, when he came for Andrew's first communion. Helle believed in God but didn't care about denominations. She went to PTA meetings if her schedule allowed, and when she could, went to Tuesday and Thursday morning aerobics classes at the Newtown Health and Racquet Club. She had a good image of her body and worked hard on it. Ann Glaser, who taught the classes, remembers her as energetic and well coordinated. "She was unpretentious and never talked about her work and travels. She appeared to know a lot about allergies and once recommended a natural allergy treatment for mine."

The folks at the Karl Ehmer delicatessen in nearby Danbury had been acquainted with the Craftses ever since they had opened the store a decade earlier. Helle and Richard Crafts used to come together, but by 1986 she went without him. Crafts when he came would always purchase fancy Black Forest ham; she bought basic lunch meats.

Helle wasn't extravagant about clothes, either, but looked chic in slim dresses she bought in inexpensive boutiques. But she would spend money on her hair to have the gray removed and to give herself a bobbed look.

Early in her career Helle had impishly worn a red wig to cover her hair that reached to her shoulders. Now she went to her hairdresser, Garry, every six weeks to have her hair cut so that one shock curled under her jaw. Her hair was naturally brown, but Garry colored it blond. Now that she was almost forty, she felt she had to pay attention to such cosmetic details, especially in the airline business; also, she had begun to feel around for a new man. Garry, who found her to be one of his more intelligent customers, observed that, unlike many others, she didn't bother to dress up for her appointments, but ar-

97

rived in a tennis outfit or a sweatsuit. Often she brought the children—for her they weren't an encumbrance—and little Thomas would say, watching Garry snip away, "I love you, Mommy," and Helle replied, face in the mirror, "I love you, too, honey," but her thoughts were on how ghastly she appeared under the bright lights that revealed every line and pimple. And behind that perception was the fear of growing older, exacerbated by an unstable marriage.

In addition to the hairdresser, Helle's meticulous daily calendar recorded frequent visits to Dr. John Fox. Dr. Fox was thoroughly familiar with her mouth. She had soft teeth—almost every one had been worked on—with numerous root canals and thirteen crowns, including two crowns surrounding a false tooth. Helle's last visit to Dr. Fox was on October 30, 1986, when he took a full set of X rays.

Helle paid attention to her hands—she had a dozen bottles of nail polish—not only because she wanted to look well turned out but because flight attendants' hands are so often under the passengers' noses.

As a flight attendant Helle averaged close to eighty hours a month in air time; the longest trip in 1986 lasted seven days. To that had to be added the trips to and from airports and hours spent recovering from jet lag. She was busy but without her husband. The couple lived separate lives. "The only time I ever saw them together in a car was when they brought baby Andrew to the new house," says a neighbor. Chris Warchol, who baby-sat for the Craftses from 1982 until November 1986, never saw both of them with the children.

Crafts's trips often had no announced destination. When a childhood friend came with her husband on a visit from Denmark, Helle could say no more than that Richard was at a gun show in New Jersey and had promised to call. Four days later, he still had not called. That was how Crafts lived his life. If he appeared, he appeared; if he didn't show up, he didn't. Helle accepted that as a normal part of her existence.

Helle's friends from her flight-attendant graduating class saw less and less of her as the years passed, one reason being that Richard Crafts made them uneasy—"off in a dream world, strange, awfully quiet." She seemed to need to boost his ego as well as hers. She talked about his ability as a tennis player (Crafts wasn't any good), as a horseman (he always refused to ride), and as an outdoorsman who had no peers in their circle. She told them that his Marine test scores showed that he was of genius quality, though he may have misread the results; in fact, he believed, fatefully, that he was smarter than most anybody else. Helle bragged about her own high-school education, claiming, as many Europeans do, that it was the equivalent of an American college degree because European standards are so far superior.

To please Crafts she wanted to have perfect children. Their pre-Marie housekeeper of ten years, who could feel the tension between them, told Helle that no children were perfect.

Although Helle tried to avoid fights with her opinionated husband, her friends believed that she could take care of herself as she always had, even in circumstances in which another woman would seek aid. When Crafts failed to appear for Kristina's birth, Helle drove herself to the hospital rather than ask for help.

When Crafts was ill with cancer, she started to engage in side ventures. Uncertain whether her husband would survive and apprehensive about her own future with Pan Am, fearing its financial difficulties would lead to layoffs, Helle tried to find other sources of income. She held twice-a-year tag sales, sold Shaklee products, earning perhaps $100 a month, and sold dolls and toys for Pierre Fichcroulle, who wanted to help her. With Rita Buonanno she started the lace curtain business. With Sue Lausten she was active in the Wheat Berry co-op, which bought food in bulk. She hoped one day to stop flying and spend more time at home.

Richard's mother visited at Thanksgiving in 1985, and the two women had an argument at the dinner table about Helle's extra work. Lucretia objected that Helle had "too many irons in the fire," but didn't offer money, though she was well off. That rankled, and Helle complained to Crafts, or tried to—he was never willing to sit down and listen. (After Crafts hadn't spoken to Helle for a period, Kristina said, "Mommy, maybe someday Daddy will love us and then he'll talk to us.")

How do you live a life? Poor Helle must have wondered. She had partly trapped an unwilling man into marriage and now, with those nervous mother's eyes on the children she had borne him, who consume, as children will, her existence when she wasn't flying, she paced the yard, asking herself *What have I done‘* She had hitched herself to a guy her friends considered a certifiable creep, and Richard had not played around, but had beaten her. Why didn't she leave him? Was it guts she lacked? She must have questioned herself inwardly as all the insecure reasons—money, a father for the kids—intruded in her soul. Yes, he would *change*. And, as those deceptive motherly tentacles wrapped her, Helle decided for the nth time that Richard was *all right*. With her too critical friends, she would defend him.

Helle's life turned around her children, her difficult domestic life, and her career, in that order. Between Andrew and Thomas she had two miscarriages, which she blamed on flying, and subsequently she stayed on the ground when pregnant. Crafts claimed she had an abdominal scar, and that other than that, "There was not a mark on her." But there had been marks on her more than once.

In 1977, when the Craftses were visiting the Smiths in New Hampshire, Crafts suddenly reached over the dinner table and squeezed a pimple on Helle's nose, making her bleed. She sprang up and kicked his leg with her stockinged foot. He got up and slugged her. She spun and fell to the floor. What disturbed the Smiths most was Crafts's expression, which remained impassive. Telling him not to join her, Helle slept in the guest room. Ignoring her bruised face, she said nothing about the incident, and neither did the Smiths, although after that they felt very uncomfortable with the Craftses.

In 1980 Helle had appeared at the house of her friend Gunilla Horrocks, disfigured by two black eyes. She thought her nose was broken, and she admitted Crafts had hit her so hard that he'd broken his watch and his hand was swollen.

Gunilla said, "You ought to get a divorce."

Helle said, "I'm looking into the possibility. I have the name of a lawyer." She knew of Dianne Andersen's courthouse nickname, "the barracuda," and she showed Gunilla a do-it-yourself divorce kit. Just the same, she spoke of wanting to have six children with Crafts.

Gunilla was not as astounded as she might have been by Helle's black eyes. Earlier that year when the Crafts family was visiting the Horrockses, Richard Crafts began teasing her son Kris, who was four. "What sound does a cow make?" Crafts would ask him, and when Kris replied, "Moo," he would say, "No, baa." Each time Crafts gave the wrong answer Kris would hit him on the thigh. Suddenly Crafts laid the little boy on his lap and began to pound his thighs with his fists. Kris cried. His three-year-old sister yelled, "Don't hurt my brother!" and Crafts responded, "You want some too?" Hearing the noise, Gunilla came rushing in from the kitchen and shouted, "Richard, stop it! Don't touch her!" Helle, who was sitting next to her husband on the couch, simply shrugged her shoulders. Without a word Crafts rose and left, his face wooden. Helle apologized to Gunilla but seemed embarrassed rather than surprised, as if his actions had not been extraordinary, at least for him. She avoided the subject for years, finally saying, "Richard was wrong and I told him so."

Crafts's Aunt Hazel was present when he struck Andrew on the rump so hard that the welts still showed when Helle returned a few days later. Helle swore to a friend she'd call Hazel as a witness if her husband tried to take the children from her. On another occasion when Andrew and other little children threw mudballs containing stones at the backhoe, Crafts said nothing, but at lunch he grabbed his son and dragged him screaming down the hall.

When little Thomas flew into a rage and tried to hit Helle, Helle said, "I hope he doesn't have Richard's genes."

Richard Crafts was private beyond normal limits, seeming to occupy a universe of his own. His sister Karen and her husband had long ago learned not to pry into his affairs. His response to a question was to get up and leave. He bitterly resisted live-in help and appeared to resent workmen in the house. When his despairing wife hired a carpenter, Crafts wouldn't speak to him.

Yet he was not willing to keep his place in good order. After neighbors complained about his backhoe, in 1981 he began construction of a detached garage for it to forestall town zoning action; but he stopped with the foundation. He also started but never completed a trench around the house to drain ground water. The sun deck outside the family room was rotting and broken. The rain gutters required repairs. Crafts would start tasks, but he bored easily and would fail to finish them.

"He turned a nice home into a slum," said a neighbor. Helle hated the appearance of her house.

Crafts could be generous, but not with Helle. Earning three times more than his wife, he made her pay for household expenses, the children's clothes, most of the nanny's salary, and her Toyota Tercel. He insisted that she buy the car for cash instead of with a loan from the Pan Am credit union.

"Gifts for Helle from him were a rarity," David Smith says. "The sorts of presents he gave her were luggage and sleds for the kids. That may have been the reason she was thrilled as a kid in a candy store when he presented her with fifteen hundred dollars for a diamond ring during his cancer convalescence."

Crafts's own equipment was top-of-the-line, the best tools, a Hasselblad camera with several lenses, expensive guns.

Like many introverted individuals, he was an equipment buff. Besides the clutter of vehicles in the driveway, he had a $20,000 International Harvester backhoe, two Gravely riding lawn mowers, three Stihl chain saws, a snow blower, a cement mixer, a tractor, a $1,000 log splitter, an air compressor, a generator, welding equipment, and many tools.

In the spring and summer of 1986 Crafts purchased some $5,000 worth of firearms to add to his score of weapons, together with two gun safes, at $700 each. He also had tools for reloading ammunition and would shoot through the open garage door and on the Currituck Road property at cats, barrels, and piles of dirt, and sometimes in the cellar at targets shrouded in paper.

"Richard liked to be one of the guys," says a realtor who had dealings with him. "He was popular with the kids on the street because of his machinery. He had lots of tools to repair bikes and motorbikes with." Crafts fixed go-carts for two neighborhood teenagers, who found he welded the frames better than the factory did. He had time for his children occasionally and if he cooked out-doors, the neighborhood kids were invited to share. He seemed to need their admiration. He took Cub Scouts, of which Andrew was one, on a tour of Bradley Airport.

Perhaps Crafts related better to adolescents than to adults. With adults he displayed contradictory behavior, helpful sometimes but downright nasty at others. If Helle wanted a towel bar hung in a certain place, he'd deliberately put it a few inches off. If she planted flowers, he'd dig them up "She doesn't know her ass from a hole in the ground," he said.

Just as in childhood he would never throw anything away, Crafts amassed odds and ends; he even had a collection of empty toothpaste tubes. Helle would sometimes sneak to the basement and get rid of what she could, nervous in case he noticed.

He was especially retentive about money. "There are two kinds of people I won't handle," a Connecticut accountant declares, "schoolteachers and airline pilots. They have too much spare time on their hands. They're constantly doping out angles on how to avoid taxes and save money. Pilots, in addition to being notoriously slow bill payers, prefer to do the work themselves, whether or not they know how."

By the cellar stairs Crafts had a cardboard box into which he dropped every single sales slip in order to deduct the sales taxes from his income tax. He scooped up receipts from store counters to add to the total. He would drive miles to avoid a toll station—his way, perhaps, of thumbing his nose. He admired a man he knew who sold stationery supplies and only put 750 paper clips in boxes labeled for 1,000.

Nobody could get close to Crafts, who rarely showed his feelings. When he cried at Andrew's birth Helle noted and remembered. But he never demonstrated much affection for her, other than applying a macho slap to her behind. She seemed eager for love. Crafts had lost his pilot's license when he had cancer; a photo taken at Christmas, 1985, when his license had been reinstated by the FAA, shows an elated Helle close to fawning on Crafts, who stands stolidly, as if he doesn't want to be touched.

Though it bored him, domestic life gave Crafts the children and a cheap and convenient base of operations. And though he didn't like to be controlled or regimented, he found escape in girlfriends, flying, and being a cop.

Crafts joined the Newtown police force in 1982 as an unpaid officer, a "hobby cop" or "rent-a-cop" as the regulars call them, without informing Eastern Airlines. He was not allowed to make arrests; he was used primarily to inspect vacant houses, to provide a police presence at public functions, and to accompany officers on patrol.

"He was the only guy I ever rode with," says Newtown officer Robert Tvardzik, "who never smiled." Once, when directing traffic outside a church on Sunday morning, Crafts got into an altercation with a motorist, cursed, and placed his hand on his gun, for which he was reprimanded by Michael DeJoseph, who thought Crafts suffered from "Wyatt Earp syndrome, bravado and machoism. Lots of cops have it but most grow up. He didn't."

In February 1986, Crafts joined the police in neighboring Southbury as a seven-dollar-an-hour auxiliary constable. The other men marveled at his Ford Crown Victoria, equipped with two citizen-band radios, antennas front and back, a red light in the outside grille and another that could be placed on the dash-board. He was seen and heard speeding down the street in the dead of night, siren screaming. For target practice at a range Crafts appeared with the rear of his pickup filled with refreshments, though refreshments had been provided. He had the only perfect score in the unit.

Some of the Southbury police did not want Crafts on the force. "He lacked common sense," says Officer Richard Benno, who played an important role in the Crafts case. "Every incident became an emergency he radioed in."

He regularly attended the municipal police training sessions given at the Newtown PD on Thursday evenings. In 1985, he went to a five-day course in Long Beach, California, given by the Lethal Force Institute, and another in New Hampshire in 1986, paying his own fees. Typical of the courses were Knife Counter/Knife, Advanced Combat Pistol, and Lethal Management for Police.

Crafts took his police work with utter seriousness. He was attracted to uniforms and organizations bound by strict rules: the Marines, Air America, the police, the airlines.

Crafts worried about exhausting his medical leave if cancer returned and about the safety of his nearly $300,000 pension fund. He didn't believe his future with Eastern was secure, a concern shared by many of the pilots after Texas Air's takeover of Eastern. Eastern pilots struggled unsuccessfully to acquire the airline themselves—maneuvers were under way in November 1986. To a study group the union helped fund, pilots reported severe emotional distress, lack of camaraderie, and feelings of helplessness. Some pilots vented their frustrations on their families.

If Crafts's world seemed to him precarious, so did Helle's to her. A friend from the old days who ran into her in July 1986 says, "Maybe she'd been flying too much—she'd gone New York-London-Frankfurt that trip—but she was tired. She wasn't the glowing Helle I'd

106

known." (This same friend received a Christmas card from the Crafts family in December. Though she had disappeared by then, Helle's name was on it.)

Helle agonized. Divorce looked like failure to her and she valued family life, at least for the sake of the children. When her friends said they couldn't understand how she put up with Crafts, she would spring to his defense, pointing out how good he could be with the children, how helpful around the neighborhood, that he held a steady job. She invariably found reasons not to divorce. Her friends had to wonder if she actually wanted the marriage to end.

In August 1986 she had finally decided to go ahead, but felt guilty and anxious. "Am I being disloyal?" she would say. "Am I hurting myself and the kids? What about his health benefits for the children? And where could we go?" Such fears had grounds in reality. She had no family in the United States to turn to and her job required frequent travel: if she stayed home she would lose her income.

In September, before Mayo's surveillance, Helle came to see the Ficheroulles, expressing an urgent need to talk. She told Lee, English by birth, that she had begun divorce proceedings because she and Richard didn't get along and she strongly suspected that he had another woman. She resented his keeping loaded guns in the house. Lee was surprised. Normally self-contained, Helle had seemed to her almost an ideal, a woman able to maintain a flying schedule, take care of her children, and find time to make soups and cookies. Lee realized, as she hadn't before, that Helle's life had a sad side.

Alone in the room with Lee's husband, Pierre, who was French and an importer, Helle went further. She said suddenly, "If I disappear it won't be an accident."

Pierre was shocked. Helle appeared to be telling him someone had to be aware that Crafts was capable of murder. "If you think that guy could kill you," he said, "let's do something. I'll find a place where you and the kids can hide."

Helle replied that Crafts, a policeman with many contacts, would find her wherever she went. Pierre tried to argue the point, but Helle, apparently resigned to her situation, countered with, "If I go somewhere, he'll accuse me of kidnapping the children."

When Lee returned, Pierre suggested that Helle take legal steps to protect herself and the children if she was so frightened, but Helle rejected that advice too. She said it was better not to do anything drastic. Wrapping herself in a bright smile, as if nothing serious had been talked about, she departed.

The Ficheroulles went over what had been said, which was quite different from anything Helle had told them before. Lee couldn't understand why Helle was suddenly so concerned about Crafts's guns, since she'd lived with them for a long time, and neither could understand her attitude toward the danger she seemed to suggest Crafts represented. They were used to thinking of her as an independent woman who didn't require looking after, and on this occasion she had certainly rejected their advice and offers of assistance. They concluded that her words reflected a temporary lapse of spirit; she would rebound. If she needed help, she knew the Ficheroulles were her friends.

In mid-September, Helle spent a few days with Betty Bell in Florida without the children. She wanted to relax. She had almost stopped eating, and had lost weight. She was deeply worried, not about Crafts's violence, Betty believed, but about money. Would he withhold payments after the divorce? Would she and the children be able to survive? Helle felt she had to be nice to him.

As though thinking of divorce but not quite saying so, Helle had discussed financial and tax matters with David Rodgers--the two identified with each other as outsiders in the Crafts clan—expressing anxiety about the future. But Rodgers identified with Crafts more than with Helle. Crafts didn't say a word about marital difficulties to his brother-in-law, but in October, in his offhand manner, he asked Rodgers about the divorce he had gone through years earlier. Rodgers began, "Oh, friendly," and then, unable to suppress the remembered anger, said, "I mean, it started out friendly until the lawyers got into it, and we ended as total enemies, even using our child to hurt each other." Rodgers related horror stories about money and visitation rights, and, realizing Crafts had his own situation in mind, he reminded him that though he had substantial assets, he had little cash, especially for a man accustomed to throwing money around. Divorce, with its combination of division of property, alimony, and child support, would put him in a financial straitjacket. Rodgers suggested ways of hiding assets.

Crafts said, "No, it'll work out."

Crafts must have spoken to other divorce-scarred men who very likely warned him how much a divorce could cost; and he was discriminating in how he preferred to spend his money.

Helle was extremely upset over a lie. Though her husband's chemotherapy had ended, Dr. Robert Cooper had continued to conduct tests every three months. The most recent was made in early October 1986, and when the medical report came in Crafts told her that he was going to die and that he would not take any more medication. At Jette's urging she called Cooper, who informed her that her husband was medically sound at the present time—in fact, he was one of Cooper's star patients—and his chances for survival had improved. Helle wrote her mother, relating the incident, "I can't trust him anymore." Crafts told the lie for sympathy and to delay service of the divorce papers.

In early October, as Helle was leaving after a visit to the Buonannos' farmhouse on Pond Brook Road, she said to Rita, "I told you I hired a detective. I've seen the photos he took. Oh God!" Suddenly she was close to screaming. "The woman looks so much like me! Same color hair, same way of wearing it! If Richard knew about the photos he'd kill me!"

"Is that a figure of speech?" Rita asked.

"No."

Rita begged Helle to say more, but she wouldn't. Distressed and frustrated, Rita was convinced that Helle had saved this ominous statement until the end of her visit because she didn't want to be told she shouldn't live in the same house as her husband if she felt so scared.

A tragedy was taking shape that Helle's friends couldn't avert. When it came to her husband, Helle was deeply divided. Her fervent hope was that something magical would happen to make him change from being a distant, unfaithful, manipulative, and occasionally abusive man into a loving husband and dutiful father of her children.

Jette Rompe says, "Helle was so blind and naïve when it came to him. If you tried to tell her anything, a curtain came down. You didn't want to make her sadder than she already was. It wouldn't have helped."

In October, when Crafts went camping with the boys, Helle brought Kristina to Jette's house. The two women had a long talk. Helle had just learned that, in May, Crafts had been promoted from flight engineer to copilot. Jette found it outrageous that he hadn't told her until recently.

Helle said, "If anything happens to me, don't assume it was an accident."

Jette replied somewhat scoffingly, "Oh, Helle, what is going to happen?" But then she started wondering whether Crafts was capable of tampering with the brakes on Helle's car or something of that kind. Could Crafts really be crazy? She blurted, "You read in the papers about guys who shoot the whole family and then themselves."

Helle answered, "Yes, but he'd never hurt the children."

As Helle was about to go—she wouldn't drive in the dark with Kristina in the car and preferred not driving in the dark at all—Jette dug a begonia from her garden for Helle to take home. As she handed her the plant, Helle said, "You know how I feel about Richard?"

"I know, you love him." Helle nodded, tears streaming down her face.

When Sue Lausten pointed to the oddities of Helle's marriage, she said, "Yeah, weird, isn't it?"

Sue Lausten has two degrees from Duke University, and extensive community activities have given her a good deal of experience in assessing people. She had frequent and intimate contact with Helle. Her opinion is that "Helle was a very feeling person, almost childlike in her trust. She was not worried about the children—Richard hit Andrew hard only once that I'm aware of, and he never specifically threatened her that I know of. When she said 'If anything happens to me, do something,' she wasn't referring to this week or next. She meant that Richard might be dangerous in the long run—the guns, his macho aura—if he wanted custody of the kids. She was vague about what she really feared. She only hinted, and you couldn't pin her down. And she only made the statement once to me, though I saw her or talked to her on the phone almost every day she was in town.

"Richard was baffling. He could be amiable, but he never showed emotion. I never heard him say anything positive or anything negative. He was very private. Of course, after she began the divorce action, he was afraid she'd upset his apple cart—wife and kids in Newtown, girlfriend elsewhere. He liked things as they were.

111

"Helle may have been frightened, but she didn't really believe Richard would kill her. If Helle was involved in extreme pathology it was behind closed doors."

In late October Helle and Karen Rodgers went to a toy fair in New York City. Helle was talking about the divorce in very definite language. Her mind was set; there was no room to negotiate.

Crafts wanted to invite the Rodgerses for Thanksgiving, and they and Helle had planned the ski trip in January. How did Karen and David feel about socializing with her, when she was on the verge of leaving the family? "Hey, no problem," Karen said.

Helle told Karen that Crafts was being a model husband. He was behaving as though he couldn't do enough for her. She seemed unimpressed by the performance and she didn't strike Karen as frightened.

Even after Crafts's lie about his imminent death, Helle had been forgiving. They had formed a pact. If he would agree to attend the children's parties, repair and maintain the house, and keep his distance from his girlfriend, he could stay on the premises without a fight from her until the divorce. But sex between them was out of the question. He appeared to comply with her demands.

On the afternoon of Friday, November 14, however, Helle called Sue Lausten, furious. Any concealed hope she might have had of saving the marriage had abruptly ended that morning, when she and Crafts had a serious fight.

Helle had taken to noting where Crafts secreted his papers and had begun to go through them furtively, replacing them exactly as they had been. She had come upon an insurance slip for a VW Rabbit Crafts had purchased without telling her ("Why does he need another car?")

and, more important, a recent Visa receipt showing he had bought gifts to the tune of $222.44 at Child World in Hazlet, New Jersey. New Jersey was where the girlfriend lived, and that Crafts must have been with her when buying presents for the children was too much to bear, especially as he had sworn to stop seeing her.

Helle had stood up to him for once; for the first time she didn't care if the children heard about the divorce.

Helle's friends had been aware that, in September, she had hired a private investigator who had taken photographs of Crafts and Nancy Dodd, and that the investigator had sternly advised her not to tell Crafts about the surveillance under any circumstances. Now, in a fit of a temper, she blabbed about the detective, though without mentioning the photographs.

Crafts begged her to leave the girlfriend out of the divorce action, but Helle adamantly refused—Dodd was her ace in the hole if he attempted a custody fight. He had followed her into the kitchen from the bedroom and tried to put his arms around her, but she turned away, Helle related to Sue Lausten, who sympathized.

That was the same day Crafts eluded the sheriff who tried to serve him divorce papers.

In Frankfurt on Sunday Helle told the same story to Rita Buonanno and Trudy Horvath. She said, "I just can't predict what he might do."

9

The Woodchipper

On New Year's Day Helle Crafts's *1986 Working Women's Calendar* advised, "A day to resolve that you'll keep your home life and work life in perfect balance . . . until to- morrow!" and ended with "Whew! I made it through an- other year."

Helle had already scheduled numerous activities on her *1987 Joys of Motherhood Calendar* and had marked birthdays with flags, a Danish custom. If she disappeared of her own volition, as her husband claimed, the decision must have been made at the last minute and prompted by a mysterious inner urge — a lover with whom she'd agreed to vanish, a call from God to join a convent from which there was no return.

Her daily routine provides not a hint of straying from established patterns. Almost every quotidian square is filled with neat jottings. A devoted mother, she arranged her life to be home for the children's birthdays, gave them parties with games, a pony, and a clown. If anything, to judge by her entries — swimming, school, birthday parties, dance classes, pediatricians, Sunday school — she over-

114

mothered, perhaps from guilt because she and Crafts were away so much.

Crafts's November was structured toward a different end. He must have begun planning during the previous month, because on October 29 he went to the Danbury Volkswagen-Audi dealer, where he bought a silver 1980 VW Rabbit with 103,017 miles on the odometer for $2,500, $300 cash, the balance due on delivery. (The book value was a little over $1,200.) The car required work, but the customer asked the salesman not to call his home; he'd be in touch. If he paid too much, he may not have cared. He told David Rodgers, "I'm playing for the biggest stakes in my life."

He returned a few days later, but the car wasn't ready — a wrong part had been sent — and he did not collect the automobile until November 17, when the dealer registered the vehicle. Crafts paid the balance of the money with a cashier's check from the Union Trust Company of Danbury. It bore the date November 3, which suggests that he was prepared to accept delivery two weeks before. Even so, the Rabbit wasn't brought to the house right away. Around Thursday, November 20, Crafts notified neighbors, the DeLorenzos, that he'd be parking a small car and a dump truck on Newfield Lane. Marie Thomas found the VW in the driveway on Saturday morning, November 22, when Crafts gave her the keys.

He later said he'd bought the car because Marie parked badly and had dented all four sides of the Tercel and the pickup, but if murder was on his mind, he would have had to obtain a car for Marie, since Helle's had necessarily to be found in the Pan Am parking lot to indicate that she'd left on a trip.

On November 1, 5, 9, and 11 Crafts flew "turn-arounds" — one-day trips. On Monday the tenth, a day on

115

which his wife was flying, he purchased a new Ford 350 dump truck for $15,000 from McLaughlin Ford in New Milford, to be delivered on November 13. It was to be used for spreading gravel on his Currituck lot's driveway, he said.

Crafts asked Anthony Kalakay, who sold him the truck, to install a hitch called a pintle hook for towing heavy equipment; it cost an extra $350, which was paid in cash. (He wouldn't have needed the pintle hook to lay gravel.) Kalakay drove the truck to Bridgeport to have the job done, since McLaughlin couldn't handle it, but on the return a fuel line leaked and the dump truck had to be towed. Kalakay notified Crafts that the delivery would be delayed, but promised it before November 18, as Crafts requested.

On the tenth as well, Crafts phoned Lavely Tree Service in Norwalk to inquire about large woodchippers. Dan Lavely had two large ones but rented only to close friends; he recommended Darien Rentals. Crafts didn't inquire about average brush-size chippers or whether a woodchipper could be rented closer to Newtown.

On November 13, from Zemel's T.V. Appliances in Danbury, Crafts ordered a $375 Westinghouse chest freezer of particular dimensions, paying a deposit of $100 in cash. That day, he also drove to Brewster, New York, where he paid cash for a flathead shovel and a pair of fireproof gloves at a Lloyd home and building store, ignoring several other stores (including another Lloyd) that were closer.

On Friday, November 14, Crafts reserved a large woodchipper at Darien Rentals in Darien, to be picked up on Tuesday, November 18.

That night he worked as a Southbury constable from 10:00 P.M. to 2:00 A.M., leaving home again between six and seven in the morning for Newark Airport. He flew a "sequence group," which paid overtime: first Newark-San

116

Juan-Miami, where he spent the night and called Nancy Dodd, then on November 16 (when Helle left for Germany) Miami-Newark-Fort Lauderdale-Newark, arriving home at 9:55 P.M. He had remarkable stamina.

On November 17—the same day he picked up the VW, probably parking it near Zemel's—Crafts went for the freezer. The buyer wished not to give his name, said Howard Levinson, the manager, who couldn't remember a similar cash transaction for a major appliance in his sixteen years in the business. Only the receipt recorded that a freezer had been purchased. "Put it down to Mr. Cash," Crafts said. In almost all such sales, Zemel's delivers the new freezer and picks up the old one, dropping it at a landfill. This customer elected to take away the 183-pound freezer, crated, in his Toyota pickup, with assistance at the loading dock. He must have brought the freezer home when the children were still in school and Marie Thomas was out. He was ready in time to take Andrew to his three-thirty appointment with Dr. Fox, the dentist.

On the morning of Tuesday, November 18—Helle returned in the early evening—the manager of Darien Rentals, Peter Groesbeck, phoned the Crafts residence about the woodchipper Crafts had reserved, leaving a message with Marie. When Crafts appeared at Darien Rentals, Richard Cenami, the owner, happened to wait on him. Crafts said he wanted the chipper to clear some land. Cenami told him the Toyota pickup wasn't large enough to tow the machine, which weighs 4,220 pounds; he would need a heavier pickup or a dump truck.

Crafts insisted the chipper be held for him, even if he had to pay $260 a day. Cenami didn't want to agree—he disliked taking money for nothing—"but he pushed me to hold it and I did," said Cenami, who couldn't recall another occasion when a customer (not a commercial customer or from the area at that) had agreed to pay for equipment he wouldn't be using. With his MasterCard as security, at 12:59 P.M. on November 18 Crafts rented a Asplundh Badger Brush Bandit 100 with a badger painted on the side. The machine, not considered suitable for use by the normal homeowner, could chip logs twelve inches in diameter

Back on the phone with McLaughlin Ford, Crafts leaned on Tony Kalakay about the Ford dump truck, which still had not been delivered. He said he "needed the truck to tow things, and needed it to tow a woodchipper and said it was costing him a lot to rent the chipper and we were holding him up."

Crafts owned a portable Honda AC/DC electric generator that could power the water pump, refrigerator, and furnace, and more, but he did not use it in the early morning of November 19 when the electricity went off. In January 1987, when Crafts was in jail and his children were living with Lewis and Sue Lausten, he phoned there prior to a forecast snowstorm. If the Laustens' electricity failed, he said, they should feel free to borrow his generator. It had always worked, he said.

At 8:00 A.M. on November 19, Bonita Cartoun, a neighbor and friend of Helle's, came over to borrow wood, but no one was home.

Ernest Ingram plowed a driveway next door to the Crafts house at about nine on the morning of November 19. He could see over the hill in the Crafts front yard and noticed deep tracks in the snow around a spruce tree. Ingram figured kids had been joyriding.

Crafts's sister had noticed a change in him three or four years previously, and so had her husband. It seemed to them that he tended to make unfounded statements and lie casually more frequently than before. Karen thought he was lying on November 19 when he brought the children to Westport. Snow was Crafts's element; he and the children would normally have rollicked in it and made do with other sources of heat if the house had really been cold. As the day wore on, she speculated more and more that he was with another woman. Nor did she believe him when he phoned that afternoon to say he was stuck in the driveway. She was sure that her brother "could maneuver a car out of anything, even if he had to use levers."

Crafts left Westport at 9:00 A.M. and encountered his buddy, Eastern pilot William Goldstein, and Goldstein's wife on the road in Newtown at about eleven. Goldstein had hoped to use his bathroom, since his own power and pump were not working, but Crafts stated his house was without electricity, too. He said the same to Marie Thomas on the phone at 12:11, though in fact power was restored to Newfield Lane at 10:44.

At 12:31 P.M., at the Newtown Banking Center, where the couple had a joint account, Crafts deposited a check for $300 for the curtain business (in Germany, Helle had told Rita about the check and Crafts would offer Rita the money the next day), and then at 1:27, at Caldor in Brookfield, he charged $257.96 to his Visa card for two blue down comforters and two pillows, queen size and king size. He had ordinary chores too, he said: put gas in the pickup, buy kerosene, bring two kerosene heaters from the basement.

Although Helle preferred not to drive in the dark, according to Crafts she left for Westport at six on Wednesday morning, November 19. (It was at 6:00 that he woke Marie Thomas.) He did not appear to be worried when he found Helle was not with his sister or when he told Rita Buonanno on the following day that Helle was en route to Denmark. Instead, his anxieties lay with hauling the Badger Brush Bandit.

At 9:10 and 9:37 A.M. on November 20 he telephoned McLaughlin Ford to inquire about the truck Kalakay had promised to lend him in place of his dump truck, which still wasn't ready. He knew the loaned truck would have a towing ball, because he'd requested it, and at 9:41 he called Darien Rentals about an adapter for the ball. At 9:44 and 9:50 he called McLaughlin and again at 12:28. He became irritable and threatened to cancel the purchase of the dump truck if a substitute was not made available immediately.

But Kalakay had found one, a Ford 50 U-Haul, white with orange markings and Ohio license plates, rented by McLaughlin for the occasion. At around 2:00 P.M. Kalakay delivered the vehicle to 5 Newfield Lane, accompanied by a man in a car to drive him back to his office.

Crafts loaded his police equipment into the truck and went via routes 25 and I-95, he said, to Darien, where the woodchipper was attached to the U-Haul. Louis Braun of Darien Rentals remembered the event because it was the first time he had hooked anything to a U-Haul. It was now after three o'clock.

Road conditions remained poor, and Crafts wasn't accustomed to driving the U-Haul, much less to towing a woodchipper. He testified that he reached Newtown at 5:45 for the Thursday evening municipal police training course scheduled from six to ten at the Newtown police department, but the class had been canceled because of the weather.

Here Crafts had a choice and time. From the station to

120

Newfield Lane was a bare five minutes, and he might easily have gone there to check on the children—Marie Thomas, who didn't show up for work at McDonald's, was with them—or to exchange the cumbersome U-Haul and chipper for a more convenient vehicle. Perhaps he didn't care to be spotted, for he failed to return home or even to phone. Instead, in his version of events, he sipped coffee at the Blue Colony diner and went to work at the Southbury PD wearing jeans. His duty commenced at ten, but he arrived, he said, at seven-thirty or eight o'clock. But there is another clear possibility: that Crafts went neither to the Blue Colony diner nor to his home, but drove the U-Haul and chipper directly to his Currituck Road lot.

At around seven on the evening of November 20, Joe Williams, hearing a loud noise, noticed a truck and woodchipper on Silver Bridge over the Housatonic between Newtown and Southbury. The chipper was in operation. Visibility was not of the best, and there was mist in the car.

Tempted to offer help because the truck's hood was open, Williams refrained. A car was coming from the opposite direction, and besides, Williams, a fisherman, resented people chipping wood into the Housatonic River and maybe harming the fish. He edged by. The truck's sliding rear door stood open about three feet; inside he saw two piles of wood chips and bags of plastic or cloth.

Joe Williams also saw a man who, it seemed to him, was cowering between the truck and the chipper as if not wishing to be observed. The man wore an olive-green poncho and a wide-brimmed boonie hat (as worn by the police). Williams drove on.

* * *

Danny Lewis, a Southbury roads-department driver, saw the U-Haul and woodchipper circle the equipment-packed municipal lot and, after failing to find a parking place, leave. Lewis put the time at about 9:00 P.M. He couldn't discern who was driving the U-Haul and thought no more about the incident or of noticing the unusual tandem again at 11:00 P.M. under a streetlight at the Rochambeau School, two hundred yards away from the municipal lot.

Southbury constable Richard Wildman had had his vacation cut short because of the weather, which turned into a three-day storm starting on November 19 and changed from snow to heavy rain. On the graveyard shift on the twentieth, from eleven to seven, he reported for duty and encountered Crafts, who was in uniform. They discussed the increasingly heavy rain. Wildman started patrol, on the lookout for disabled cars. Crafts had patrolled too — his log said he had inspected nine empty houses and responded to a call about a prowler just after ten.

At 4:00 A.M., checking the Rochambeau School lot, Wildman discovered a U-Haul with a woodchipper attached and a Southbury patrol car behind them. At first Wildman thought the car belonged to another officer, but then he saw Crafts, in a reversible police raincoat, orange side showing (the orange for directing traffic at night), loading his police equipment into the passenger side of the truck. Wildman assumed Crafts hadn't been able to find a place to park the cruiser in the crowded yard. There was space now, and Wildman offered a ride to Crafts after he parked the police car.

When Wildman gave Crafts a lift back to the U-Haul, he asked, "What the hell are you doing with a woodchipper?" Crafts claimed that the Wednesday morning snowfall had brought down tree limbs at his house. "Limbs!" Wildman said. "They must be awfully big."

According to Wildman, four o'clock was late for Crafts to be heading home, though from time to time he would hang around after two, when his duty ended. Crafts later said that he had written his report, filled out a new pay sheet, checked part-time work openings on the bulletin board, and at 2:30 had gone home without stopping, by a route that didn't take in Silver Bridge.

But Wildman observed the U-Haul and woodchipper again at 4:30 A.M. in a commuter parking lot. He didn't see Crafts. In the report he filed, Officer Wildman neglected to mention the second sighting. He didn't believe it important. He swung by a half hour afterward, but the U-Haul and chipper were gone.

Crafts said he parked the U-Haul and chipper on the Currituck lot, and at eight or eight-fifteen—he couldn't recall if the children had school that day (they had)—drank some coffee or tea, and headed for the lot with the purpose of clearing brush.

He was not there long, however, because at nine he phoned his mother in Florida. At about 10:30 Tony Kalakay saw the U-Haul and chipper at McLaughlin Ford, where Crafts inquired about the dump truck. Crafts maintained that the trip from Newtown to New Milford took twenty minutes, but with the U-Haul and chipper, it would have taken more like forty minutes. If, as he stated, he returned from New Milford to Currituck Road, almost two hours of the morning had been spent on the phone call and the round trip, leaving little time for him to use the woodchipper on his own land—the ostensible reason he'd rented the machine. (It's useful to remember that he hardly expected his movements to be carefully scrutinized later on.)

He left Newtown at about noon. At 1:29, as established

by Darien Rentals's time clock, the woodchipper was checked in. Peter Groesbeck, charging Crafts for three and a half days, rounded off the amount to $900, plus tax, and Crafts paid on his MasterCard. Groesbeck, needing the third leg of the chipper, which supported the machine when it wasn't attached to a vehicle, raised the U-Haul's rear door. Inside he saw a pile of wood chips a foot or two deep and mounded toward the front, as well as rakes, shovels, a gas tank, and a medium-sized chain saw with a blade. He recognized the saw's brand, Stihl, because Darien Rentals had carried it for years.

Groesbeck attached no significance to this display. Woodchipper operators often shoot the pieces through the spout into a receptacle. It was true that almost $1,000 was a high price for a day's use of the machine, but Groesbeck couldn't realize that the time available to Crafts to use it was limited to the late afternoon of November 20 and the early morning of the twenty-first.

Returning to Newtown, Crafts, removing the tools Groesbeck had noticed, put the U-Haul in the Grand Union parking lot — he left it there, he said, because of snow-removal problems on his street — and proceeded home on foot. Bonita Cartoun, seeing him on the road, offered him a lift. He informed her that he was walking for the exercise and to inspect the storm damage. She asked him where Helle was, and he said Helle was in Denmark.

Crafts talked to Kalakay, who at 5:30 P.M., four days late, finally delivered the red-and-white Ford dump truck. They drove to the Grand Union parking lot, where Crafts handed over a cashier's check for the remaining $11,408.80, and Kalakay departed in the U-Haul. The gas tank was almost empty, but though the customer was supposed to fill it, Kalakay didn't complain.

Wearing his uniform, Crafts went to work in Southbury again as a policeman.

On Saturday, November 22, he was airborne. He "deadheaded" as a passenger to Miami, then worked a flight to San Juan and returned to Kennedy Airport at 9:00 P.M. the same day. Another night with Nancy Dodd in New Jersey. On Sunday he flew the 4:30 P.M. flight from Kennedy to San Juan and came back at 12:40 A.M. on Monday morning. Home.

It was, or would have been, business as usual.

Part III

Investigations

10

The Newtown PD

At 4:15 on the afternoon of December 1, when he finished taking statements from Marie Thomas and Rita Buonanno, Patrolman Henry Stormer had little doubt that Helle Crafts was dead and her husband had killed her, though he kept his thoughts to himself. Detective Robert Tvardzik made neat notes that afternoon of what Stormer told him and obtained the Craftses' birth dates from the FBI's National Crime Information Service, which carries the date of birth for everybody with a U.S. driver's license. Hooked on the occult, Tvardzik conferred with an astrologer—the wife of a Newtown police dispatcher—whose charts revealed that Crafts was not guilty of murder and that Helle had a boyfriend and "she walked"; Helle was secretive and erratic, an "airhead," while her husband was depressed, not violent.

Detective Noroian, whose views often reflected Chief Marchese's, was extremely skeptical that a homicide had been committed, but Crafts's conflicting accounts required action. Lieutenant DeJoseph instructed Noroian "to get in touch with Crafts and have him come into the station house." Noroian left a message at Crafts's home, and at 8:30 A.M. on December 2, Crafts arrived. The conversation among Crafts and Noroian, and DeJoseph, who went in and out of the room, lasted an hour or more. Noroian was, he told Crafts, very concerned about statements made by Marie Thomas and Helle's friends. DeJoseph wanted to know why Crafts hadn't reported his wife missing, and Crafts said calmly, "She's done this before. She's left for a week or two."

Asked why he hadn't made a statement in light of the seriousness of the allegations, Crafts replied, "I was going to do it today," but DeJoseph's hunch was that he would have said the same thing the following week or even year if DeJoseph hadn't "prompted" him. Noroian took down Crafts's words, and Crafts signed the statement.

I, Richard Crafts DOB 12-20-1937 residing on Newfield Lane, Newtown, CT. make the following statement.

On Tuesday November 18, 1986 at about 6:00 pm my wife Helle Crafts returned home from a trip. Helle is a flight attendant for Pan Am Airlines. That night she was happy and showed no sign of being depressed or upset.

On Wednesday November 19, 1986 at about 6:00 am she was up and dressed and said that she was going. I told her that I was going to take the kids and go to my sister's house in Westport because we had no power due to the storm. She left the house about one hour before I did and left with her car. I have not seen or heard from my wife since November 19, 1986. When she left she was wearing a dark brown skirt and brown sweater. . .

I have read the above statement, have had it read to me. I say it is the truth. I know that if I make a false statement to a police officer in the course of his duties I will be in violation of the Connecticut penal code.

Richard B. Crafts

The detectives didn't ask whether Helle had plans for a divorce, but they fastened on Crafts's remark that she had a large Danish bank account — the inference being that she might have gone to Denmark — and listened attentively while he claimed she'd run off with an Oriental lover, or was in the Canary Islands, or with her mother, or with Betty Bell in Florida. DeJoseph wondered how she could be in so many places at the same time. At his suggestion, Noroian urged Crafts to take a polygraph exam and Crafts agreed. "He seemed willing, even eager," DeJoseph says. The detective expected that weeks would pass before Crafts could take the test, because the polygraph unit's time was heavily booked for screening applicants for state employment.

Crafts's statement constituted a missing-person report, and so before he went on vacation at the end of the day Noroian filed an all-points bulletin over the FBI's computer system, a routine step when the circumstances of a disappearance are mysterious.

On November 25, a calm-seeming Crafts went to the Carpet and Furniture Center in Newtown and ordered, from Marjorie Horvath, carpeting for three bedrooms, also ordering replacement underpadding. The total cost was $1,500, of which he paid a third on his Master-Card. Horvath said the carpet would be ready for installation in a week — she knew it would not be ready, but always gave customers optimistic dates so as not to lose sales—and asked for his business number. He said he'd be at home. On November 26, a man went to the house to measure the rooms. On about December 2, Crafts came into the store with his son Andrew. The carpet had not yet been delivered, but without being told to, which Horvath found strange, Crafts paid another $500 in cash. She asked him if he'd like the old carpeting removed, and he replied, "No, I'll do it myself." Unknown to her, the measuring man had noted that the old carpeting had already been removed. Marjorie Horvath never heard from Richard Crafts again.

On December 2, DeJoseph's daybook records, he received a call from a man he identified only as a state police lieutenant, who warned him that the state cops were aware of the Crafts case and might want in. Even that early in the case, conflict loomed on the detective's mind. Bob Brunetti's call the day before in Keith Mayo's behalf was the first time DeJoseph could remember that the state's attorney's office had expressed interest in a case so early. Usually it simply waited for a local police department to provide facts.

Square-faced DeJoseph, then forty-one, is proud and prickly. After serving with U.S. Army counterintelligence, he joined the Newtown police, and while working full-time at the station, spent eight years obtaining a degree in criminal justice at Western Connecticut University, graduating in 1978. In 1982 he did graduate work at the FBI academy in Quantico, Virginia, by no means an easy place to get into.

DeJoseph was considered a good cop and a mature one. He was intensely loyal to his boss, Marchese, who had been a friend of his father's. In January 1988, he succeeded Marchese as chief of the Newtown police, and he runs the department with a steady hand.

DeJoseph lifts weights, reads books, and collects antiques when he can afford them. He defends himself against accusations that he moved too cautiously in the Crafts case. "I've been criticized for bearing in mind the rights of the accused, but it's part of the job."

He dreads watching guilty people escape conviction. His cousin, a cop with whom he was close, was shot in the back and killed; the man accused of the murder was freed because of insufficient evidence. DeJoseph believes in careful investigations even if they have to be slow.

On the morning of Wednesday, December 3, DeJoseph met with Brunetti and two inspectors, Robert Blumequist and Anthony Dalessio, in the state's attorney's office. Inspectors work on bringing cases to trial and serve as conduits for information and evidence between the state police and local jurisdictions. Walter Flanagan leaned against the door frame.

"What've you got, Mike?" Blumequist asked, and DeJoseph, explaining the Crafts matter, gave them copies of the few statements he had. Dissatisfied with Crafts's, DeJoseph brought up the question of a search warrant for his house, but state's attorney Flanagan, as DeJoseph relates it, said that probable cause was lacking.

At Darien Rentals that Wednesday morning, Crafts rerented the Badger Brush Bandit, using his Master-Card. He planned to return it the following afternoon. He made inquiries about a steam cleaner and may have obtained one.

A cancellation had occurred at the state police lie detector center, and DeJoseph was able to schedule Crafts for the following day (he would later conclude that Crafts had counted on the long delay). He left a message for Crafts, who not long afterward appeared at the station house, boots and trousers covered with mud. No, Crafts said, he didn't care to take the test on Thursday because he'd rented expensive equipment to use on the Currituck Road property, but DeJoseph pressed him to comply, and Crafts agreed. Crafts displayed anxiety and DeJoseph wondered why.

A few days earlier, Southbury constable Richard Benno had received a call from a friend who had been in contact with Trudy Horvath, the flight attendant who had dropped Helle at home on the night she disappeared. The friend informed Benno that Trudy feared Helle Crafts had been murdered, and then on Sunday Benno, who'd been waiting for a chance to question Crafts, caught him in a lie.

Crafts had come into the station house before reporting to a four-hour privately paid shift as a guard at an IBM construction site. His children were with him. He told Benno that the family possibly would be getting a dog at the nearby pound, and that his wife would be along for the children. Benno assumed Helle had come back. He saw the children playing with skateboards and then happened to observe them, from an upstairs window, with Crafts in an old police cruiser. Benno radioed Crafts to return, and he complied, without the children. Benno informed him he'd broken the rule against having civilians in a police car. "I told Richard, 'You know better,' and he told me it would be all right, his wife would be along to get them."

A half hour later Benno noticed the children, scantily

134

dressed for the cold, playing alone on a sandpile nearby. Crafts had left them there. Benno asked Andrew where Helle was, and the boy said she had flown to visit her mother in Denmark. With another officer, Benno drove to the IBM site and confronted Crafts about his statement that Helle would collect the children. Crafts said he'd had trouble with his wife "and didn't want to air his dirty linen with us." Benno noted that Crafts was using his red Toyota pickup instead of a police car, but neglected to mention until later that there was a black fifty-five-gallon drum in the rear. It might have contained the burned remains of the personal effects Helle was supposed to have taken with her.

When Benno passed the sandpile again, the Crafts children had disappeared. Marie Thomas had fetched them, as she told the Buonannos.

Coming off duty that afternoon, Benno reported this episode to Trudy Horvath, as well as to a member of the Western District Major Crime Squad, another state policeman, and the Newtown PD; though DeJoseph learned of the call, he failed to pursue the matter.

Not so the state's attorney's office. Blumequist's responsibilities included Southbury and Newtown. After meeting with DeJoseph and also having heard something of what Benno had reported, Blumequist and Dalessio decided, on the spur of the moment, to make an informal inquiry to learn what sort of person Crafts was. Dalessio was friendly with Benno, and on the afternoon of December 3 the inspectors drove to Southbury.

Benno described the events to them. While they thought that Crafts's "not wanting to air his dirty linen" might have been true, the two inspectors concluded that Crafts had at least acted suspiciously. They feared he might have buried his wife's body under the concrete foundations being poured at the IBM site. With Michael Smarz they discussed sinking a methane probe or using infrared photography from a plane with FBI assistance, but they didn't have enough to go on.

On their return journey Blumequist and Dalessio detoured by Newfield Lane and observed a woodchipper in the driveway of Crafts's house. The machine meant nothing to them.

The inspectors neglected to notify Newtown that they had been to Southbury. "There was no need" is Dalessio's opinion. "We don't have to tell local departments when we go on fishing expeditions." But DeJoseph became furious when he learned of their activities. He considered them a violation of protocol and contrary to a directive issued by Flanagan, who was in charge of liaisons with local police, about sharing information.

The potential for a rift existed between Newtown and the state's attorney's office, which did not regard chief Marchese as trustworthy.

Sometime in the investigation's first week DeJoseph, worried about Marie Thomas's statement and remembering she had indicated that Helle had a bad cough when she left for Germany, asked her on the phone if she'd heard any coughing on the night of November 19. Marie replied that she'd heard coughing at three in the morning. Asked how she had known the time, she said she was a light sleeper. (But she also told Mayo she had not heard coughing and was a sound sleeper.)

Henry Stormer, who had been with the Newtown PD since 1980, figured Richard Crafts as weird—why else would a man with a pilot's income need to play cop,

136

carry a gun, and wear a police uniform? Stormer wasn't happy in his. He hoped to make detective: detectives don't wear uniforms. Originally assigned to the Crafts investigation, he was annoyed when the chief put him at the dispatcher's desk on December 2. Nonetheless, on that day and the next, he interviewed Betty Bell in Florida by telephone. She reported that, concerned about Helle, she'd made a date to see Crafts, who was to have been in Miami, but he had failed to keep the appointment.

Lee Ficheroulle brought in a typed six-page statement, and Jette Rompe told Stormer about the fur coat and the phone lists that Crafts alleged—falsely, in Jette's view—Helle had taken with her. Crafts had told Jette he'd waited all day in Westport for his wife to appear. That story, at least, could have been easily checked, but wasn't.

Crafts's statement that Helle had a Danish bank account, which Stormer related to Jette on December 3, disturbed her far more than everything else he had said, because she was certain he'd lied. Unable to sleep because of what the falsehood might imply, Jette phoned Helle's mother just after midnight on December 4. Mrs. Nielsen was profoundly upset, more so than by the other calls from the U.S.A.; Crafts must have known her daughter had no such account.

Truth was the business of the six-man polygraph unit at the Meriden state police complex, which performed two kinds of tests, screening for employment and "specific issue"—meaning crime—tests.

On Thursday, December 4, Crafts arrived at the Newtown PD, where, shortly before 8:00 A.M., he wrote and signed a statement.

137

I have been informed by Lieutenant Michael Dejoseph that serious allegations have been made against me in regard to the whereabouts of my wife Helle. He further informed me that it is my best interest to undergo a Polygraph Examination. Lt. Dejoseph has also told me that the only time available for the examination is 9 AM 4 December. If this date is not met the next available time is not until January. I have therefore agreed to accompany Lt. Dejoseph to undergo this examination in a spirit of cooperation. I have not had the opportunity to consult legal counsel concerning the wisdom of this undertaking.

DeJoseph then drove him to Meriden. They got there around nine. Crafts seemed calm and confident.

He was left downstairs in the reception room while DeJoseph conferred with Sergeants William Dyki and Joseph Palombizio. They were highly trained. Examiners take 264 hours of courses at the National Training Center of Polygraph Science in New York and submit the results of twenty-five tests conducted by themselves at Meriden; if they passed, they were certified. More training, lectures, and seminars on techniques new and old followed. Dyki, who had been with the section since 1974, had administered over a thousand lie detector tests. He didn't expect this one to be different.

Crafts said he'd taken a polygraph on joining the Southbury police, and so Palombizio checked the file and conferred with the examiner who'd given it. The polygraphist said, "You'll see he doesn't show any response. I've had only one other subject whose response was so flat."

DeJoseph related the facts of the case as he understood them, so that questions could be prepared. A woman was missing; serious allegations had been made that Crafts either knew where she was or had disposed of her; Crafts's stories made no sense. Dyki said he couldn't administer the test properly with so little knowledge and he inserted questions relating to murder so as to cover all the bases. Then, alone in the small polygraph room with Crafts, who had already been read his rights and had signed a release, Dyki asked questions unsuitable for polygraph purposes, with Palombizio and DeJoseph watching through a one-way mirror. The examiner wished to determine, among other things, whether Crafts could sit still long enough to have the test administered, a necessary condition that some 25 percent of subjects can't meet and may be gauged psychotic as a result. The reactions of 3 percent of polygraph subjects defy accurate analysis.

Police consider the lie detector not foolproof but a method for assessing whether an investigation should be started, what direction it should go in, or whether it should be ended. "The polygraph's success," Dyki observes, "is based entirely on a person's fear of being caught. The greater the fear, the greater the reliability." The examiners have two types of questions: control questions, used to establish the subject's normal level of response, and criminal questions, which are interspersed among the rest. Crafts read the questions in advance. He was then attached to a Stoelting machine, which produces four graphs measuring heartbeat, blood pressure, respiration, and sweating. The questions were:

1. Were you born in the U.S.?
2. Was Wednesday the 19th [of November] at about six A.M. the last time you saw your wife?

139

3. Do you know for certain your wife's present location?
4. Did you kill Helle?
5. Did you in your entire life ever hurt anyone?
6. The last time you saw Helle was she all right?
7. Did you have someone kill Helle?
8. Have you ever told a serious lie?
9. Have you told me the complete truth about Helle's whereabouts?

Obviously, the criminal questions were 3, 4, 6, and 7. No, no, yes, and no were Crafts's responses. (To number 5, he answered yes.) Further to study his alertness and ability to continue, Palombizio administered a doubt-verification test, consisting of cards bearing numbers, about which Crafts was told to lie. Then the nine questions were presented again, and then a third time with the order juggled in order to prevent him from establishing habitual responses.

Unless Dyki and Palombizio agreed, the result would be deemed inconclusive. They concurred: "It is the opinion of the examiners based on the polygraph examination that no deception was indicated when Richard Bunel Crafts answered the above relevant questions." To Dyki, cool Crafts was the sort of person you'd like to have as a pilot.

Maybe too cool. As would later be recognized, other possibilities existed. Since Crafts had taken the polygraph before, he might have been familiar enough with the test to control his responses. He knew the results were inadmissible in court, which might have served to diminish fear of being detected. And if he really believed he'd committed the perfect murder by destroying the body, he might not have been frightened at all. In answering questions 3 and 9 about Helle's whereabouts, he genuinely did not know. Her remains might have been anywhere in the Housatonic River. The answer to number 7 was truthful; he hadn't had someone kill Helle. Question 6 was easy to psyche himself through, leaving only number 4 to give him any trouble in being convincing. Because the police had only superficial knowledge about the case, the questions were simple.

DeJoseph called Brunetti to tell him the result, and Brunetti, who had learned about Crafts's CIA-Air America background from DeJoseph and speculated that he might have swallowed an exotic substance to lower his response level, advised him to make Crafts urinate into a bottle and watch him while he did it. DeJoseph complied and mailed the specimen to the state toxicology laboratory for urinalysis, but the results proved negative.

At the state's attorney's office they grumbled that Crafts might have taken the exotic drug early enough in the day for the stuff to have left his system by the time he peed into a bottle. But such talk was useless. The man had passed more than urine. They had hoped he'd flunk or at least display enough nervousness to provide leads, but he had sailed through.

That Thursday afternoon, December 4, Crafts returned the woodchipper to Darien Rentals, withdrawing his MasterCard and paying $419.26 in cash. As on the first occasion on which he had rented the machine, he'd had scant opportunity to use it, since the morning had been consumed by the lie detector test at Meriden.

That evening Crafts attended the regular police training class at the Newtown PD. After he was seated, Jean Hoover, a part-time Danbury policewoman who found him intelligent, thoughtful, unassuming, and quiet, entered the room and noticed two deep parallel scratches from wrist to knuckle on the back of his left hand. They had begun to heal. Asked what had happened to his hand, he said he'd been clearing brush and had one more patch to go. Hoover thought he was lying, because she didn't think anyone would be clearing brush after a storm. From Crafts, who seemed sad, Hoover had heard that his wife was divorcing him but not that she had disappeared.

DeJoseph didn't necessarily trust polygraph exams — "I'd seen guys beat them when I knew they lied" — but the examiners had raved about the results and considered Crafts a textbook example of veracity. On Friday he told Brunetti on the phone that he would treat Helle Crafts as an ordinary missing person; no special effort would be undertaken. DeJoseph wrote in his report, Crafts "continually stated the same scenario which he had provided detective Noroian with when he made his initial statement. I did not get the impression that he was lying to me. It is my feeling at present, based on the polygraph examination and my numerous conversations with Mr. Crafts, that he does not know where his wife is."

On the back of the report DeJoseph scribbled notes from a telephone interview with a neighbor of the Craftses, who, though she did not know Helle well, described her as highly ambitious and not such a very good mother. DeJoseph was all but convinced of Crafts's innocence.

* * *

Over the weekend DeJoseph reconsidered. "I kept thinking things didn't add up. The inconsistent stories, the Benno lie, the wife's failure to reappear for Thanksgiving. I looked at it through the eyes of a parent." As he notified Tvardzik by telephone on Monday, December 8, before he went to work at 4:30 P.M., DeJoseph was ready to pursue the investigation, though his small staff was already shouldering a big load in preparing two murder cases for trial. Both defendants were later convicted, and if Flanagan felt dissatisfaction with Newtown's work, he failed to tell DeJoseph.

That day, at three in the afternoon, Tvardzik met with Rita Buonanno at the Newtown Banking Center. Tvardzik wished to inspect the contents of the safe-deposit box she and Helle shared. The bank wouldn't give him access to the box, so Rita made a list of the contents: birth certificates and passports for the children, savings account passbooks for two of them, last will and testament of Helle L. Crafts ("I hereby appoint my beloved husband . . ."), stock certificates in small amounts and in the children's names. The jewelry included bracelets, a silver cross, a gold locket, a double strand of pearls, three gold chains with crosses attached to a turquoise necklace. Crafts had claimed his wife had taken her jewelry with her, which clearly wasn't the case. Rita said to Tvardzik, "If you don't believe Helle's dead, you're a fool."

Tvardzik, who had been on the Newtown force since 1974, later claimed he veered toward Crafts's guilt from the time of the polygraph exam, believing the result to be too perfect. Something had to be wrong.

During the previous week, using numbers Rita had

143

supplied Stormer, DeJoseph had begun a credit card check, which was routine for mysterious disappearances, through a "snitch in a financial institution." By December 9, DeJoseph's cramped handwriting listed locations at which Crafts had made purchases in November, including one for $257.96 at Caldor in Brookfield that would prove an important lead, though it wasn't followed up for almost two weeks.

On December 9, as well, Tvardzik spoke with Jens Holch, the Danish vice consul in New York, asking for help from the Danish police in locating Helle. Holch wrote a letter confirming the conversation and agreeing to cooperate. Tvardzik also discussed Helle's car with DeJoseph. Stormer verified that it was still in the Pan Am parking lot, and DeJoseph wanted to inspect the vehicle, ask questions about who had left it there, and if necessary obtain a search warrant. Brunetti had the same idea. He told Tvardzik he'd obtain a letter authorizing the search from Dianne Andersen, Helle's lawyer—Brunetti couldn't intervene directly, because the case was Newtown's. But Chief Marchese, cost conscious, refused to authorize a search, because he didn't believe the forensic results would justify the expense. Stormer snorted, "To Louie, if a case couldn't be solved on the phone, it couldn't be solved." Brunetti asked Pan Am security to look at the car. The body, if there was a body inside, had been there long enough to smell. (Brunetti did not realize Tercels have no trunk.)

The next day, December 10, while at the courthouse on another matter, Tvardzik explained Marchese's position on the car to Brunetti and Blumequist, who gave him Benno's report. Tvardzik had begun to suspect the state's attorney's office had a strong, even proprietary interest in the case.

Returning to Newtown, Tvardzik wondered if the case

could be marked closed.

A teletype arrived on the National Crime Information Service from the Placerville, California, police. An unidentified white female homicide victim had been found on November 29: blond shoulder-length hair, blue eyes, five-foot-five in height, weight 115 to 125, approximate date of birth 1936 to 1959 (the body was decomposed), abdominal scar. At 11:45 Tvardzik teletyped Placerville for more information. The victim had been wearing a turtleneck sweatshirt, red plaid pants, and a gold cross and could be described as having a prominent nose. Helle's nose was sharp but not exactly prominent. Placerville had fingerprints and dental charts and would send a photograph. Newtown had neither prints nor dental records for Helle Crafts.

The next morning, December 11, Tvardzik spoke with Smarz about Crafts's police schedule, learning that he had worked the nights of November 20 and 21 and had reported in for work consistently. Tvardzik also checked the municipal police training course records at his own PD. Crafts had a near-perfect attendance record, and no class had been held on November 20 because of the weather.

Sue Lausten called Tvardzik during the afternoon. She suggested finding Helen Dixon—Crafts had said Helle might have gone to visit Helen Dixon in London or the Canary Islands—but she didn't have her address or married name. (Lis Nielsen, assisted by Helle's friend Helle Meyendorf, had already located Helen Dixon Bond and established that she hadn't heard from the missing woman.)

On that day Tvardzik, assigned by DeJoseph to full-time work on the case, became temporarily excited. Information arrived that the Toyota Tercel was gone from its position in the Pan Am lot. Had Helle Crafts returned? Tvardzik hastily called a Pan Am security agent, who reported that the car had not been moved.

Tvardzik conferred daily with DeJoseph. The two had been compiling questions that they believed needed answers, and on the evening of December 11 DeJoseph called Southbury and asked that Crafts be sent to Newtown forthwith.

Crafts arrived at 9:20 P.M. in his police uniform, fifteen minutes after DeJoseph's summons. "He indicated to me that he would answer all my questions," DeJoseph wrote, and scribbled Crafts's responses.

Q. Richard, did you know that your wife hired a private investigator?
A. I had no idea, but I thought she might have.
Q. Did you know that a private investigator has documented your relationship with a New Jersey woman?
A. No.

"Now does," DeJoseph noted. He had shown Crafts the surveillance photos Mayo had left with the Newtown PD.

Q. Who is your girlfriend? How long have you had a relationship with her?
A. Nancy Dodd. On and off for the past twenty years.
Q. Does she [Ms. Dodd] know of your wife's disappearance?
A. No.
Q. Did you argue with your wife over some Visa

146

charges made in New Jersey?

A. Yes, that's true.

Q. Why would your wife tell her friends she was afraid for herself . . . tell them to check on her if something happened?

A. I cannot imagine her saying this. It is completely out of character for her to say this.

Q. On November 18, when Helle came home, when and why did she leave?

A. Those answers are in my statement.

Q. Did you know that she was leaving?

A. Yes.

Q. What might she have taken with her?

A. A blue garment bag, blue canvas suitcase. She has a new set at the house, exactly like the one she took with her.

Q. Are her flight bags in the house? Passport? Bank or any checking accounts?

A. No.

Q. Was she ever fingerprinted?

A. Yes, Pan American airlines and Capital airlines.

Q. Can we get a copy of her dental records from Dr. Fox?

A. Yes, no problem, I will get them to you.

Q. What is the story with your bedroom rug? Apparently you removed it, or cut some pieces out of it. Can you explain this to me?

A. All the rugs in the house are being removed, replaced.

Q. What was spilled on the rug in your bedroom?

A. Kerosene.

Q. Who replaced the rug? When? By whom? When was it ordered?

A. Rug place at Rt. 6 & 25 [Newtown], 10 days ago.

Q. Did you cut pieces out of the rug?

A. Yes. Two feet at a time. It's easier to take out that way.

Q. In Southbury, your kids were in the car. Why did you tell Officer Benno [Southbury] your wife was picking them up? Who picked them up?

A. I told Benno my wife or babysitter. The babysitter picked them up.

Q. Why have you been telling everyone different things about Helle being missing? Like her mother being sick, that you called Pan Am.

A. I didn't want to say my wife was gone and I did not know where she was.

Q. Who is Helen Dixon?

A. An old friend of my wife. I can get her address for you if you wish.

Q. On the day of the storm, when you dropped your kids off in Westport, where did you go?

A. I left my sister's about noon, got back to Newtown about 1:00. The power was still out. I got two kerosene heaters out of the basement. The power came back on about 3:00 or 3:30.

Q. What did you do with the rug you took out of your bedroom?

A. Dumped bedroom rug in the Newtown landfill one week ago. It was blue in color.

Q. Has Helle received any mail since she has been missing?

A. No. She has gotten no letters since she left. She usually gets about two letters a week.

Q. Did you know that Helle has a separate safe-deposit box?

A. No. (Surprised)

Q. Does Helle go by any other name?

A. Helle Lorck, used this name on occasion.

DeJoseph also asked Crafts, as an aside, and didn't write the answer, "What happened after you got home? Stay there all day?" and Crafts said yes, he had.

In DeJoseph's view, Crafts had told three possible falsehoods—"I cannot imagine her saying this," "I told Benno my wife or babysitter," "She has gotten no letters since she left"—and he found removing the rug two feet at a time odd. Because a resident of Newtown Lane had told him that power had been restored on November 19 later than it had in fact been, he did not check Crafts's statement that it had been restored at about three or three-thirty.

On the morning of Friday, December 12, DeJoseph was off duty. When he came to the station after lunch, he and Tvardzik had a strategy session. He thought of himself as playing a chess game with Crafts; his plan was to keep gathering facts and asking the man questions until Crafts was caught in enough lies to elicit a confession. But the Newtown Police Department was not ready to commit itself fully, because the chief continued to regard Helle as an ordinary missing person. DeJoseph was more than reluctant to criticize his boss, but would later admit, "I could have used five or six more guys," and though Marchese's austere budget all but excluded overtime, DeJoseph "would somehow have found the money." And yet, when James Hiltz of the Western District Major Crime Squad called that day to offer help, DeJoseph turned him down.

Lou Marchese was a chief's chief of the old-fashioned kind. He arrived at the station at eight in the morning and departed at four-thirty. In the fifteen years he'd been in charge he had never taken a vacation or a sick day. He worked on Thanksgiving and Christmas Eve. He was diligence personified, staunch and inflexible.

The chief, who insisted on being informed of everything and refused to delegate authority, made the decisions for the twenty-eight-man force, and he could be intimidating. "Come in here," he'd shout at Harry Noroian, "and I mean now." Noroian would quake. If there is such a thing as a police personality with an autocratic element, one that enjoys pushing people around, revels in the ability to have orders obeyed, loves to demonstrate power, Marchese embodied it.

"I guess you can say I always wanted to be a cop," Marchese told Pat O'Neil during an interview on the occasion of his seventieth birthday in 1984. Marchese was a complex personality — stubborn, well read, a connoisseur of food and wine, a man who gave to the down-and-out from his own pocket at the station house. "Hard to put a handle on," says DeJoseph.

Born in 1914 in Bridgeport, Marchese passed a competitive examination for the state police in 1941. He was decorated for rescuing five people from a burning house, rose to captain in 1965 (at a time when there were few captains on the Connecticut state police), and became commanding officer of the Western District. Marchese was like a god to DeJoseph, but a god discriminated against for his Italian name by the Irish who ran the department.

Behind him Marchese had many firsts: first state police public-relations officer, developer of its first public-relations kit, first police representative on TV and radio in and out of the state, innovator of a bureau for notifying parents of kids found driving around late.

Though he had a background in public relations, Marchese failed to pay attention to his own. In the 1960s, when he took charge of a case in New Milford, then a constabulary run by the state police, he shocked the local cops by sprawling at a desk, lighting a cigar — he smoked thirty-five a day until he quit, and even then he always kept one in his hand — and snapping orders. A senior member of the New Milford force has hated Marchese for his arrogance ever since.

Marchese became chief assistant to police commissioner Leo Mulcahy, a demanding leader who tried to instill a sense of mission and superiority in his men. Marchese resembled Mulcahy in his ideas. When a new governor was elected in 1970 and Mulcahy was obliged to step down, Marchese told a number of people the position was his, but instead the post went to an obscure man whose family had supported the governor's campaign. One of the new commissioner's first actions was to demand the resignation of a half-dozen top officers; Marchese learned of it on his car radio. While he claimed he had no regrets, others believed him badly disappointed. Thereafter, certainly, he displayed no love for the state police, for which he'd worked successfully for three decades.

That same year, 1971, Newtown, hitherto a constabulary, formed its own department and advertised for a chief. Marchese got the job. "Whatever else can be said about Lou," explains Newtown's then first selectman, "not a whiff of scandal occurred when he was in office."

But there were complaints from the townspeople of negligence and incivility, and there were conflicts with the state police; Marchese did all in his power to keep them off his turf. By 1977 the ill will between Newtown and the state police was electric.

In March of that year a move to replace the chief got under way. Nearing the end of his contract, Marchese had indicated he might quit and then changed his mind because he had divorced — he grumbled that his wife took all his money and he was generally down on women, which may have affected his attitude toward the Crafts case. Robert Connor of the state police (who later worked on the Crafts case) wanted the job, and a meeting was held at Connor's house to discuss the matter. Four of the five members of the police commission attended the meeting.

The Newtown PD had developed a reputation for uncooperativeness just short of mutiny, and questions were raised about the force's alienation from the state police, its effectiveness, and that of the chief.

The meeting was supposed to be a secret, but Marchese learned of it from a reporter and went to the newspapers. Blasted by the Newtown *Bee* for violating the sunshine provision of the Freedom of Information Act, the four commissioners backed off. The chief would reign for another decade.

Nonetheless, state police resentment against him continued high and on a personal level. During his early days on the force Jim Hiltz had been forced by Marchese to accept a reprimand he thought he didn't deserve. Marchese was the only one of his commanding officers who saw fit to punish Martin Ohradan, who had to work overtime several nights without extra pay for being late for roll call. On one occasion Tony Dalessio, presenting himself at Newtown to collect a file on a shooting indictment about to be taken to trial, was not admitted beyond the PD's reception area and was refused the file by Marchese personally; Dalessio had started to draw up a subpoena for Marchese, but the chief responded to a threat made by the state's attorney of being held in contempt of court. Walter Flanagan recalled that incident and others.

The chief's attitude could be neatly summed up: the state police couldn't be trusted and must be kept in the

152

dark.

DeJoseph says that Marchese knew "the state cops would hog the credit and screw the locals. His policy was to learn everything you can but tell them as little as you can. He considered the major crime squad glory boys, best at giving press conferences." DeJoseph secretly shared Marchese's bias.

Returning to work on Friday, December 12, Tvardzik received a call from Rita Buonanno first thing. It was a long conversation and not entirely without acrimony. Tvardzik had been told that her flight-attendant friends used the post office box shared by Helle and Rita as a mail drop. Tvardzik was thinking of love affairs, and Rita bridled. Not true. Neither Helle nor anyone else used it for such correspondence. And no letters for or from Helle had come to the box.

Tvardzik would sometimes say goodnight to Marchese, go home, and call DeJoseph with a report on the day's progress or lack of it, so that the chief wouldn't realize how much time the detectives were putting into the Crafts case. In the same fashion Stormer, breaking a self-imposed rule against talking to news people, met Pat O'Neil behind the town hall to avoid Marchese's eye. Stormer was guarded and didn't have much to report, but he let on that the Newtown Police Department's belief in Crafts's guilt went up and down like a malarial temperature. His own, too. He remained convinced Crafts had murdered his wife, but sometimes his faith wavered.

It wavered on the afternoon of December 15, when he spoke with Betty Bell, who had called to inquire about

153

the progress of the investigation. Stormer told her that the police had no new leads. She responded that she had spoken with Richard Crafts several times and did not believe that he was involved in any foul play, but added that if Helle hadn't returned by Christmas, she could be assumed dead.

For two weeks now Helle's friends had been pestering the Newtown PD for answers, but all they got were bland assurances such as Tvardzik's to Lee Ficheroulle on December 15. "We're not letting it ride," he said. "We need evidence. We have to sit on the fence."

To Lee, Tvardzik sounded like someone from a complaint department — evasive. Helle's continuing absence, Crafts's contradictions and lies — what further evidence was required for an arrest? Helle's friends, constantly on the phone, received no understanding or empathy from the police and felt abandoned. Lee phoned the governor's office to say Newtown wasn't doing its job, but the call wasn't returned.

On the sixteenth Tvardzik got another false lead. He called Peter Daccolti of the Newtown roads department, who had plowed Newfield Lane on the morning after the snowstorm. Tvardzik noted to DeJoseph, "He saw a woman — long coat — maybe a silver or gray car??? at 7:00 A.M. Not sure. He talked to this woman who was walking. He might remember her. He'll stop in to see you. Look at pictures! Rahhhh." Daccolti stopped by the next day, but the woman he'd talked to, probably on the morning of November 20, was not Helle Crafts.

Of his own volition Daccolti had also phoned Ernest "Juny" Ingram, a private snowplow operator, and In-

Helle Crafts's Pan Am flight attendant graduating class, Miami, June 1969. Helle, wearing a red wig, is third from left, second row. (Hanne Schneider)

Helle and Richard Crafts, Christmas,
1985. She almost had to force him to pose.

Crafts cut wood and sold it.
The chain saw is the same
found by the police under
Silver Bridge.

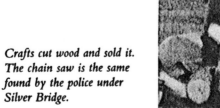

Helle Crafts a few years before her disappearance. (Betty Bell)

Career Day at Newtown kindergarten, March 1986. Crafts explains airline routes while Helle and the children listen. One child wears Crafts's pilot's cap.

The Crafts house on Newfield Lane. Snow fell the night Helle disappeared. (Betty Bell)

Crafts working on wood, 1979.

Helle (left) with Rita Buonanno at the Taj Mahal. (Rita Buonanno)

Crafts with two of his children and David and Karen Rodgers, Thanksgiving, 1986. Helle had disappeared.

Keith Mayo's surveillance photos of Crafts and Nancy Dodd.

Keith Mayo outside his detective agency in Danbury, Connecticut. (The News-Times, Danbury, Conn.)

Patrick O'Neil, intrepid journalist, dogged the Crafts case for the Danbury News-Times. *(Benedict C. O'Neil)*

The woodchipper at Darien Rentals.

The Ford dump truck that arrived too late to tow the chipper.

Police "mud monkeys" searching for evidence along River Road. (The News-Times, *Danbury, Conn.*)

Crafts being brought to Danbury courthouse the morning of his arrest for murder. (The News-Times, *Danbury, Conn.*)

Forensic expert Dr. Henry Lee testifying at the murder trial in New London. (The News-Times, *Danbury, Conn.*)

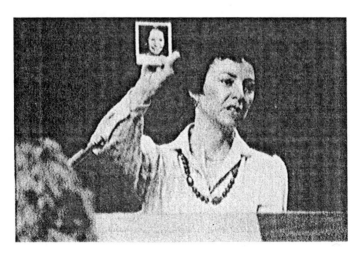

Sue Lausten on the witness stand showing Helle's photograph. (The News-Times, *Danbury, Conn.*)

Daniel Sagarin with his client. (The News-Times, Danbury, Conn.)

The lone dissenting juror, Warren Maskell. Behind him is St. Joseph, the patron saint of carpenters. (The News-Times, Danbury, Conn.)

gram called Tvardzik to say that he had seen no vehicles or persons he wasn't familiar with on the morning of the nineteenth. (He failed to mention the tire tracks he had seen around the spruce tree in the Craftses' yard.)

On December 17 the Danbury *News-Times* published O'Neil's article on Helle's disappearance. The Newtown PD had supplied him with material, and DeJoseph was pleased to have done so, because publicity might bring forward people with useful information. Only one lead turned up and it wasn't of any help.

That day DeJoseph gave Stormer the name of Albert Horrocks, a United pilot whose wife, Gunilla, was a close friend of Helle Crafts. Horrocks (who hadn't been present during the incident) told Stormer about the episode in 1980 when Crafts had lost control of himself and struck one of his children and also about the occasion on which Helle had appeared at his house with two black eyes. He informed Stormer that his wife had called the Crafts residence some weeks before and spoken with Richard Crafts, who had told her Helle was on the point of coming back from a trip.

Stormer said to him, "People involved with this case have been watching too much television," and Horrocks thought the remark so uncalled-for that he considered contacting the state's attorney. Stormer's response is that he didn't want to "put off" potential witnesses.

Noroian, returning from vacation on Monday, December 15, was impressed with the department's progress. But though he was at Danbury almost every day, he failed to sense the negative attitude in the state's attorney's office toward Newtown's endeavors.

On Thursday, Mayo's magic carpet surfaced, as Noroian learned from the Eastern District Major Crime Squad. He and DeJoseph picked up the smelly object and took it to the state police forensic laboratory at Meriden, which took samples but refused to accept it, though DeJoseph asked them to do so twice. The detectives returned to Newtown and placed the rug in the town garage, grumbling about the state cops as usual.

DeJoseph's investigation was based on psychology — Crafts had to be outfoxed — and patience. Unfortunately for him, Walter Flanagan's ran out.

11

State Police
Enter the Case

Almost from the moment **Keith Mayo** and Dianne Andersen told Brunetti about Helle **Crafts**, the disappearance had intrigued the prosecutor's office. A Danbury woman had vanished some months earlier, having reported that her husband had threatened her life, but she had reappeared after six days. Helle had been gone much longer. She had children and a responsible job for which she hadn't shown up. Her husband was a highly paid "airman," as Eastern described pilots. His stories sounded fishy and — especially unsettling in that bastion of law and order — he was a part-time policeman.

Richard Crafts's successful passage of the polygraph discouraged the state's attorney's men, but doubts lingered. He had certainly lied to Officer Benno. Statements by Marie Thomas and Rita Buonanno strongly suggested deceit and raised the specter of foul play. Still, the jurisdiction was Newtown's, and Danbury awaited developments.

On Friday, December 12, after speaking with trooper Mo, who relayed to him Mayo's accusation of foot-dragging on the part of the Newtown Police Department, James Hiltz phoned DeJoseph on a hunch. DeJoseph flabbergasted him. He described the case as "bullshit" (even though, the evening before, unknown to Hiltz, he had subjected Crafts to sharp questioning) and pointed out that Crafts had passed a lie detector test. "Jimmy," he suggested provocatively, certain that the lieutenant would do no such thing, "why don't you talk to Lou?" Hiltz was out of line in sticking his nose into Newtown's business, and Marchese could be brutal.

Hiltz found DeJoseph defensive and protective, and his mind went back to 1973 or so, when DeJoseph and Noroian had met secretly with him, then an undercover officer, behind a school house to exchange information. The Newtown boys had been worried the chief would learn of their perfidy in dealing with the state cops. In Hiltz's view, Marchese had "a passionate hate for the state police. Everything else was secondary." So perhaps DeJoseph was stonewalling in loyal deference to his boss. Perhaps he believed Newtown could solve the case before the Western District Major Crime Squad could get into it. Perhaps he really believed in Crafts's innocence.

"Smelling a rat," Hiltz phoned Bill Dyki at the polygraph center. Had Richard Crafts taken a lie detector test? Indeed he had: "It was almost like talking to a control tower. Methodical, without emotion." Now, given the facts, as relayed by Hiltz, Dyki said, "I wouldn't be surprised if you told me he killed his wife."

Quiet but determined, Hiltz wished his unit to shine at Hartford, headquarters for the eleven-hundred-odd state police, and he could be aggressive about getting police business. Not that he was short of cases or ever would be—every sixty hours Connecticut had a murder, every twelve a rape, every ten a suspicious fire—but a case that required good detective work never hurt. Apart from considerations of justice, Hiltz had an institutional imperative: results the state legislature could read about and translate into figures in the budget. So he wouldn't easily pass up an interesting homicide, as the Crafts case certainly looked to be.

Born in 1942, Hiltz, like DeJoseph, had worked in U.S. Army intelligence. He enlisted in the state police in 1966 and had had an exciting undercover career infiltrating the narcotics trade and radical student groups (with whom he came to sympathize) and a quieter one as a youth officer when, in 1976, he became serious about his police career. He returned to college part-time and studied on his own for a sergeants' qualifying exam, which he passed easily.

About then an episode occurred that deeply affected the state police and indirectly Hiltz. In September 1973, Peter Reilly, eighteen, was accused of murdering his mother, Barbara Gibbon, in their Falls Village home. Upon finding her body, Reilly had called for medical assistance. Questioned and searched, he was regarded as a suspect. He volunteered to take a lie detector examination. He got a four-hour rest after twenty-five sleepless hours and was then given the test and interrogated by four police officers for eight hours. The interrogation was tape-recorded. The state police said that he failed the test, and at 11:00 P.M. Reilly confessed he had jumped on his mother's thighs, breaking them, and slit her throat with a straight razor.

After nearly five months in jail Reilly was released on $50,000 bond raised by his supporters. Five Canaan families put up property to secure the bond. Though Reilly now denied killing his mother, a jury found him guilty of first-degree manslaughter, and he was sentenced to six to sixteen years in prison. Efforts on his behalf by the Lakeville *Journal*, by Joan Barthel, whose article in *The New York Times Magazine* strongly questioned Reilly's guilt, by Arthur Miller, William Styron, and other figures from literature and journalism continued through 1975.

A hearing began in January 1976. A leading psychiatrist said Reilly's confession was the result of police coercion. A judge granted a new trial, saying a "grave injustice has been done." The state's attorney who had prosecuted the case had died, and his successor, Dennis Santore, found evidence in the files that was favorable to Reilly. Finally, after squabbles that reached the governor, Reilly was cleared of the murder.

The furor raised by the Reilly case led to proposals for three changes in the Connecticut justice system. The first two have not always been observed in practice. The state police would rely far less on confession and much more on evidence. The police, local and state, would exercise less influence over the state's attorneys. And the state would create three major crime squads of highly trained officers independent of police departments. They would employ scientific techniques of gathering and handling evidence and would be backed by an up-to-date forensic unit.

Police embarrassment over the Reilly case—Hiltz agreed that the state cops had "grossly violated the rights of the accused"—led to a shakeup at the Canaan barracks, where Hiltz had again been assigned to narcotics, and he became platoon sergeant. He was then sent to the newly formed major crime squad, where he headed criminal investigations in the northwest corner of the state. Intelligent, resourceful, competitive—he was proud of winning four gold medals in the state police olympics—he rose rapidly to become commander of the Canaan barracks and in 1985, as a lieutenant, commanding officer of the Western District Major Crime Squad.

Hiltz is amiable and soft-spoken, but the quotations on his office blackboard are: "An ounce of loyalty is worth a pound of cleverness," and from coach Vince Lombardi, "A good loser is still a loser." Jockstrap stuff, but the commander was always telling his men that they were a team. What is a team meant to do? To win. The first goal of the police is supposed to be crime prevention, but that wasn't Hiltz's territory. His job was to produce evidence for convictions.

On December 16 he spoke with Officer Benno—on that day Crafts had been suspended from the Southbury force, officially for having driven with his children in a squad car but also because he was suspected of murder—who, like a growing number of police acquainted with the case, believed Crafts was guilty. Hiltz called DeJoseph, again seeking permission to assist, but DeJoseph said no. "Newtown holding back," Hiltz noted in his daybook.

160

DeJoseph hadn't invited Hiltz to the party, but he wanted to come. He thought he could make a contribution even if he wouldn't be popular. Major crime squad efforts didn't cost the locals a dime and freed manpower to pursue leads, not that Hiltz really believed Newtown could compete with his unit, the investigatory abilities of which, he proudly believed, surpassed those of the FBI. He did not believe the major crime squad had to be in the public eye. On several occasions it had been in and out of forensic investigations without press or public knowledge. *Forensics* would prove the key word in the tempest that followed.

Having spoken to DeJoseph, Hiltz called Flanagan to complain that the detective wouldn't tell him anything. He met with Flanagan the following day. The state's attorney was irritated by what he regarded as Newtown's incompetence — their failure to retrieve Helle's car rankled — and he was irked though not surprised by Marchese's failure to request the Western District Major Crime Squad's help. Still, though Hiltz pressed him to choose sides, he was reluctant to lock horns with the unpredictable chief. If the state's attorney intervened, other police departments in his jurisdiction might be resentful. Marchese might be defiant and threaten court action, take the battle to the newspapers, make accusations against him. Flanagan told Hiltz to hang in. Hiltz says, "I had my doubts he'd flip it to us."

On December 18, after Dianne Andersen had expressed concern about Marie Thomas's safety, Flanagan felt he could wait no longer. He was the top law-enforcement officer in the district and ultimately responsible for its justice system. Newtown appeared remiss in its investigation, and he decided to force Marchese to cooperate with the state police. He wrote a letter, which was hand-delivered by Blumequist, requesting Marchese come to Danbury the following morning.

The Newtown police insist that the letter laid out a deal: investigation would remain Newtown's responsibility; forensics would be the responsibility of the Western District Major Crime Squad. Oddly, Flanagan's copy of the letter has disappeared from his files. Marchese told DeJoseph he couldn't find his.

On Friday the nineteenth, Keith Mayo brought Marie Thomas to Flanagan. Mayo had never met the prosecutor before but was quickly convinced that Flanagan had become a believer. By then only two attitudes mattered to Mayo: whether you believed Richard Crafts had killed his wife or whether you didn't.

After earning a law degree from the University of Connecticut in 1963, Flanagan had practiced with William Lavery — the judge who would sign Crafts's arrest warrant — for about five years, then became an assistant prosecutor in Bridgeport. In 1979, he was appointed state's attorney in the newly formed Danbury district. Many gauged him among the best of the twelve prosecutors in the state and admired his ethics and judgment.

A tall, gray, professorial, and usually jaunty forty-nine, Flanagan looked somber when Mayo showed him the surveillance photos that quite possibly figured in a murder motive. Dianne Andersen arrived and paced around, smoking cigarettes; energetic Dianne often preferred to stand.

Flanagan agreed the case appeared serious and expressed concern about the publicity that could spring from articles such as O'Neil's. He was worried that the investigation would be affected if Crafts had too many clues to what the police were thinking and also that the newspaper reports would influence potential jurors. On the latter point his fears were well founded.

Marchese was expected. Flanagan, having talked with Marie about her knowledge of the case, told Mayo to take the girl to another room, not wanting the chief to infer from seeing her that a deal had been struck with the state police before Flanagan had discussed it with him. And wasn't it strange, Flanagan went on, that while Crafts required weeks to report his wife missing, he'd informed the police of Marie's departure the day after she left his house.

Flanagan decided that Marie should phone Crafts without revealing where she was. In the presence of Blumequist and Dalessio, who taped the conversation for possible clues, Marie told Crafts that she had not felt comfortable spending the night in the house without another woman there and alluded to the newspaper reports.

Crafts told her he had reported her missing and asked her to call the Newtown police and "tell them you're okay."

He also told his sister Karen that Marie was missing and complained to her, in what the police would come to believe was most revealing language, "They think I've chopped off Helle's head."

Marchese brought Noroian to the meeting in Flanagan's office. Brunetti, who was also present, recalls Flanagan saying that Marchese needed the state police, which had more manpower and expertise than he had, and summarized Flanagan's message as: "The state police would take over the forensic side and Newtown would continue gathering physical evidence. The two should cooperate. It would be a joint investigation."

Noroian summed it up matter-of-factly in his report: "Mr. Flanagan stated that he was dissatisfied with this case investigation and that he was calling in the state police major crime squad. This concluded our meeting with state's attorney Walter D. Flanagan." The meeting was not unfriendly, and on the drive back, according to Noroian, Marchese said, "We have to cooperate."

In the early afternoon another gathering took place in Flanagan's office. Present were the state's attorney, Brunetti, Dalessio, and, from the major crime squad, Hiltz, Martin Ohradan, and Robert Connor. The meeting lasted about an hour. Flanagan said nothing about seeing Marchese, and Brunetti said nothing at all. Flanagan said the Western District Major Crime Squad would lead the investigation in the Crafts case.

Mayo had been waiting to talk with Hiltz. Flanagan had told him he could leave and Hiltz would telephone him, but Mayo, on edge as usual, had elected to stay around. Mayo's faith that the rug from Canterbury would match the sample from the Craftses' bedroom had a Holy Grailish quality, and others were carried along by his assurance. Flanagan also believed the rug would provide evidence of murder, but during the meeting Hiltz called Dr. Henry Lee, chief of the Meriden forensic laboratory, who, comparing samples, had tentatively determined that they did not match.

When Hiltz passed this on to Mayo, he flared up and accused Hiltz of lying so as to cut him out of the case. Hiltz said soothingly, "We still need details and a strategy for a search warrant" and asked Mayo to come to Waterbury headquarters in the morning.

That night Mayo called to apologize, but Hiltz knew that Mayo had called him a liar to other people as well. Weary of Mayo's explosiveness and unwilling to have him associated with the case because it might not look good in court, he told him, "We'll run with this, thanks a lot, and don't call me at home again."

DeJoseph compared what followed to the battle of Thermopylae in 480 B.C.; that he should go to Thermopylae for a parallel provides a solid clue to Newtown's thinking.

Leonidas, the Spartan king, determined to hold the pass at Thermopylae, key to central Greece, against the invasion force of Xerxes, the Persian emperor. Leonidas had seven thousand men, three hundred of them Spartans. Xerxes waited for the Greeks to retreat from his vastly larger force. They stood firm. When he attacked, the Greeks repulsed him. A traitor named Ephialtes told the Persians of a way over the mountain, and a Persian battalion, the Immortals, took the path at night to flank the Greeks and attack them from the rear. The Greeks had just enough time to retreat, but Leonidas chose to remain, because the laws of his country required him to conquer or die. The Spartans and hundreds of other warriors stayed with him. They fought heroically, but all were killed except one man who escaped to Sparta. He was received with contempt because he hadn't shared the fate of his comrades. A monument to the dead Spartans read, "Go, stranger, and tell the Spartans that we obeyed the laws, and lie here!"

DeJoseph relates the story with a grim cackle. For him, Mayo was Ephialtes, Flanagan Xerxes, the major crime squad the Immortals, the Newtown police the Spartans who wouldn't retreat and got slaughtered.

A third meeting took place that day. At four Hiltz, Ohradan, and Robert Connor arrived at the Newtown Police Department under the inquisitive eyes of Pat O'Neil.

Noroian said to them that Crafts was as American as apple pie and they would like him; he liked the police. But the detective didn't exactly rule out the pilot's guilt.

Hiltz remarked to Noroian that while the effort was to be a joint one, the major crime squad would call the shots.

Noroian replied, "Well, it's good that you'll do the forensics and we the investigation."

Hiltz smiled. "Harry, that's not what I said. We'll be working together on the investigation, but Marty Ohradan will be in charge." Noroian seems not to have wanted to understand.

Marchese came in but remained on his feet. He kept referring to Mayo as that son of a bitch who tried to embarrass him. Hiltz recognized from the profanity, which Marchese employed only infrequently, that Lou was upset about Mayo. In Marchese's eyes, Mayo had no business approaching the state's attorney's office, circumventing Newtown's investigation, and bragging about his rug on television, and he couldn't have been much of a cop because he'd left law enforcement early.

"Give them what they want," Marchese said, meaning Newtown's reports, and agreed, twirling an unlit cigar in his mouth, that Ohradan would work out of Newtown. Because

Ohradan had served under Marchese, he thought he understood his mannerisms. Marchese wore a little smile, but his eyes sparkled with anger. Ohradan predicted there and then that Newtown would balk. Indeed, the file for which the three men had come to Newtown wasn't ready. Ohradan was told to return for it the following morning.

O'Neil, who talked to Marchese after the meeting, found him low in spirits. "Marchese was the glummest I'd seen him. He said, gnawing his cigar, 'Do you believe this? All those guys used to work for me.'"

The major crime squad men emerged, laughing and frustrated. Hiltz wrote in his daybook sarcastically, "Louie was awfully nice."

After they had left, Marchese authorized overtime on the Crafts case.

Mayo came to Waterbury at the appointed hour of 8:00 A.M. to lay out what he knew about the case. Although the major crime squad and Newtown had seemingly agreed to cooperate, Newtown wasn't asked to attend because, mindful of the friction between Mayo and the Newtown police, Hiltz wanted to avoid a shouting match.

Mayo, transmitting an idea put forward by Jan Rieber, his polygraph expert friend, suggested that the major crime squad should search for a witness who had noticed Crafts on the road on the night of the great storm. Everyone now involved in the investigation presumed that Crafts had somehow disposed of his wife's remains during those hours.

Noroian had expected Ohradan at 8:00 A.M. on Saturday, December 20, but it was 2:00 P.M. before he arrived, having previously interviewed Mayo for four hours. The two groups of cops continued to pull against each other then and in recollection.

Noroian remembers Ohradan thought that Helle's dental

records, which had been obtained from Dr. Fox at Crafts's request, had been destroyed by Crafts, but Noroian said, "Here they are." The Newtown detective was out of the room only a few times and made copies of the whole file, and handed a complete one to Ohradan, with whom he made arrangements to seize Helle's car on Monday. He believed Ohradan left in "good spirits," and he phoned DeJoseph at home to tell him, "We're going to get the car."

Ohradan remembers Noroian leaving the room repeatedly to take phone calls that he believed were from Marchese. (Noroian remembers that the calls, one from his wife, were private and not from Marchese.) When asked for the dental records Ohradan recollects Noroian excused himself, returned, and said that DeJoseph had them. The dental charts were not furnished to Ohradan. (The major crime squad didn't get its hands on them until the following week.) Ohradan left with a meager collection of documents, partly because many case reports had not yet been typed.

Ohradan—nicknamed "Porky" because during investigations he wore a porkpie hat—didn't really want the Newtown PD around his neck. He hadn't believed in cooperation from the start, and Noroian gave him a way out. If he was running the investigation, as he thought had been agreed, Noroian should not have been checking his every move with Marchese (Noroian denies having done that). So, working himself into a rage, Ohradan called Hiltz at home, described his encounter with Noroian, and said, "I'm not going back to Newtown."

Always supportive of his troops, Hiltz stood behind Ohradan, who he felt was straightforward, shared information, and never tried to steal anyone's thunder. Hiltz felt indignant at the news that Noroian wouldn't even talk on the phone in the same room as Ohradan. As far as Hiltz was concerned, the joint investigation ended the very day it began.

Notes from DeJoseph to Noroian dated December 20: "Harry—call American Express and MasterCard—check on

167

bank activity. Anything new. Check with Hertz and Avis in Danbury to see if Crafts returned car to them on the 20-21-22-23-24 Nov. Talk to preacher at Trinity church. See if Helle spoke with him. Call Danish embassy and see if they can get info on bank account. How much in account. Any recent activity . . ."

Without the knowledge of the state police, the Spartans of Newtown prepared to defend the pass.

On Saturday night Mayo attended a Christmas party, glum, restless, withdrawn, convinced that Crafts would not be accused of any crime.

Which arm of the investigation had the right to retrieve Helle's car remained unclear, and Ohradan refused to set foot in the Newtown PD; Noroian waited for him all day Monday. Ohradan delayed for a few days, and when he sent men to Kennedy, the Toyota Tercel had been driven away.

Mayo was among those who watched Dr. Henry Lee examine the rug spread out on a lawn in Meriden on Monday. Lee knew instantly that the rug had never belonged in the Craftses' bedroom; theirs had been a wall-to-wall carpet and this rug had not been fastened to a floor. Nonetheless, a bit of a showman, he announced for the benefit of his audience, "We'll have to look under a microscope, but on first impression, though the carpet and Mr. Mayo's samples have similar backing, the weave is different and the substance doesn't appear to be blood."

Official word that the rug was the wrong one reached Newtown on the same day, causing a chuckle, because it seemed that Flanagan had lost face. DeJoseph wrote in his daybook,

"Interesting case. Rug turned up negative. Haha!"

Hiltz wrote in his daybook, also on December 22, "Problem with Newtown, it's conducting its own investigation. No sharing. They seem to be going one hundred miles an hour." He had begun to receive reports from inside the Newtown Police Department. He learned that Marchese had told his men, "Let's get that SOB [Crafts] before those guys do."

DeJoseph claimed that Newtown's efforts accelerated only because its investigation had reached a critical point, but the timing indeed suggested that the department was engaged in a race with western major crime.

On Sunday, December 21, first thing in the morning, De-Joseph told Stormer, now on the case full-time, to "continue" the investigation, and Stormer started at once. He canvassed Newfield Lane, talking to eight families. John DeLorenzo had seen tire tracks in the Craftses' driveway the morning after the storm but couldn't recall if there had been one set or two. The Rasekhs reported that power had been restored at 11:00 A.M. on the nineteenth. Ann and John Moran would not have been surprised if Helle had decamped, leaving the children, because she had always been away from home a great deal. Ann Moran said that some time in the past Helle had told her she was very happy to leave her children with Crafts, because he was a good father, and added that during the past summer she had seen the couple walking around the yard holding hands. Chris Warchol, sometime baby-sitter for the Craftses, said they got on fine. Richard Crafts had asked her to sit with the children in early December but she had had to go to a dance. Several neighbors had seen a dump truck and a small silver car parked in the Newfield Lane cul-de-sac after November 19. Nothing much.

Obtaining the name of Helle's doctor from Rita Buonanno, Stormer called Dr. Donald Evans at home to ask for Helle's blood type. Evans, on reading of the case, had examined his file, which lacked the information, but promised to check

169

Helle's medical history further.

Stormer discussed the case with DeJoseph. They thought Crafts might have rented the car seen in the cul-de-sac to return to Newtown after dropping Helle's Toyota at Kennedy. (No record of a car rented by Crafts turned up.)

That Sunday DeJoseph, telling Crafts that he knew he wasn't divulging everything he should about Helle's disappearance, urged him to come in for more interviews. Crafts replied that he was leaving for Florida and intended to stick by his story.

On Monday Stormer reached Helle's gynecologist, Dr. Gerald Foye, who said her blood type was O positive. The Connecticut Motor Vehicles Department told Stormer, as did the New York state police, that neither Richard nor Helle Crafts had a record of traffic violations. Stormer had wondered whether Helle had incurred one recently. At town hall he obtained deeds for the Craftses' properties and the next day a survey of the Currituck Road lot, which, as it turned out, had once contained a mica mine, raising the interesting possibility that Crafts might have put a body in a shaft.

DeJoseph wrote Placerville, enclosing a copy of Helle's dental records, though absolutely certain that Placerville's murder victim was not Helle.

He went to the Currituck Road property, looking for holes, and noticed there a pile of wood chips, a foot high and three or four feet in diameter, covered by branches. He saw a man working on a backhoe but did not identify himself to him. DeJoseph had been wearing a raincoat; soon a rumor spread among the state police about a man in a raincoat on Crafts's property. Who could it have been? Why had he been there?

DeJoseph had already fastened on one of Crafts's ingrained habits: credit cards. He suspected that Crafts charged purchases, even ones that might point to murder, because he could deduct them from his income tax. None of this had been passed on to the state police.

Now, finally following up on the information that Crafts had purchased $257.96 of merchandise at Brookfield Caldor in November, DeJoseph drove there and made a discovery. The detective located a charge slip at Caldor showing that Crafts had purchased the bedding on November 19. The find was important in two respects. Crafts might have been replacing objects bloodied during a murder, and he had told DeJoseph he'd stayed home all afternoon after returning from Westport — he had been caught in one more lie.

DeJoseph worked deep into the night at the station house. The next day was his last before he went on a vacation that had already been delayed by the Crafts case.

On Saturday, December 20, Karen Rodgers had gone to Newfield Lane to collect the three children from Marie Thomas, who was about to leave for the West. Marie showed her brownish stains on the mattress in the master bedroom and on a piece of cloth, neatly folded and washed, in the laundry. Karen, though very suspicious of her brother by now, felt she couldn't involve herself against him. She suggested that Marie call Sue Lausten. Sue Lausten phoned Ohradan, who, then interviewing Mayo, wouldn't advise her on the propriety of entering the house but felt certain that if Marie had made the request it would be legal to go in. Sue's husband, Lewis, went in her stead, and Marie showed him the mattress, which, without frame or boxspring, lay on the floor. Mattresses from the boys' bunk beds had been put on foundations. Since November 20 or so, she said, Crafts and the three children had spent many nights in the same room, his implausible reason being that he'd removed the rugs from their rooms. The children had helped put the rugs on a rock pile in front of the house. Crafts said to the kids, as if giving them a pep talk, "We do fine without Mommy, don't we? See? We don't need her."

Lewis Lausten told Stormer that he had seen quarter-dollar-sized brownish spots on one side of the mattress, smaller spots, and a smudge that looked as though something had been wiped off. Naturally he couldn't determine if the stains had been made by blood.

171

Through the source for Crafts's credit card charges, Noroian received information that sent astonished whispers through the PD corridors. On November 18, Crafts had rented a woodchipper from Darien Rentals. He had returned the machine on November 21 and rerented it for December 3 and 4, as Noroian learned by calling the rental agency. That evening Noroian told his wife, "You'll never believe it, but looks like the Crafts guy put his wife through a chipper." For the first time, Noroian said, he felt certain Crafts was guilty.

That day, Ohradan and Detective T. K. Brown interviewed Jette Rompe, while detectives Joseph Quartiero and Shaun Byrne took on Rita Buonanno. The police had only superficial knowledge of the case and they were surprised by the number of inconsistencies in Crafts's statements that the women pointed out to them.

On Tuesday, December 23, Walter Flanagan concluded that Marchese's men had failed to follow his order for a joint investigation, though he'd muddied the waters himself by not establishing a clear line of authority. Still, even if Newtown believed the state police had been confined to forensics, they couldn't do that job properly without investigative knowledge, which Newtown had failed to provide.

Flanagan instructed Hiltz to establish probable cause and draw up a search warrant for the Crafts house. DeJoseph was not informed.

Noroian, Tvardzik, and Stormer worked on the case that day. Stormer was on the track of David and Floortje Smith, who had seen Crafts hit his wife. He spoke with Bonita Cartoun, a neighbor, who had been into 5 Newfield Lane within the past few weeks and was shocked by the mess. Crafts had always been negligent about the outside of his house, and now he was giving the same treatment to the inside.

Also on the twenty-third, with DeJoseph and Tvardzik on Christmas vacation, Stormer phoned neighbors he hadn't reached before and also called Rita Buonanno, Lena

Johannsen-Long, Lee Ficheroulle, Trudy Horvath, Jette Rompe, and Betty Bell. He talked with most of them, but nobody had anything new to report except for one development: the state police had begun to interview the women. Stormer also learned that Hiltz's unit had made the same request of Jens Holch, the Danish vice consul, as Newtown had already made. The two law-enforcement outfits were moving on parallel tracks.

Undeterred, Stormer reached the mail carrier for Newfield Lane. Crafts had said his wife had received no mail in her absence, but in fact she'd had letters from Copenhagen and many letters from England. Stormer went on to Father Frank Dunn, of Trinity Church, who denied having seen any signs of abuse on Helle or the children.

In Waterbury on Tuesday, the major crime squad detectives assigned to the case, a growing number, reviewed the Marie Thomas tape and their interview notes and the statements supplied by Newtown. They banged out paragraphs that were retyped and inserted into the search warrant. To double-check on Lis Nielsen, Ohradan phoned Holch, who, bewildered, called back to say Newtown had told him not to speak with any other law-enforcement agencies. (Newtown denied the allegation.) Hiltz reported the incident to Flanagan; his impression was that Flanagan had already decided to excommunicate Marchese and his men.

Although the state constitution contains a hoary amendment empowering a chief prosecutor to remove a case from a local department, no one could remember it having been used, and taking the case away from Marchese required considerable soul searching on Flanagan's part. But he proceeded because he believed only the major crime squad could investigate adequately. Also, he was infuriated by DeJoseph's report of December 5, made after the polygraph test, clearing Crafts of murder. Flanagan insisted it wasn't the detective's job to make such a judgment, especially so early in the case.

On December 24, Hiltz, Quartiero and Byrne applied to Judge Frank McDonald for his signature on a search warrant for Crafts's house. The judge, a former prosecutor, said, "This is one of these cases where you're damned if you do and damned if you don't." Somewhat to Flanagan's surprise, he signed the warrant.

The probable cause, meaning justifiable grounds, established in the warrant remained completely circumstantial. Hiltz's superior, Major John Watson, anticipating repercussions if the major crime squad failed to advance the case, told him, "Watch yourself."

One more step remained. At three in the afternoon of December 26, Flanagan arrived at the Newton PD with Blumequist and Dalessio. He delivered his own letter affirming the state police would have exclusive jurisdiction and said to Marchese bluntly, "You're off the case."

The chief twirled an unlit cigar in his lips and argued, "I think you're making a mistake."

Flanagan said stiffly, "I may be wrong, but I feel I have to do this in the interests of justice."

Harry Noroian said with bitterness, "You're questioning my ability and integrity."

"Not your integrity," said Tony Dalessio.

Henry Stormer went home and cried real tears for his wasted efforts. Mike DeJoseph brooded on the professional humiliation.

12

Searches

The warrant McDonald signed revealed how little the state police had to go on. Helle Crafts had hired Keith Mayo to obtain proof of Crafts's infidelity. Helle had planned to divorce Crafts. Helle and Crafts had had a fight before she went to Germany. A dark patch had been seen on the bedroom rug. Helle had made statements that seemed to have predicted an attack on her by her husband. Crafts had lied to Benno. Helle's car had been found at Kennedy Airport. "That based upon the foregoing facts and information the affiants [Quartiero and Byrne] have probable cause to believe and do believe that evidence of Murder will be found. . . ."

In Hiltz's mind, a fine line exists between morality and the criminal justice rulebook. With clear indication that Crafts had killed his wife, "We let morality sway us," he says.

The Western District Major Crime Squad began to assemble at the Crafts residence at 4:00 P.M. on December 26, 1986, immediately after Flanagan's meeting with Marchese, who was not told about the search.

First into the house was Ohradan. Though Crafts claimed in court that the garage door could not be locked because of a "frost heave"—he was far more precise with technical jargon than about time—Ohradan found it could not be opened. He gingerly removed a pane of glass from the kitchen door and got in, followed by Flanagan, Brunetti, and Dalessio. One of the first items encountered was a note, dated December 23, fastened to a cupboard: "Helle, I'm at mother's with the children. Please come. We love you. R. I have your car with me and keys for the truck and the Rabbit are on the stairs. The Ford is out of commission."

The four men in the kitchen surmised that Crafts had expected the search. Hiltz wrote in his daybook, "He knew we were coming and he left a note." But the facts were odder than that. On December 22 Crafts had left Westport for Florida with the children and their clothes. Would he have returned just to write a note for his wife? On the twenty-third he made a credit-card charge at a drugstore in New Jersey — Thomas had an earache. Moreover, since Helle had learned of the purchase of the Volkswagen only by rifling her husband's papers and hadn't divulged her knowledge to him when she left for Germany — unless she told him on the night she vanished — this reference to the Rabbit would have been meaningless to her. As for the Ford Crown Victoria, it performed when seized by the police.

The crime-scene van pulled up a short time later. The procedure called for the site first to be videotaped and then photographed with a hand-held camera to establish the exact position of objects and help avert charges by criminal defense lawyers that the police had planted evidence.

Then the premises were carefully examined. The first link in the chain was to establish so-called life-style, or an interruption in life-style that might indicate a major event has occurred. Many signs of that existed in the Crafts house. The chaos astonished the investigators: dining room table in the kitchen, kitchen table in the dining room, which was also filled with bunk beds, knocked down and leaning against a wall, and boxes and a bureau stuffed with toys. Another chest of drawers lay on its side in the family room, where the hearth (which had not been used on the night the power failed) overflowed with ashes of burned paper. Mute testimony to better days, a photograph of a smiling Crafts family hung on the wall of the family room. A closet contained unopened Christmas presents, one of which bore a card

"From Richard to Helle"; according to Crafts, it contained Danish licorice, hard to obtain in the United States.

Across the foyer lay a narrow hall. The first room on the left belonged to Kristina, they correctly guessed, rugless and empty except for a child's bed. A police uniform hung in the closet. The first door on the right led to a bathroom, where they found rumpled towels and in the tub a bucket containing washcloths. The second room on the left was the boys' room. Also rugless, it contained a single bed.

Marie Thomas told about Crafts having taken up the rug in the master bedroom (even though, earlier in the year, Helle and Sue Lausten painted the room and the hall with colors to complement it). Marie Thomas had seen a dark patch. But she had neglected to mention that about two-thirds of the padding beneath, including the place where it was presumed the patch had been, had also been torn out. The remaining strip, which was in good condition, led into the alcove that housed Helle's vanity and into the bathroom. Why had the rest been taken? Because blood had seeped through?

A woman's neat touch was conspicuously absent. The boys' mattresses lay on foundations, but the queen-size mattress lay on the floor. Kristina's toys seemed to announce that she had been sleeping there with her father. (The collapsible frame that had once supported the queen-size mattress had been spotted by Marie under the cellar steps, but now it was gone.) Clearly the family, or what remained of it, had been sleeping in the same room, causing Dalessio to mutter perceptively, "They're like a clan under siege."

Flanagan and Brunetti left. Remaining, besides Dalessio and Ohradan, were Byrne (the evidence officer on the case), Quartiero, James Craig, Robert Connor, William Kaminski, Joseph Destefano, James White—the Western District Major Crime Squad's forensic unit. Elaine Pagliaro, a member of Lee's staff, among whose forensic specialties was hair, joined them. The omnipresent O'Neil showed up and the police let him stand outside. "What are you doing?" the reporter asked, and was told, "Oh, nothing." A deathly quiet shrouded the neighborhood.

Using their regular procedures, the detectives segmented the house into areas, and those areas into smaller areas, teams of two then examining the smaller areas twice for a murder weapon, bloodstains, signs of violence, and so on. Downstairs, Kaminski shouted, "Look at the guns! This guy's a nut." When an officer from a different unit began to disassemble an armed grenade, Kaminski ran, not realizing the man was an ordnance expert.

They worked until ten that night and returned in the morning, Saturday, when Kaminski, photographing the house from the outside, observed deep tire tracks curving around a spruce tree. He also photographed two dirty kerosene heaters on the front porch. Then he went to the Currituck Road lot, where he discovered the Ford Crown Victoria parked behind a backhoe. He had taken the keys, which had been hanging by the cellar stairs, and now opened the trunk. The mat was missing but woodchips were present. To Kaminski they were still meaningless.

Seized that day were most of the 113 items to be listed in the warrant: the note addressed to Helle, fibers, washcloths, carpet samples, an open box of Shop Rite plastic trash bags, blue comforters, family photos, a safe-deposit box key, a pair of men's tan crepe-sole shoes, nine pieces of mail, Helle's calendars, ashes from the fireplace, Crafts's flight logs, the Toyota pickup, hand grenades — one with firing mechanism — a crossbow, loaded clips for assorted guns, a folding buck knife, and fifty guns, which included Smith & Wessons, a Walther PPK, a Colt, Rugers, a Sako (Finnish), Remingtons, a Winchester, a Heckler and Koch, a Nanurrn Pistole (French), a Browning, a Beretta, a Thompson — enough to warm a gun collector's heart. The weapons were taken as a matter of routine. One of them might have been used in a homicide and might be needed for tests. They failed to seize the two chain saws in the garage, because nobody yet suspected Helle had been dismembered.

Hiltz and Ohradan concurred that in moving objects around, Crafts had aimed at distorting the evidence. It was harder to look for dried blood, say, on furniture not in its proper context.

Lee came to the Crafts house on Saturday. Until then, though the towels, which had been washed, had promise, nothing of real evidentiary significance (and nothing that would be used in the murder trial) had been discovered. The search looked to have been wasted.

As a last resort Ohradan asked Sue Lausten to re-create the room as it had been when Helle lived there. Sue noticed that a dust ruffle that had been draped around the mattress was missing and that the blue foundations under the boys' beds were new. The police now placed the foundations beneath the queen-size mattress to replace the missing box spring and put the bed in its proper position, to the left of the door, with bed tables on either side. Women's magazines indicated that Helle slept on the side nearer the bathroom. The dark patch on the rug reported by Marie Thomas appeared to have been off the foot of the bed on the bathroom side. Bare floor lay between the bed and the remaining padding.

Now it was Lee's turn. Armed with three cases of equipment, he prowled the room, searching for telltale signs on the walls that furniture might have been removed and looking everywhere, including the ceiling, for traces of blood. The spots on the mattress were examined with a magnifying glass, and he performed on them what is known as a presumptive test, using orthotolidine solution (tolidine, ethanol, glacial acidic acid, distilled water), in which a bright blue color indicates a reasonable possibility of blood. Result positive. Lee deduced the droplets had landed with medium velocity, striking at an angle of about 10 degrees (Hiltz believes Lee can do trigonometry in his head). Lee would say only that "something happened," but he deduced that Helle Crafts, if she had been murdered and murdered in that room, had been kneeling on, sitting on the edge of, or stooping or standing close to the bed. She had not been lying down.

That blood fell directly on the surface of the mattress when "something happened" indicated that intervening materials—blanket, sheets, mattress pad—had been pulled back.

Lee directed the police to remove a 76-by-79-inch section of the mattress cover for analysis at the laboratory. (There was no blood in the innards of the mattress.) He also examined washcloths from the bucket in the bathroom and newly laundered towels. They too tested positive for blood and went to Meriden.

That night Hiltz and Ohradan joined Henry Lee at another crime site — assuming 5 Newfield Lane was one. A middle-aged couple had been having an affair for years. The woman was married. She had met her lover in his van to exchange Christmas presents, and perhaps he didn't like his, because he had shot her, then shot himself. Lee had still a third possible homicide that weekend, a baby that had been left outdoors and had frozen to death.

When the search of the house ended at 5:30 P.M., December 28, on Sunday, forty-eight hours after it had begun, a copy of the warrant was deliberately left on top of the microwave oven.

Ohradan was inclined to believe that Crafts had killed his wife in the bedroom and had contrived to remove, in the dead of night, box spring, comforter, sheets, and other items that might have had blood on them, and had taken his wife's car. But Ohradan had little to crow about. Even if Lee established, as he did, that the blood on the mattress cover was human, comparatively recent, and of Helle's type, that wasn't proof of murder. Ohradan needed a corpse, he thought.

The next day the theory of the case was altered almost beyond recognition.

On Monday the twenty-ninth Ohradan, who had changed his headquarters to Troop A in Southbury, because it was nearer Newtown, attended a staff meeting there. Later that morning he traveled to the Currituck Road lot to inspect a water-filled mine shaft that had been camouflaged with branches. The hole was drained, and he brought in a bloodhound named Lady that sniffed both properties for a body, finding none. (Lady had a bad temper. A few days later she bit Kaminski.) Ohradan saw wood chips but they made no more impression on him than they had on Kaminski and DeJoseph.

The Ford was seized, driven to the road, placed on a flatbed truck, and taken to Troop A. Here the major crime squad blundered. As would soon be known, its trunk contained important evidence, but the search warrant did not cover the car when it was off the lot.

Ohradan's conviction that Newtown was withholding information remained unshakable, and at one o'clock he sent Quartiero and Byrne with instructions to get tough with Noroian. When Noroian left the room to make copies of documents, Quartiero proceeded to pick through papers on his desk. Noroian caught him and was angry. "You wouldn't like it if I went through stuff in your office," he complained, and Quartiero said, "Hey, Harry, I'm only a grunt. A worker. I do what I'm told."

Byrne reported, "Detective Noroian stated that to the best of his knowledge the reports he had given us represented all the investigative work done on the case by the Newtown Police Department." It wasn't so. Noroian neglected to tell Western Major Crime about the chipper Crafts had rented and about the bedding purchased at Caldor, both of which were vital to the investigation. Noroian insisted that he had provided the report about the woodchipper (DeJoseph's on the bedding had not as yet been typed), but the state cops hadn't read it; still, Noroian might have *said* something.

Thus far, the major crime squad couldn't claim to have proceeded much further than Newtown had. They'd seized materials that tested positive for blood, but the laboratory analyses weren't in yet, and nobody could say for certain whether the results would be any good in court, supposing they got that far. The problem remained what it had been from the start: no cadaver and no clue to how a body might have been disposed of.

That afternoon, at Hiltz's urging, Ohradan, feeling a little desperate, stopped at the Southbury PD and asked Smarz and Benno if anything unusual had been observed on the night of the great storm. That Richard Wildman had seen Crafts with a chipper was brought to Ohradan's attention for the first time. That the incident had not been reported earlier was totally and understandably attributable to absence of a lurid imagination among the Southbury police. A man chop up his wife? Ohradan was incredulous, too, until Benno told him that Joey Hine, a roads-department driver, had spotted a chipper after midnight on River Road.

They can show you some pretty disgusting photos at Marty's Waterbury bailiwick, but this one got to Ohradan. He had

181

grown up on a farm with an apple orchard; he had a bachelor of science degree in horticulture from the University of Connecticut. His first love had been fruit trees, wood.

A woodchipper!

Ohradan instantly remembered an episode that had taken place the previous summer. Twenty-five-year-old Steven Serfillipi had knocked out (he said) a young German shepherd named Duke, whose barking annoyed him, before putting the dog through a chipper along with wood. (Letters from dog lovers poured in to the Danbury *News-Times* — "grisly," "ghastly," "horrifying," disgusting" · -but none were sent later about the disposition of Helle Crafts.) "If he did it to an animal," opined Judge McDonald, raising Serfillipi's bail to $20,000 (he finally received a suspended sentence, a year's probation, and mandatory psychiatric counseling), "he perhaps might do it to a human being."

Had Serfillipi provoked an idea in the mind of Richard Crafts? Could something so horrific really have happened? But Ohradan had to remind himself that the answer to the question of where the body was might lie at hand.

Ohradan instructed T. K. Brown and Patrick McCafferty to interview Joey Hine in the morning.

At 4:30 P.M. Henry Stormer, invited by Ohradan, arrived at Troop A, his mood a reflection of the Newtown detectives'— angry, resentful, and somber. Stormer was worried Marchese would learn of the visit, but he went with DeJoseph's knowledge. Stormer confirmed that Crafts had rented a woodchipper in Darien. By then the cops were aware that they had stumbled onto a potentially explosive story and that the news media had to be kept in the dark to prevent Crafts from learning about the new development.

Brown and McCafferty found Hine, a brawny fellow in his late thirties with tattoos on both arms, at the town garage after noon on Tuesday. Yes, Hine had seen a chipping machine on River Road in the early morning hours of November 19 while he was clearing snow from the road. He was positive the sighting had been on that night because he had already worked his usual shift, from 7:00 A.M. to 4:30 P.M. His wife had had to get him out of bed. Snow had not been expected that early, so he had had to rig up his plow. He had completed clearing River Road, a normal route, and then proceeded up Purchase Brook Road, where he encountered a fallen tree and had to turn back. But for that, he never would have observed the chipper attached to a "box-type" truck "partially off the shoulder, partially off the road" between 3:30 and 4:00 A.M. on River Road. Hine couldn't pinpoint the time exactly; he had been tired, and was not wearing a watch.

Hine headed south on River Road toward the truck. A car was coming from the opposite direction. Hine said he'd seen a few strange things in his eight years on the job but what he saw then was the strangest. A man in an orange poncho emerged from behind the truck, holding up one hand to the car and motioning Hine with the other, like a traffic cop.

The woodchipper was light in color; no, he hadn't been able to tell whether it was in operation (though judging by the absence of noise, it wasn't).

He'd seen the machine again at five-thirty down by the bridge, and heading toward the garage in daylight, he saw half-inch piles of wood chips, barely visible, in four to six locations on River Road.

Brown and McCafferty had trouble suppressing gasps.

In Brown's car, Hine led them unerringly to a culvert on the bank of Lake Zoar. As the detectives got out of the car they could see wood chips an inch thick, apparently spread with a pitchfork or shovel, on both sides of the culvert. They noticed paper and pieces of stained bright-blue material mixed with the wood chips. Climbing down the bank, they discovered an envelope with a nick in it, marked "American Cancer Society," which they thought might have significance, since Crafts had had cancer. Then Brown, on hands and knees, saw through the envelope's glassine window the name of the addressee: Miss Helle L. Crafts. McCafferty exclaimed, "Something's definitely wrong here."

While McCafferty stood guard, Brown gave Hine a lift to the town garage and then drove on to Troop A. He shouted to Ohradan, "I found her fucking name on a piece of paper!"

Hiltz, Ohradan, and Quartiero, led by Brown, were at the river site in minutes, and right away happened on return-address mail stickers, also nicked, bearing Helle's name and address. "Can you just imagine a chipper?" said Ohradan, in his porkpie hat, kneeling over them. "I'll retire if this guy put her through a chipper." (Hiltz recorded the remark in his daybook and would kiddingly remind him of his words.) Ohradan could not accept that Crafts had actually shredded his wife. He says, "I thought Crafts was jerking us around, trying to make us think he had done such a thing."

It was then about 1:00 P.M. Detectives Kaminski and Joseph Destefano, on Stormer's information, had gone to Darien Rentals that morning and confirmed that Crafts had rented a Brush Bandit on November 18. The machine was in the rental agency yard and was to be towed to Troop G in Westport, where Detective Craig waited with the crime-scene van to examine it. A hurried call came from Troop A; Kaminski and Destefano were to come to River Road as quickly as possible. Kaminski broke speed laws. Snow threatened, so the eight men from the major crime squad worked fast—photographing, sketching, inspecting the riverbank for a mile in both directions, finding objects in plain view, tagging them, and placing them in manila envelopes or garbage bags: the letter, the stickers, fabric, strands of blond hair, many tiny fragments, and wood chips—the staples of the forensic meal—and also a Shaklee vitamin label (the police were not aware that Helle sold Shaklee products).

The evidence was formally seized by Kaminski, and the thirty-some bags taken to Troop A, where they were placed in a locked office to defrost.

Crafts's lawyer, trying to establish that evidence had been planted, harshly criticized Hiltz for not sealing the area afterward with a round-the-clock guard; but snow, branches, and leaves covered the ground, no one but the police knew of the search, and Hiltz believed everything of significance had been removed. A parked police car would have attracted attention.

* * *

184

On January 2, from 3:00 P.M. to midnight, Destefano, Kaminski, and Craig labored in the garage at Troop A with Ohradan helping now and then and Hiltz going in and out. The assignment was unpleasant and received with groans. Inside the thirty-odd bags was not silver but substances unknown and under investigation. The floor was covered with butcher paper, leaves were discarded, and the rest was laid out on the plywood table supported on sawhorses for minute examination. The items embedded in the wood chips—lacerated blond hairs, for example—were tiny. Some hair was found in clumps of ten or twenty strands. Skeptical Ohradan insisted that bone fragments scored by the marks of a machine were steak bones, but the largest piece had furrows strongly suggesting calvarium bone from inside a skull. The major crime squad men believed they'd seen more interiors of craniums than most brain surgeons.

Kaminski found a small piece of grayish metal. He would have given odds that it was a dental crown and would have won.

On January 2 Dr. Lee examined the trunk of the Ford. He found, amid the wood chips, hair, human flesh, bone fragments, and blue fibers. On the morning of January 5 the first River Road evidence went to Meriden.

Every homicide that has water nearby requires a diving team so that the state police can't be accused by the defense of dereliction, and Hiltz requested one. On the afternoon of January 5 state police divers appeared at Troop A. Hiltz instructed them to look for body parts and he offhandedly told them to look for a chain saw as well. He assumed Crafts had directed the woodchipper's spout toward the lake (the bits that had been found might simply not have made it as far as the water) and that he had cut up the body before he inserted it into the machine.

The dive team, nineteen troopers in all, had received five weeks of U.S. Navy training in Florida and more training after that. They were Navy certified. On January 6, at 9:00 A.M., five

185

of them assembled near Silver Bridge on the Newtown side of the Housatonic River and launched a Zodiac diving sled with an outboard motor. They had not been informed which bank to search, and they weren't about to ask at Troop A, where they imagined everyone was drinking hot coffee while the diving team froze in the river. In any case, the current was too swift for much to be accomplished under the bridge, and the water too cold — 34 degrees — for them to remain immersed for extended periods, despite long-john underwear, a dry suit, and over that a Viking cold-water exposure suit.

The next day, having been shown the site, they searched along the bank with the sled, a slow and boring job, but the first find came on land. Sergeant Daniel Lewis, whose regular job was in the state police public-relations office, spotted a small shiny red object in the snow; a polished fingernail, it had to be. A small piece of flesh was attached.

Since the water beneath the bridge was swift enough to rip off face masks, the power company reduced the volume released from the dam and lowered the level. Early on January 8, while performing a line search — two divers wearing forty-pound belts working off a rope — Sergeant Scott O'Mara found a large green plastic bag filled with meaty bones. O'Mara marked the bag with a Pelican float and left the water with a nosebleed.

Hiltz asked Lee, who was about to testify in Hartford court, to come back immediately, but weather delayed his flight.

A Southbury mortician who was an auxiliary state cop provided a body bag, and about noon the bones were raised. Lee arrived soon after and quickly ascertained that the bones had belonged to a deer, no doubt shot out of season by a hunter who then sank the evidence. But there was more. Sergeant Paul Krisavage, on the line search with O'Mara, had spotted an orange flash thirty feet down in the water. Flippering there, he raised a chain saw, chain wrapped around the housing. It was a Stihl, serial number filed off.

The divers knew what they had to look for next and experimented with stones to see how far an object could be thrown from the bridge. On January 9 Krisavage found it protruding four inches from sand: a chain-saw bar. He carried the blade to

Quartiero, who was standing on a rock and deftly slipped the bar beneath his feet to avoid detection by a TV news helicopter that was hovering overhead. The bar went into a bucket of water so that it wouldn't rust in the air.

The police diving team, a proud and dedicated all-volunteer group, had good cause to be pleased with themselves.

The weather remained freezing, and so Hiltz asked the National Guard for a tent, which was erected on January 9. On the tenth began one of the most intensive forensic forays in history.

Involving as many as eight "mud monkeys," as the detectives called themselves, the search lasted a week for up to ten hours a day. Portable Salamander heaters, powered by a generator, were used to thaw the ground. Whoever had deposited the wood chips had spread them in three areas, and the alien material, scraped from the earth by rakes, trowels, and hands, was brought from them all. Under floodlights inside the tent was a plywood table on sawhorses, at which three men worked. After the leaves had been removed, the pieces were put on a screen supported by two chairs and rinsed in water pumped from the culvert. Suspicious items were examined under a lighted eight-inch magnifying glass. Hundreds of bits and pieces, some already photographed with a Polaroid in the crime-scene lab van, were placed in cardboard boxes for shipment to Lee's laboratory.

As in an archaeological dig, some finds proved more important than others. On January 10, Quartiero uncovered what Meriden would decide was a human toe joint. On the twelfth, Destefano touched something too smooth for wood. Magnified, it was part of a human finger. This finger couldn't be mistaken for anything else and finally convinced Ohradan, who had remained squeamishly dubious, that a human being, or parts of one, had been subjected to the chipper.

Dr. Constantine Karazulas, dentist and forensic odontologist partly employed by the Meriden forensic unit, had identified the piece of metal brought from Troop A as the crown of a human tooth. On Saturday the tenth, Lee, who had concluded other dental evidence might be found, asked Karazulas to come to

River Road. All day Karazulas stood in muddy cold water, picking up loose material, placing it in a barrel, running it over the sifter. No luck. On Wednesday, January 14, examining a new area, he slipped into the river and filled one of his boots with water. Cursing, he threw a pile of debris on the table. He said, "Something has to be here because I'm not staying much longer with a wet foot." And then he found an object. "I looked at it and felt immediately it was the cap for a human tooth." The tooth had porcelain and bone attached.

Through McLaughlin Ford, Detective David Carey located the U-Haul with Ohio license plates at the U-Haul Center in Danbury and impounded the vehicle at Troop A. He could see nothing of interest inside, but Destefano, using a magnifying glass and tweezers, succeeded in finding bonelike material and blue fibers in a corner, hair under a metal plate, and a reddish substance on a wall. The truck had a ramp with a loading arm, in a bracket of which were the same blond hairs and blue fibers. Destefano turned up blue fiber yet again in the housing of the chain saw.

On January 13 Richard Crafts was arrested on the charge of "Murder."

13

The Arrest

Since Helle had invited them for Thanksgiving, Karen and David Rodgers were surprised that she was not at home that day. Crafts, however, appeared in a good mood as he cooked the two turkeys under damp cloths. While he told Karen that Helle was in Denmark, when David asked him where she was, he simply shrugged, so Rodgers assumed that Helle was so seriously angry with her husband that she'd abandoned him or had been scared to the point of hiding.

After the meal, the Rodgerses volunteered to remove from the master bedroom floor the staples that had secured the rug padding. Neither told the other what he thought, but Karen was slightly confused as to why the rug had been taken up along with the padding in Kristina's room, which had been in perfect condition.

Over the next few weeks Karen and David would live in different worlds on the question of murder. Both knew full well, however, that Helle would never leave her children for very long and that Crafts would never pay to replace good padding, especially when he was on the verge of losing the house. Unless, of course, he had a vital reason to do so.

Rodgers, in his mid-fifties, former U.S. Navy commander, head of the naval reserve in his area, marine surveyor, and semi-retired businessman, had intimate knowledge of Helle and Richard Crafts. He believed Crafts automatically lied when confronted with something uncomfortable, though until then the lies had concerned other women. Rodgers judged Crafts capable of vindictiveness and vengeance.

Karen was slower to cast Crafts in a villain's role. She wanted to think of him as he had always been, her big brother.

In the next few days, Rodgers mulled over his impressions and came to suspect that Crafts had had something to do with his wife's disappearance. He had killed her by accident or in a fit of rage and had gotten rid of the body, or he'd had somebody else do the killing and disposal of the body, or somebody had tried to frame him. In any case, Crafts clearly did not want to go to the police.

Rodgers kept his dark thoughts from his wife.

In early December, Helle having failed to materialize, Rodgers called Crafts. He said, "What can I do to help? You can bullshit everybody else if you want, but don't bullshit me. I think you're in deep trouble." Crafts didn't even try to deny the accusation. He wouldn't talk at length on the phone because he believed his line was tapped; he suspected the listener was the private investigator Helle had hired, whose name Crafts didn't appear to know. Rodgers wondered if his own line was tapped too—he thought he heard clicks—and he and Crafts would speak by prearrangement from pay phones.

When they met a few days later, Crafts reinforced Rodgers's suspicions by seeming to fish around for a defense. "It's known she had familiarity with handguns," he muttered. "Maybe we can find her prints on one. Maybe she threatened me with a pistol. But I don't know where she is." But Rodgers detected grim humor in his expression.

They discussed the polygraph examination Crafts had now passed, which he shrugged off in such a way as to suggest that he hadn't been frightened—possibly, Rodgers thought in retrospect, because he knew the police couldn't produce a body. Rodgers decided that, like himself, Crafts belonged to the old school, brought up to believe that to obtain a conviction a prosecutor required a corpse.

* * *

On December 19 — the day Ohradan and Noroian discussed seizing Helle's automobile — Crafts asked Rodgers for help in bringing Helle's car to Westport. Anticipating trouble, Rodgers refused, but Crafts assured him he had the necessary permission from the police, who would have taken the car already if they wanted it. Rodgers agreed to assist him.

On December 20, his forty-ninth birthday, Crafts, as part of his Newtown municipal police training course, attended a field exercise at 8:00 A.M. To Jean Hoover, he looked distracted, depressed (unusual for him), and had poor posture and dirty hair. In one drill Crafts sat in a police car writing a ticket with a car stopped in front of him. A cop playing the driver left the other car, walked in front, alongside, and then around the rear of Crafts's vehicle, appearing at the pilot's window, revolver in his hand. Crafts never looked up. "Bang, bang," the cop said. "You're dead." Richard failed to react.

That afternoon Crafts and Rodgers drove to Kennedy Airport in Crafts's pickup. Crafts was to fly that day.

Without trouble Crafts found the Pan Am lot and Helle's car, which Rodgers then drove to Westport. Karen Rodgers didn't want the car put in her driveway for fear that the Crafts children, who would stay with them until they went to Florida with their father, would believe their mother had returned and be badly disappointed; so Rodgers parked it at a motel that was a New York airport-limousine stop. His rationale was protective: if an all-points bulletin on the Tercel was issued and the cops spotted it, Rodgers, who was no longer sure the car had been removed with police permission, could claim he'd left the Tercel where Helle could easily get to it — not that he had any expectation of her doing so. The next day he moved the car to a church nearer his house. The police were less likely to find it there.

Crafts reappeared in Westport at midafternoon on Monday,

191

December 22, his children's clothes messily piled on the front seat of the dump truck. He and the children left for Florida in the Tercel from the church parking lot. Crafts had made up his mind about the trip only at the last minute and had been unable to obtain airline reservations, he said.

Karen had always had an excellent relationship with her brother. If she wanted a piece of furniture moved or the children picked up at school, he would obligingly drive from Newtown to Westport, where he felt free to invite himself for dinner. While David told her little or nothing about his covert dealings with Richard, and Karen didn't ask questions, she was deeply divided inside about Helle's fate.

When Karen had gone to Newtown the previous Saturday, December 20, to collect the Crafts children, Marie Thomas told her about the spots on the mattress. Marie had also seen a photo on TV of the rug Mayo had found, and was convinced it was the rug from the Craftses' bedroom and had had blood on it. As much as anything else, the rug convinced Karen that Crafts had killed Helle, though in her heart-of-hearts she begged that he hadn't. Her hopes were briefly bolstered when a few days later the rug was dismissed as evidence, but in her mind she knew that her brother was guilty.

David, as Karen knew because he had told her, didn't want the burden of the Crafts kids and hoped Crafts would go free. She thought her husband was wrong to make such a statement out loud, and tension between them was high.

The Newtown police hadn't bothered to interview her — and Karen was afraid to go to them because she was certain they'd tell Crafts — but on Monday evening Quartiero and Byrne of the major crime squad came to the Rodgers house, to Karen's intense relief: something was being done. Karen spoke little, but hearing the facts from the detectives confirmed her worst fears. She also believed that David was evasive with the police.

Late that night or the next — Karen wasn't quite sure — she and David sat at opposite sides of his desk and she screamed at him, "Look! He's guilty as hell. Watch out! You'll be put away yourself."

Rodgers told her not to worry, but she did.

During the Christmas holidays, Karen kept her eyes on the driveway, half convinced that her brother "could slip another cog" and kill all of them. Indeed, he arrived with a gun in a holster, but it was his Southbury police .357 Magnum, which he stored in David's safe. If Karen felt almost resigned as to her brother's guilt, she couldn't entirely rid herself of the prayer that someone else had murdered Helle, who was almost certainly dead, and lost her temper at Quartiero for not having investigated Mayo.

Crafts and the children stopped at Nancy Dodd's place in Middletown. In Florida they stayed at his mother's house in Boca Raton while she went on a cruise. The still scrappy eighty-one-year-old Lucretia always left home over Christmas because that was the season during which her husband had died. She wouldn't admit he was dead, only that he was away.

The children spent some nights in Boca Raton, cared for by Lucretia's sister Mildred, going to Crafts's other sister, Suzanne, and her husband, Malcolm, in Delray Beach during the day. Crafts claimed with paternal piety that even when he flew out of Florida over the holidays he always managed to spend the nights with the children, but the statement, though backed by Suzanne Bird, wasn't true. He spent at least one night on the Rodgerses' couch during that period, and on December 26, before returning to New York, he and Rodgers drank beer for two hours at the Westport VFW. (The state police searched his house that night, but if Crafts knew of that he made no mention.)

The pair was fairly drunk but not to the point of incoherence. Rodgers had opposed taking the Tercel to Florida; by so doing, Crafts showed that he had no expectation that his wife would return for Christmas. Now Crafts said he would remove the insignia, and her Pan Am sticker from the windshield, obviously intending to dispose of the car, but Rodgers opposed that, too, on the same grounds. (Crafts did so anyway.)

193

He said he'd received a call in Florida from the Connecticut state police but intended to ignore it. "That's stupid," Rodgers said. "It'll look suspicious." Crafts then had the idea of returning the call when he knew nobody would be available to question him and did so on New Year's Day, during a football bowl game.

Rodgers pushed Crafts with questions. Any chance blood might be found in the pipes or cistern? Could they find anything on the lot? Crafts answered no to both questions. And then, when he thought Crafts was verging on a confession, Rodgers said, "I don't want to know any more." Rodgers still believed that while his brother-in-law had killed Helle, the murder had not been premeditated.

Rodgers was in an uncomfortable position. He says now that while he disliked Crafts's "habitual evasiveness and how he used people for his own ends," they'd gone target shooting together, bird hunting, shark fishing on Rodgers's boat, exchanged gifts and favors, and had some sexual adventures together, and he remained deeply fond of Crafts.

He had a choice: to go to the police with his unprovable suspicions or not. He thought, If Helle is dead, I can't bring her back. If Richard is jailed, I'll have the encumbrance of his three kids right off the bat. I don't want him locked away. I want him around to support them. One parent will be better than none. He's no threat to anyone else. He's likely to be all shook up and scared inside. I'll offer him a shoulder.

In Westport on December 29, Rodgers and Crafts spoke again. By then, Crafts knew his house had been searched but didn't seem alarmed. Rodgers advised him to hire a lawyer, which he immediately did. Rodgers also suggested hiring a private investigator at least to go through the motions of searching for Helle. Crafts agreed but didn't act on the idea.

Crafts spent the night of December 29 with Nancy Dodd. At La Guardia Airport on December 30 he ran into an old flame, Judy Kurzner. Recently, he had spent the night with her but had said nothing of Helle's disappearance. Since then she had read about the case and now she questioned him. He said he'd phoned all over the country looking for his wife, but Kurzner found Helle's absence at Thanksgiving and Christmas odd. He replied flippantly, "Maybe she didn't want to cook two turkeys."

Newtown continued to receive Crafts's credit-card receipts. One showed that on New Year's Eve he took someone, undoubtedly Nancy Dodd, to dinner in New Jersey.

Sergeant Quartiero left a message on Dodd's machine, asking her to call back, which she did. She claimed that Crafts did not try to prevent her from returning the call; but he could not have done so without making himself look guilty in her eyes. Crafts had told her that he was looking for Helle and repeated his never-verified assertion that Helle habitually left home for weeks at a time.

Just after New Year's, in the course of questioning by the major crime squad, Rodgers learned about the woodchipper rental, and he brought up the subject with Crafts after he returned from Florida.

"Oh? They found out about that?" Crafts said. "I'm going to tell them I got it to clear brush on my lot on Currituck Road, and that'll be a dead end for them. It's as far as they can go."

Learning that the police were busy in Lake Zoar, he told Rodgers, "Let them dive. The body is not there. It's gone."

On Tuesday, January 6, Ohradan received a call from Francis X. Shea, the lawyer Crafts had hired through a large advertisement in the yellow pages. Shea inquired on Crafts's behalf what the state police wanted with his client. Carefully avoiding any mention that Crafts was under suspicion of murder, Ohradan pointed out that Crafts's wife was missing and naturally the police thought it important to talk with him. He offered a meeting with Crafts whenever he wanted.

Flanagan had instructed Ohradan not to reveal what had already been discovered on River Road, where even then divers were probing beneath Silver Bridge. One purpose of interviewing Crafts was to force the man to commit himself to a story, so that the facts he stated could be checked. Another was to assess Crafts's personality and try to gauge whether he was capable of what the evidence appeared to indicate. Maybe he would suddenly confess. It had happened before.

At 1:00 P.M. on Tuesday Crafts arrived without his lawyer at Troop A, where Ohradan and Quartiero interviewed him. When asked, "Did Sergeant Ohradan advise you we are calling this an investigation?" Crafts simply said no. He asked no questions and showed no surprise. During the interview his voice was so soft as to be almost inaudible.

When Crafts reviewed the events of the night of November 18–19, he had a little trouble recalling the dates, as though they were far behind him.

He had risen, as he generally did, at about 2:00 or 3:00 A.M. because he had a stomach problem, and noticing the house was "real" cold, discovered the power had failed. (It failed at 3:44 A.M.; while the detectives did not know the precise time until months later, they suspected the house wouldn't have turned cold all at once.)

Helle departed at about six, Crafts related. What had she worn? "I couldn't give you stitch and embroidery," but he remembered the colors: brown and purple. She failed to say where she was going, but he assumed it was to his sister's house in Westport.

You haven't seen her since?
No.
It didn't bother you?
No.
How many times in the past has she done this?
To a varying degree I would say twice a year.
For how many days at a clip?
It varies from two or three days, and she has been gone as long as ten days.
Other than her job?
Now you got me. . . .
You did not have any suspicions at all that she might be, for want of a better word, playing around?
I considered it, but I think I decided that she either wasn't or she was and would tell me and what would be

196

would be. I cared about it, but I didn't become unglued.

Crafts mentioned the various places his wife could have gone, the same ones he had told Helle's friends about.

> I called Pan American and made up some cock and bull story and told them she had some personal emergency. She needed a vacation, and I talked to Dana Dalton, male, and he told me she was already on an emergency leave, which I presumed that she had in fact called and arranged for herself. [Dalton told Crafts that Helle herself had to ask for an emergency leave.]
> *So you were worried here a little bit, right?*
> I was kinda curious. Nosy.

Ohradan raised the issue of the children.

> *Are they asking about Mommy?*
> (Crying) They want to know when Mommy is coming home.
> *What have you been telling them?*
> Telling, I don't know, the police are looking for him, for Mommy, and we don't know where Mommy is. (Whispers) She has got to come back.

"Looking for him" struck the detectives as a curious slip.
As to the missing carpet:

> I had ordered the new carpet and they wanted $1.75 per yard to rip up the old carpet. So I told them I would rip it up myself.

As to the prospective divorce:

> *Have you discussed the divorce with her?*
> We discussed it. We (inaudible) there was no animosity and (inaudible) discussed various aspects of what would occur. She just didn't want to be married to me

197

anymore. She wasn't even going to throw me out of the house. (inaudible) continue to reside at 5 Newfield Lane. Danish standards are a little different than ours. Helle herself, Helle's parents were not married until Helle was about 25 years old [When, in fact, they had married for the second time]. She went to her mother's and father's wedding. And they don't place a high degree of importance on marriage and divorce as we do in this country

Why does she want a divorce from you, Mr. Crafts?

I guess she got tired of me fooling around. Or maybe she wanted to do some fooling around herself.

Did things turn into heated arguments?

No, we have never argued.

Crafts said he and Nancy Dodd had speculated about Helle's whereabouts. Asked what those speculations were, he replied:

Helle wanted to drop out for a while. Disappear for a while. She wanted to get away and think things over.

Crafts's reaction to the albeit legal invasion of his privacy was mild. An innocent individual almost certainly would have rebuked the police, they thought. Instead, he complimented them on their professionalism, as one cop to others.

Ohradan and Quartiero might have lacked psychology degrees, but they were shrewd and knowledgeable and had a great deal of experience. Crafts had briefly shed real tears about his children, but what especially struck them during the three-hour interrogation was the mumbling (they considered that a ruse to foil the tape recorder) and Crafts's lack of emotion about the disappearance of his wife. Even if you were estranged from the mother of your children, they reasoned, you'd worry about them and about her when she had been absent for six weeks. And Crafts's story was hole-ridden. Ohradan told Hiltz the airman had the wrong stuff. He was capable of murder.

The discoveries at River Road seemed to support the theory.

The next day Judge McDonald signed another search warrant for the Crafts house, but Flanagan canceled it because the fingernail was found. The first search warrant might not have held up in court, but a new one, based on physical evidence of a woman's destruction — a *polished* fingernail — would. The document was drawn up and on January 9 McDonald signed again. The search and seizure was conducted in the early evening; removed were "clothing with light colored hairs, hair brushes, combs, a roll dispenser of white plastic material, nail polish and fingernail and/or toenail clippings."

Shocked that Shea had let Crafts be interviewed by the state police, Rodgers preferred another lawyer, J. Daniel Sagarin, whom he had learned about from attorney friends, library research, and reading the newspapers. Brilliantly, in Rodgers's view, Sagarin had just successfully defended a young man named Mark Iorio, who had admitted shooting a rifle into a car's rear window. A young man in the car had been killed.

The state had taken an all-or-nothing position: the defendant was guilty either of murder or of nothing. Sagarin attacked the ballistic evidence (the bullet had been badly mangled), and the jury found Iorio not guilty because the prosecution had failed to prove that the bullet causing the death was the one Iorio fired.

Sagarin looked to be the sort of no-holds-barred defender his brother-in-law might need if he were guilty of accidental or spontaneous murder and especially if the crime had been premeditated, a possibility Rodgers had begun to weigh. He arranged for Crafts to call Sagarin, and the two met briefly at Sagarin's office in Milford. Crafts gave Sagarin a $5,000 check as a retainer in case of arrest.

Convinced Flanagan would order an arrest warrant to be prepared, that Saturday and Sunday Hiltz and the major crime squad began work on it. They joked about Crafts's last weekend.

* * *

That weekend the Rodgers and Crafts families — the Crafts children having returned to live with their father — went to Ludlow, Vermont, to ski, staying in the apartment they had occupied the year before. This year the party was different by one person, Crafts instead of Helle, although the trip, long planned, had been noted in her 1987 calendar.

Arriving with Andrew a day after the others, Crafts must have left his house at about the time the police were preparing to enter it, but he made no mention of police activity in the neighborhood. In Ludlow he claimed not to have been reading the newspapers.

And Crafts may not have felt too apprehensive. He had a vacation scheduled until the end of the month, by which time he expected his troubles with the police to have ended. His job remained safe, unless he was convicted, as he strongly doubted he would be. If a death certificate were issued, he had Helle's assets to look forward to; otherwise, if she remained classified as a missing person, he'd have to wait seven years to collect.

Her brother's knee hurt, he didn't feel like skiing, he looked exhausted — all of which Karen put down to his flying schedule, girlfriends, and three children without a nanny. Karen, taking a brief respite from reality, concentrated on the kids in her charge.

After everyone else had gone to bed, Crafts and Rodgers had another long conversation. Crafts, who seemed to enjoy playing games with the police, claimed to have been followed when he drove to New York with one of the children in the car, and took pride in losing the cops on the return trip.

He said, "A man has to do what he has to do."

Flanagan rose at 5:30 A.M. as usual on Monday, January 12, to putter around his Fairfield house and prepare for the courthouse. He had almost decided to arrest Crafts, but the question was whether he had enough evidence to prevail. The affidavit had to substantiate the charges fully and bridge the gap between probable cause and a case that could and would be successfully prosecuted.

Flanagan again reviewed the evidence. Damning as it was, he considered waiting for more, because he wanted no chance of an acquittal. But other factors weighed in the balance. Crafts's Southbury police Magnum was unaccounted for; might he use it on his children and himself? How unstable was he? That Crafts had recently made a bad landing in Miami in clear weather and had received a reprimand troubled Flanagan. Suppose, emotionally stressed, he crashed with a plane-load of passengers?

Flanagan spoke with Henry Lee several times that day and they determined on a meeting to examine the evidence from all points of view. The key to the decision would be H. Wayne Carver II, the state's acting medical examiner. (Carver's predecessor had lost her job partly because her Dobermans had been discovered in the autopsy room, licking blood from feet and floor.) Improper disposal of a dead body constituted only a misdemeanor; unless Carver agreed Helle Crafts had been murdered, no arrest would occur.

Returning from Vermont and learning from the newspapers how grimly serious his brother-in-law's situation was, David Rodgers suggested Crafts should bring the children to Westport and leave the state until matters were clarified, but Crafts seemed more concerned about his phone being tapped than anything else. He was still relying on the absence of a body to see him through and wanted no incriminating remarks made on the telephone. He did not believe he'd be jailed, or if he were, not for long.

At 6:00 P.M. a large group assembled at Meriden: Carver and a staff pathologist; Flanagan, Brunetti, Dalessio; Hiltz and Ohradan and their boss Major John Watson; Lee and criminologists from his staff.

The two most sustainable pieces of evidence in court were the thimble of a dental crown, which Karazulas and another forensic odontologist, Dr. Lowell Levine, stated categorically had once been fixed in Helle Crafts's mouth, and the bit of calvarium or parietal bone from a human skull. This piece of bone had been disconnected in a barbarous fashion.

Hiltz suggested DNA testing. To prove Helle's identity, Lee could use the portion of finger found on River Road and blood samples from her mother and the children. These should be sufficient to show that the DNAs (the underlying genetic structure) corresponded, but one of the forensic team objected that such tests, still in their infancy, were a two-edged sword. Fatal errors in proof could be made. Lee agreed. (DNA tests were tried later, but the results proved inconclusive.)

The forensic evidence alone, even with human blood of Helle's type, was not enough. But Carver, declaring that he had taken into account the state police evidence as well, got to his feet, all six feet seven inches of him, and wrote on a blackboard the necessary word: *Homicide*. Lee and the others put together a report for the state's attorney.

Dated the following day, though Crafts's lawyer and Helle's relatives and friends could not verify or obtain it for many weeks, the death certificate was a strange document: "Helle L. Crafts: date of death 1-13-87; town of death, Meriden; cause of death, undetermined." Officially, Helle had died in Meriden in January.

Karen Rodgers had spoken to a friend who had heard on the radio that Crafts might be arrested. She hurried from Westport, arriving at Newfield Lane at 8:45 P.M.

Nobody was home, but Pat McCafferty and T. K. Brown were parked nearby, watching the house. Karen introduced herself to Brown and asked him to let her take the children away if an arrest was imminent, but he replied that they were there only on watch. Karen gave him her card and begged the detective to call her if the worst happened. He wouldn't and couldn't have done so, Karen later realized. She was, after all, the suspect's sister, and the police wouldn't have let her take the children.

The Meriden meeting ended at about 9:30 P.M. Ohradan returned to Troop A to complete the arrest warrant and affidavit with Quartiero, who delivered it to the home of Judge William Lavery, which was across the street from the Newtown PD, where the investigation had begun. At Lavery's were Flanagan and Hiltz, who, after the judge signed, brought the document to the police at Newfield Lane.

At about eleven, Ohradan phoned Crafts from Troop A and informed him an arrest warrant had been issued. "Come out into the light," he said, "and someone will approach you."

"I'm tired. I'll take care of it in the morning," Crafts responded.

"I'm not asking you, I'm telling you."

Crafts hung up, saying, "Don't call me back." Ohradan did call again, but the line was busy. Crafts was calling David Rodgers, Shea, and Sagarin, but only Rodgers was reachable.

Ohradan radioed Hiltz, who was in a police car outside the Crafts house, to say that Crafts refused to obey. Hiltz, Flanagan, and Quartiero went to Judge Lavery's; he wrote an order in longhand giving temporary custody of the children to Sue Lausten, who was a friend of his.

Hiltz phoned Crafts and said, "Richard? This is Lieutenant Hiltz. Please don't hang up. We have an arrest warrant for the murder of your wife and we'd like to get it over with as quickly as possible."

"I'll take care of it in the morning," Crafts said again.

"I'm concerned about the safety of the kids. That's why I don't want to wait until morning," said Hiltz. "If we do that, we'll have helicopters all over the house, news media, news people, and it'll be a spectacle. You don't want to expose your kids to that sort of thing, do you?" Though unstated, Hiltz's fear was that Crafts would choose to shoot, and harm might befall the children.

Crafts hesitated. "I want to thank you for being honest with me. And professional," he added, still the correct cop. He was calmer than Hiltz, who at the moment respected him for it. "I'll be out at twelve-fifteen."

Flanagan, Hiltz, and Quartiero returned to Newfield Lane.

Crafts had been in touch again with David Rodgers, who had offered to come to him. Crafts declined. "I told them to go away," he said, but then called back to say, "It looks like I'm going to be arrested." He wanted his brother-in-law's presence for help and to look after the children. "Hold out for three-quarters of an hour, and I'll be there," Rodgers said. He set out from Westport at high speed, making the usual fifty-minute trip in thirty-five.

O'Neil liked to poke around and ponder. He'd been driving on a hill overlooking Lake Zoar on the night of the great snowstorm, when Helle Crafts vanished, and his thoughts, like those of everyone else knowledgeable about the case, went to the lake. Bodies usually waited for summer warmth to float up, like that of Joyce Stochmal, stabbed to death, which slowly bobbed to the surface in August 1985. The mysterious fate of Helle Crafts prompted gruesome reckonings. O'Neil's were not so far from the truth. He told himself, If I'd killed a person, I wouldn't dump the cadaver into the water just like that. I'd put holes in it so the decomposition gas would escape and maybe the body would stay at the bottom where nobody would ever find it.

When Henry Stormer informed O'Neil that Crafts had destroyed his wife's body in a woodchipper, O'Neil felt revulsion but not surprise, except at the ingenuity displayed by Crafts, who had certainly solved the problem of a reemergent body, assuming his wife's remnants had indeed gone into the lake.

O'Neil was drawn to the water, and at seven and eight-thirty on the evening of the twelfth he checked the River Road site, where a policeman was watching TV in the crime van. Nothing else was going on, so he returned to his apartment, trying to figure out who could have seen Crafts with a woodchipper in the early morning of November 19. Someone had, he had been told.

At 11:50, the *News-Times* received an anonymous call from a distraught woman, who said, "The police, with guns, are surrounding the Crafts home." The paper phoned O'Neil, who drove to Newfield Lane. He saw unmarked cars and a cruiser or two lined up in front of the house and on Currituck Road — maybe six vehicles. O'Neil left his car, surprising a uniformed officer, Sergeant John Delavope, who put his hand to his side but for a flashlight, not a gun. He asked O'Neil's name, wrote down his license number, and told him to leave if he didn't want to be arrested.

O'Neil borrowed his brother's car, drove back, and parked some distance away. He returned to Newfield Lane on foot, and, terrified the police would mistake him for an escaping Crafts and open fire, hid beneath some bushes, dropping the ballpoint pens lodged behind his ear into the snow. Crafts's was the only house with lights on.

The police were edgy, and Flanagan too. When Quartiero's car slid down the icy driveway of the Crafts house, Flanagan muttered to himself, believing Crafts was attempting to escape, "I'm not paid well enough for this." He started his engine, ducked, and moved slowly down Newfield Lane.

Delavope, using the public-address speaker in his cruiser, had ordered Crafts to come out with his hands up, but the only response was frenzied activity inside the house. Lights were turned off and on. Crafts would appear at a window and then drop out of sight. At one point he opened the front door and shouted, "Leave me alone."

At midnight, somebody yelled to Dalessio, who was stationed behind the red-and-white dump truck, wearing a bulletproof vest, to come to the front of the house. Dalessio had been a marksman in the army. He had the only long gun, his own Heckler and Koch .223 assault rifle with a telescopic sight.

If Crafts had continued to resist arrest and had acted provocatively — showing a gun, say — the police might have acted too. Hiltz was a civilized soul, but he could not allow a murder arrest warrant to be flouted, and threats of force had to be answered by force.

Bloodshed was a possibility the police accepted. Crafts might have had a gun—they'd seen his arsenal, and in fact there was one they'd missed, a collapsible rifle. He probably wouldn't have fired, they believed, but they couldn't be sure of that and had to consider the danger to themselves and the consequences to their families.

If Crafts had begun shooting, Dalessio would have used his rifle and the police would have stormed the house, though Crafts would have had an advantageous position behind the windows beside the front door. Dalessio worried because his bullets could penetrate interior walls and hit a child.

Crafts had agreed to emerge by twelve-fifteen but didn't. Hiltz walked across the street to the Morans and asked to use the phone. "Richard," he said, "you and I made a deal. What the hell are you doing?"

"I want to say goodnight to the kids," Crafts replied. "I'll be out in five minutes." He was stalling for Rodgers, but Rodgers, though he broke speed limits getting there, failed to arrive on time.

Five minutes dragged by. A neighbor, watching from a darkened house, saw Crafts putting on clothes in his bedroom. Hiltz approached the porch, apprehensive about the windows. The door opened and Crafts came out at 12:34 — O'Neil, hidden in the bushes seventy-five yards away, recorded the time. Hiltz ordered him to put his hands against the wall. Guns were trained on him. Crafts complied and the police frisked him. Led to Quartiero's car in handcuffs, he passed Sue Lausten on her way in. "Thank you for taking care of the kids," he said.

Undressed and in bed, the children slept through the entire event.

Crafts was taken to Troop A, where the police, having read him his rights, attempted to grill him, hoping for a confession, but he wouldn't respond. Quartiero asked Dalessio to watch him while he went upstairs for FBI fingerprint cards. Dalessio realized Crafts had been a student of his at the municipal police training course in Newtown only that March, but such an unexceptional one that he hadn't remembered him. In the moment Quartiero was absent Crafts fell asleep.

Hiltz talked to Crafts in the processing room for ten minutes. He started out friendly, congratulating him for having made a sensible decision in coming out of the house and telling him that he'd made the arrangements with Sue Lausten about the children. Then Hiltz sat in a chair and tried to get Crafts to meet his eyes, but Crafts wouldn't look up.

Hiltz, falling into his tough-cop mode, thrust his face three inches from Crafts's and with only half-feigned anger hissed, "What went on between you and your wife is your fucking business, but I'm here to do a job. What right do you have to mess up the lives of your children? Cocksucker, you better not call them on the witness stand." Crafts nodded his head. "We have the facts. You were seen on River Road with the woodchipper in the fucking night. Oh yeah, we know all about it. Have you fucking nothing to say?"

Crafts had begun to sob — an innocent man would have raged against his arrest, Hiltz judged — telling Hiltz that the children were his weak spot. Hiltz rose and opened the door. Quartiero had been listening from outside. Convinced that Crafts would confess instantly, Hiltz said to Quartiero, "He's yours." Then he looked back into the room: "As fast as you could flick a light switch, Crafts remembered his position and turned off the tears."

"Have a good night, Lieutenant," Crafts said.

14

The Murder

As Helle Crafts returned home on the evening of November 18, her husband knew of three possibly complicating developments. McLaughlin Ford hadn't delivered the dump truck as promised, the Toyota pickup couldn't pull the heavy woodchipper, and the all-weather station on the radio atop the refrigerator predicted snow.

But other concerns loomed larger. Helle's divorce threat, backed by a skillful lawyer with ample ammunition, looked serious. A marital split would cost him alimony, child support, and the use of the house, even though he might have to pay the mortgage. On an income further reduced by taxes, pilot's insurance, and union dues, he'd have to finance a new establishment, unless he moved in with Nancy Dodd or reduced himself to his small New York apartment. The situation was highly inconvenient.

Far from least, he would have to endure a forced separation from the children, his wife's custody over them, and abridgment of his freedom to see them whenever he chose. He'd suffer loss of face among other men—"Your wife *left* you?"—and of the flexibility (especially cherished by him after cancer) to live it up just as he pleased. Yes, he'd be had in more ways than one.

He hated weary-faced Helle, who'd had the audacity to invade his private life by having him photographed by a private detective. If his days were medically numbered, he sure didn't want to waste any or have them spoiled by her.

But Crafts had a practical reason for haste. He and Helle had made a pact by which he had agreed to play the model husband. He'd been insincerely sweet, hoping to sway her to change her mind—she had never been resolute with him and had backed off from divorce many times—and to impress other people with his consideration if she persisted. As insurance, he had spread rumors about her character to establish a perception that a sudden departure was not unusual. The ruckus with her on Friday, before he'd flown out for the weekend—why had he been so stupid as to charge toys that he'd bought in New Jersey with his girlfriend or to let Helle find the Visa slip?—confirmed his wife's intention to proceed. In that she'd alarmed him.

And there lay the danger. Helle would continue to attempt service of divorce papers, and if the sheriff succeeded by surprise (tomorrow perhaps?), he would be in a far weaker position. It would be harder to pretend that she'd simply gone off with a lover or to think things over.

Next day, surely, he'd get the dump truck and the chipper, and proceed with the demolition of the body, as planned. Not a trace of his wife would remain. Tonight's weather wouldn't interfere with his movements, he being an outdoorsman, and might even help to cover them because potential witnesses would stay home. Turn liabilities into assets! Let it snow!

The previous day he'd picked up the Westinghouse freezer chest at Zemel's. He couldn't put it in the basement; Marie might have noticed. He parked the Toyota pickup well away from the house, leaving the freezer under the cap. On Tuesday, he uncrated it, depositing the packing in one of his black fifty-five-gallon drums for burning.

On Tuesday, the day of the murder, perhaps, he tested the freezer, still hidden in the truck, as a pilot tests the controls of an airplane before flying. He plugged an extra-long outdoor extension cord, of which he had several, into a socket in the garage and hooked it up to the freezer. After dark on Tuesday, he parked the truck behind the house near the kitchen door, where it wouldn't be seen by those inside, reattaching the cord and setting the switch for minus 10 degrees: maximum cold. His wife's icy coffin was ready.

The subject of snow might easily have been on Helle's lips at 7:00 P.M. when she dropped her flight bags in the bedroom and darted to the kitchen. She'd heard about the storm from Frank Buonanno and pronounced herself lucky her flight hadn't been further delayed, because the drive home might have been difficult. As always, the children wanted to know what Mother had brought from abroad.

If she gave Crafts a peck for appearance's sake, a question hardened her blue eyes. He tried to be affable, because she had to be completely unsuspecting. He'd fixed supper — spaghetti and meatballs was a dish of his — and Helle, with her uncertain appetite, ate some with sips of red wine. At 8:00 P.M. they put the smaller children to bed, although Andrew, being ten, received a few minutes' grace to watch TV.

As Crafts went through the motions of cleaning up, Helle hung her uniform in her dressing closet and put on a blue cotton nightshirt with pockets, having showered or intending to later on. One of her favorites, the nightshirt reached to her upper thighs. Beneath it she wore panties. She'd gathered the mail and perhaps read a note from Crafts's mother in Boca Raton, postmarked November 12, discussing the Florida weather and signed "Mother Crafts," and a letter from the American Cancer Society, addressed to Miss Helle L. Crafts, containing return-address stickers. When her husband entered the bedroom Helle stuck them in her pocket. Already there, as a reminder of some kind, may have been a Shaklee vitamin label.

The previous day in Frankfurt, after dinner with Rita Buonanno and Trudy Horvath, Helle had retired at ten. She had risen at eight—2:00 A.M. Connecticut time—and worked aboard the airliner. By 8:00 P.M. locally she had been awake for eighteen hours and planned to go to sleep at ten, as did Rita Buonanno. Perhaps Crafts kept her up with divorce talk because he had to be completely certain the children were fast asleep. Perhaps he let her pester him with the question, "Have you been in touch with Sheriff Sullivan about the papers?" No, he hadn't. In the morning he'd call Sullivan. In the morning he'd call Sullivan, he repeated. Let us fix the killing at somewhere before ten.

How did he do it? The bloodstains on the mattress told a tale. Helle was not shot, because a bullet would have produced spots of maximum velocity impact. Nor did he shove her head under a pillow to muffle the sound as he shot her, because the blood fell directly on the mattress cover. A knifing would also have produced spots of maximum velocity impact.

That the droplets of blood were not intercepted by bedding might mean that the bedclothes were pulled off during a struggle; perhaps he lunged and she tried to escape, thrusting obstacles in his way, no matter how flimsy. But another explanation seems logical. Helle was making the bed.

The Craftses' mattress was covered by a contoured bottom sheet. Over it went a comforter with a cover, and over that sometimes a knitted blanket. Crafts was not a bedmaker. Helle performed that chore. A very tidy person, having been away from home for three nights, she may have intended to change the bottom sheet or remake the bed. That would have seemed to Crafts an opportune moment, because she was preoccupied.

Creeping up from behind he struck her; and a likely suspect for a murder weapon could have been found nearby. In the bathroom, in a recharging holder, was an SL-35 "Streamlight" flashlight, one and a half inches in diameter, something less than twenty inches long and heavier than a standard hammer. Police employ such powerful flashlights to search for hidden suspects and to club assailants, and for shining in attackers' eyes. The hard surface would not be marked by a blow to the body. For Crafts the special beauty of the flashlight would have been that if Helle saw the familiar object in his hand, not raised, she wouldn't scream as she might if he held a baseball bat, say, which would have made his violent intentions obvious.

So whether she tried to struggle or not, he hit her on the head with the flashlight or another weapon. He struck her twice, the second blow driving out the blood. In between, shock paralyzed her vocal cords, but she might still have been capable of thinking, *If anything happens to me . . . me . . . me . . Is this happening to me . . .* Helle, lapsing into unconsciousness, fell onto the bed and rolled off, head or face grazing the mattress's side, leaving the six-inch smear Dr. Lee found there. Perhaps as a reflex or as a last desperate attempt to escape, she lunged onto the carpet. She bled, and on that Crafts hadn't counted.

The scene is indistinct. We want to stop it but are powerless to affect the action or reverse it any more than Crafts could have. Did he, face contorted, gasp and stare at the human devastation he had wrought? If so, not for long. This was to be—had to be—the perfect crime. He'd mentally rehearsed the details over and over. They must be pieced together seamlessly.

Crafts claimed the doors to the master bedroom and the children's rooms always stood ajar, because the children always used their parents' bathroom. But Dr. Lee testified he found semen on the mattress, and the children's toothbrushes were in the hall bathroom across from

212

Kristina's room. Andrew said that sometimes he used his parents' bathroom, but only if the door was open when his folks weren't home.

So Crafts would have opened the door and stepped into the peaceful hall. Nobody stirred. Perhaps wrapping the body in the sheet, he quickly carried his wife down the hall over his shoulder, fireman style, then through the kitchen and out the back door, where light reflecting off new snow provided ample illumination.

The pickup's tailgate had a special feature: it could be laid flat or lowered at an angle to form a ramp. Without the bumper or the two-inch by eight-inch wood plank Crafts had installed in place of the bumper, the tailgate could be dropped until it nearly touched the ground. Lowering Helle to the earth, he slid the freezer down the tailgate. He would have had to do this because inside the truck, under the cap, he lacked sufficient headroom to open it. He had lined the freezer with clear plastic, such as painters use for drop cloths. He had a quantity of this plastic in the cellar. Scrunching her a little—the freezer wasn't quite long enough to lay the body flat—he placed Helle inside, covered her with plastic, lowered the lid, and shoved the freezer back under the cap. He hid the bloody comforter and dust ruffle in the basement.

It is conceivable the Helle was not dead when she landed in the freezer. She might have come to, blinked her eyes, whimpered, and feebly pressed against the lid. If so, she would have quickly frozen to death.

To use a chain saw on a soft body would have caused an indescribable and, for Crafts, dangerous mess.

The police believed Crafts put Helle in an old standup freezer in the basement that had belonged to the Rodgerses, and maybe left part of her inside when he dumped it. The full state police diving team spent five days searching for it at Stevenson Dam the next summer. But that freezer wasn't large enough for Crafts's purpose. Besides, the body would have had to be placed in an awkward squatting position, and if for some reason it had

213

fallen forward, would have opened the door, which was fitted only with magnetic catches (though he could have taped it shut). The new freezer was the one the police should have worried about.

Crafts wiped up the bedroom as best he could with mop, bucket, towels, and airline facecloths, of which he had many. The carelessness with which he cleaned up after himself was characteristic. Besides, he never thought there'd be a detailed forensic investigation.

The bed presented a larger problem. To judge by Crafts's actions, blood must have gotten onto the pillows, the frame, the dust ruffle, and the box spring. He disassembled the frame and placed it beneath the cellar stairs. He left the mattress on the floor, presumably reasoning that the spots were small and no one would notice them. Besides, he needed something to sleep on. He gathered Helle's flight bags, handbag containing her passport, some clothes, toiletries, and other personal objects she would have taken on a trip. He took the $300 check from her wallet.

Marie went off duty at midnight or so, but she was late getting home, no doubt increasing his tension and impatience as he lurked in the bedroom. He still had much to accomplish. When she arrived at 2:00 A.M., Marie noted the pickup truck was not in the driveway—almost certainly it was behind the house, with the plugged-in freezer and Helle's body aboard. Marie entered the house through the garage and basement. When he heard her in the hall, Crafts might have coughed to imitate his wife, who'd had a cold when she departed for Germany, though she hadn't coughed during the car ride home.

After Marie had been asleep long enough, say an hour, he moved Helle's Tercel, which was capable of two- or four-wheel drive, probably rolling the car to the street before he started it. Plenty of places to park existed on Church Hill Road, from which he could have walked the mile or so home. More likely, he drove the car to his heavily wooded lot and left it there far up the hill out of sight, loping the five minutes home across lawns, unnoticeable except for the moment when he ran across Currituck Road.

At 9:45 P.M., heavy wet snow had begun to fall at the rate of about an inch an hour, five or six inches in all. Of itself, the snow didn't concern him, because both vehicles he needed had four-wheel drive.

But the long night was not without a serious snag. At 3:00 A.M., a transformer blew at a relay station in Bethel, seven miles away, filling the snowy Newtown sky with eerie green light as though from a flying saucer or as though the gods were expressing anger against a capital crime. At 3:44 A.M. power disappeared on Newfield Lane.

Since he gave the police the wrong time — between 2:00 and 3:00 A.M. — for the power failure, it is likely that Crafts was out of the house when it actually occurred. When he returned from moving the Tercel and found no electricity in the house, a disturbing thought crossed his mind: if power stays out for a protracted period, Helle will fail to freeze unless I use the generator.

He waited just over an hour from the actual time of the power failure before phoning Rodgers at 4:44 A.M. His reason for calling was not that he knew his brother-in-law would be awake, as he claimed. Rodgers happened to be nodding at his desk, but his normal bedtime was before three. Perhaps Crafts intended to establish his presence at home; he did ascertain that Rodgers had power and would be home the next day to oversee the children and Marie. Crafts probably was unaware of the problem in Bethel. For all he knew, electricity might have been restored at any moment. A more natural response would have been to wait before phoning, but the children's school would certainly be closed the next day, and the McDonald's too, and he required time alone. He hadn't expected so much of a mess in the bedroom.

Now came the chanciest part, because Marie might have woken up and looked out the window, but Crafts strongly doubted she'd leave her bed and sweet dreams, and he desperately needed the four-wheel drive pickup to get through the snow to Westport. Detaching the extension cord, he backed the truck to a position just inside the overhead garage door, which was below Marie's range of view, slid the freezer down, and put it onto a hand truck, which he wheeled to the rear of the garage. He covered the freezer to conceal it from anyone looking through the garage windows and plugged it into a socket in case power returned. Then he jammed shut the garage door. Finally he checked the fuel supply for his 2,000-watt Honda generator and laid out two extension cords in case the power failure continued. Those were the reasons he forced the children and Marie to make a unaccustomed exit through the front door and across a snowy slope in the morning.

Next Crafts executed a maneuver, the result of which was reported by Ingram, the snowplow operator, who saw deep tire tracks around a spruce tree in the yard. Heading across the lawn from the driveway in the pickup, he circled the tree to gain momentum up the hill to the kitchen door, where he hurriedly loaded the box spring, the bloodied comforter, sheets, pillows, dust ruffle, and Helle's belongings onto the truck. Lights out, sounds completely muffled by the snowfall, he returned to the driveway at low speed, emerged on Currituck Road, close to his house, and hid the evidence on his property.

At six he woke Marie. His hair was damp, the pickup's windshield almost snow-free, and the four-wheel drive locked in place, all of which suggests that he had been outside and using the vehicle. He drove the children and Marie to Westport in the pickup, fixed pancakes, and returned. By 11:00 A.M. he'd been home and out once more. He purchased kerosene, not to heat the house, as he said—the power had been restored—but to try to remove the patch on the rug. He deposited the $300 check made out to Helle at the Newtown Banking Center because she would have done that herself, and at Caldor bought replacements for the comforter and pillows he'd removed.

By late afternoon on Wednesday Crafts's wife had been in the freezer almost five hours before the power failure and six or seven after electricity had been restored. Insulation would have prevented her from thawing much in the interval without power. According to a mortician, only six or seven hours would be needed to freeze a thin woman, but Crafts probably did not have that knowledge. He could ascertain with his finger that his wife was hard as a rock. But deep inside the body? He couldn't be certain, nor could he take the risk of having soft debris in the nearly quarter-inch swath of dust a chain saw spits out. Operating on instinct, and deciding he must wait twenty-four hours before sawing and packaging, he put the new freezer and the generator under the Toyota's locked cap, the one plugged into the other, and drove the vehicle to his wooded lot. He had to run the generator only twenty minutes every six hours to keep the contents frigid. The freezer may have remained on the pickup for several days, no matter where he parked it. Marie Thomas never saw the truck again. By the time it re-emerged she had left the Crafts house for good.

He still had to remove Helle's car, a prime clue, from Newtown. Left in any one place too long, even on the Currituck Road land, somebody — perhaps the police — might notice it.

He had a scheme to handle the problem. When he had gone to the Berkshire shopping center in Danbury for the freezer on Monday he had also collected the VW Rabbit from the Volkswagen dealer who was located nearby, and parked it. On Wednesday, he drove the Tercel to the vicinity of the shopping center, where it would be completely inconspicuous, and then drove the VW to his Currituck Road property. Not enough time had passed for him to bring the VW home yet. It wouldn't have looked right to replace Helle's car too soon.

Darting home for his Ford sedan, which did not have four-wheel drive but was usable again because the roads had been cleared, Crafts realized he was very late in returning to Westport, but nobody there would seriously question him.

Since he'd reserved the woodchipper for Tuesday, the eighteenth, the original plan must have been to perform the whole job on Wednesday, but with the dump truck not available, Crafts faced a serious emergency. On Thursday, December 20, he made frantic calls to McLaughlin Ford for a towing vehicle, and at 1:30 P.M. Tony Kalakay finally brought the U-Haul. A U-Haul! Audacious as he was, Crafts must have shuddered. The truck would stand out. But there was no turning back.

After procuring the chipper that same afternoon, Crafts pulled it, with the U-Haul, to the heavily wooded Curri-tuck lot, the higher parts of which could not be seen from the road or the few nearby houses, and tested it. Only then did he chain-saw the body, underneath which he put plastic drop cloths. To slice and package his wife in dark plastic bags in addition to the clear plastic drop cloths and some of the sheeting in which she had previously been wrapped and tie the bags with rope probably took an hour. He used the tip of the gas-powered Stihl's bar to minimize the tissue spew. Other chain saws rang in the air; neighbors were continuing to clean up after the storm.

The police suspected that Crafts had severed only Helle's head and extremities, since they found bits from those areas of the body only. They thought he must have deposited the torso elsewhere, perhaps in the old freezer or in a dump with an immediate compactor.

But that the torso has not been discovered is good reason to believe that he dismembered and chain-sawed the whole body: another reason is that remnants of papers Helle would seem to have had in her nightshirt pockets were found among the River Road chips. Helle was hurriedly bagged in seven or eight parcels. Crafts went to Silver Bridge, and with wood he'd brought in the U-Haul, he chipped his wife's remains into the river, bag by bag.

He could then breathe much easier. The hard evidence had been completely destroyed, he believed.

In its belly the Brush Bandit has a steel disk, forty inches by two inches, which moves at 1,130 rpm, in excess of 100 miles an hour. The motor was larger than a Volkswagen's. Attached to the disk are two sharp, eight-inch blades set close together, which do the cutting. Six reinforced fan blades in the rear throw out material as far as sixty feet, depending on the angle, through the spout, which revolves through 360 degrees. The handbook, decorated with a cartoon of a tombstone, instructs, "WARNING: Improper use of the chipper can result in severe personal injury."

Joe Williams, passing slowly in his car, had seen Crafts on the bridge, so Crafts quickly drove to River Road for the final step. By this time, around seven, it was dark. To clean the chipper of traces of the body, he put wood through it and shot the chips into the back of the U-Haul for disposal. Some paper and small human pieces, probably from the extremities, which would have frozen hardest, fell short of the U-Haul or bounced out or scattered in the wind. Of that, working in darkness, Crafts was not aware.

The first major unaccounted-for block of time in Crafts's story is that Thursday afternoon and evening until he reported for work at 9:00 P.M. at the Southbury PD. He said he got there earlier, but nobody saw him. That he made no effort to conceal the U-Haul and chipper is understandable, since he firmly believed no evidence of Helle's corpse remained.

After completing his four-hour police duties, at about

2:00 A.M., Crafts was spotted with the U-Haul and wood-chipper by Officer Wildman at 4:00 A.M. Wildman saw the U-Haul and woodchipper again at 4:30, without Crafts, and somewhere around that time Joey Hine, not wearing a watch, saw a man with the U-Haul and chipper and noticed the equipment without the man about an hour later.

Crafts was engaged, as he had been earlier, in getting rid of chips from the U-Haul. Using a rake and the flat-head shovel that he'd purchased in Brewster, he left the chips in small piles along the road.

At some point, perhaps after throwing the chain saw and bar into the river (though that might have been later), he went home, parking the U-Haul and chipper on the Currituck Road property. However briefly, he used the chipper there; chips later found in that place had been cut by the same blade as the ones on River Road.

On the way to and from Darien, where he went next day to turn in the woodchipper, Crafts detoured to rake or shovel out more chips from the U-Haul. This day also has unaccounted-for periods of time. If the distance of every journey Crafts claimed to have made is measured, the sum is about 210 miles, yet the U-Haul's odometer read 240 when he returned it, leaving 30 unexplained miles.

He brought the U-Haul to Currituck Road yet again and swept it out carefully. Fearful that the remaining chips might be contaminated with human flesh and blood, he shoveled the small pile into the trunk of the Crown Victoria, which he'd parked there for later removal. After-ward, he noticed tiny flecks of flesh and blood and wood chips on the mat in the trunk. He discarded the mat, in-tending to replace it soon.

Careful not to be seen at his house, he brought the U-Haul to the Grand Union parking lot.

After burning what he could of Helle's things in the

220

fireplace and in barrels with charcoal—the fireproof gloves were handy for sifting materials—Crafts still had to dispose of the Tercel, which Rita Buonanno saw in the Pan Am employees' lot at four-thirty on Saturday afternoon. He owned a tow bar, but the police closely examined the bumper of the Crown Victoria—Marie Thomas said he left home in it on Saturday—and they concluded no tow bar had been attached. How and when Helle's car arrived at Kennedy Airport remained unsolved by the police. However, Crafts could have towed it with the Toyota pickup.

Crafts claimed that the pickup's bumper was broken. Two pieces of the bumper could be seen lying in his driveway. He replaced it with a two-by-eight wood plank. He later said that he had taken the truck to a shop for repairs, but no record of the pickup's having been in an auto shop was presented in court by his lawyers.

If the bumper had indeed been broken, he could have mended it himself without trouble; in fact, the bumper did not need to be repaired or replaced.

With his electric grinder, Crafts could easily have removed a corner from the bumper that was unnecessary for towing and placed it in the driveway as a demonstration that the bumper was broken; he could just as easily have rebolted the primary bumper frame that held the towing ball.

On Saturday morning, November 29, he towed the Tercel, which was never examined by state police forensic experts, from its obscure parking place to Kennedy Airport. Uncoupling, he drove the Tercel the final distance to the Pan Am lot, and walked or took a bus back to the Toyota pickup.

It could have been the perfect machine crime, well oiled. Details remained, such as the new freezer, which might have been kept in the kitchen or hidden on the Currituck Road property until after Thanksgiving, when it appeared in the basement of the Crafts house, and the master bedroom rug, which he dumped in the Newtown landfill except for the part with a bloody patch, which he must have burned. Crafts had almost completely covered his tracks. If he had not been sighted on River Road by a road worker (or if he had checked the River Road sites for debris), the remains of Helle Crafts would never have been found and Richard Crafts would almost certainly not have been arrested.

He would have been better off without the contradictory stories he told when Helle's friends asked him where she was—a single disprovable answer would have sufficed: "I don't know"--better off without using credit cards, without using his home phone and charging calls to it, albeit sometimes to establish alibis. But there was a good chance that he would have been heard through the public-address system on an Eastern flight, saying, "This is Captain Crafts speaking. The weather in Miami . . ."

He hadn't reckoned on forensic science.

But Craft's habit of not finishing tasks prevailed. He didn't return to River Road to see if any evidence had been left behind.

15

The Forensics

An extraordinary murder trial took place in 1987 in Texas. The case was authentic (a sex-related killing that had been committed in another state), the judge, prosecution, and defense lawyers played their normal roles, and the jury deliberated the fate of the accused. The object of the exercise, however, was to assess not guilt or innocence but how the jury conducted itself. The jury, unaware the proceedings had been staged, was observed through a one-way mirror by a half-dozen or so forensic experts. One was Dr. Henry Lee, who came away impressed by how much the jurors distrusted eye witnesses. Perhaps because of the influence of TV and movies, he believed, they wanted physical evidence.

As director of the Connecticut state police forensic laboratory, Lee serves the state police, 144 local police departments, 179 fire departments, and thirty other state and federal law-enforcement agencies. His job is to analyze evidence the police develop and prosecutors use. (The laboratory was also once summoned to ascertain whether a Chinese restaurant was serving dog or cat meat.) Skilled in every forensic field, Lee has an international reputation. He has been consultant abroad and called by forty states for help in solving crimes. He analyzed evidence from the 1980 murder of Scarsdale diet doctor Herman Tarnower, the 1985 assault by the Philadelphia police on the radical group MOVE, and other famous cases. He has investigated more than four thousand homicides, but Helle Crafts would prove the most difficult and challenging case in his career.

Henry Cheng Lee was born in 1938 in China, from which his family fled to Taiwan to escape the revolutionary war. Lee had a dozen older siblings, all but one of whom went to graduate school, and he too studied hard. In 1956 Lee entered the new Taiwan central police college not because he had any great desire for a career in criminal justice but because there he would receive free tuition, good training, and an education. He was a star performer on the college martial-arts team and graduated second in a class of fifty in academic rank. At school he developed his lifelong work habits: Lee rises at 4:00 A.M. and is at his desk or in his laboratory — he also has one at home — until midnight.

Lee was a Taipei police captain for three years. The victim of his first murder case had been cut up and placed in six large pickle jars; Lee wouldn't look at meat for months. When he started using his salary to aid families of victims and suspects, he deduced that he lacked detachment and should try something else. He became a reporter and then an editor of a newspaper, but, restless, decided to make good on a promise to his mother to acquire a graduate degree. With his wife he arrived in New York in 1965. The couple had fifty dollars between them and not many more words of English. Lee worked parttime as a waiter and martial-arts instructor while he earned his second bachelor's degree, in two years, at John Jay College of Criminal Justice and then enrolled for graduate studies in science at New York University. "I had been thinking about just becoming a biochemist or a geneticist," Lee said, "but police work was somehow in my blood, and I figured I could combine them." Receiving a Ph.D. in biochemistry from NYU in 1975, he joined the University of New Haven faculty, established a new and popular program in forensic science, and was granted tenure as a professor in three years, a record for the school.

In 1979, having volunteered his skills to public defenders,

224

with whom his reputation was growing, he was hired as director of the state police forensic laboratory, which then consisted of one microscope housed in a converted lavatory. Since then, Lee—slightly built, bouncy, humorous, articulate, and effective—has lobbied the police and the legislature into his current annual budget of around $2.5 million. His office in the Meriden state police complex has forty-two employees and modern equipment, such as an argon laser fingerprint analyzer, most known by arcane initials. He is trying, with the assistance of legislators and the governor, to set up an automatic fingerprint computer system and a DNA-typing program for the state. If he can raise the money, he will buy a computerized fingerprint filing system that identifies possible suspects in seconds.

Lee could easily earn two or three thousand dollars a day as an independent forensic expert instead of the modest salary he gets from the state (he does receive sizable consulting fees), but he enjoys his virtually round-the-clock, seven-day-a-week professional life as a high-ranking police official. He likes the variety of cases and tries to solve them with logic and intuition as well as by science.

A man accused of murdering his estranged wife claimed she had stabbed him, inflicting a wound four inches deep, and then had accidentally fallen on the blade when he tried to take the knife away from her. Lee analyzed the mixture of blood types on the blade. On the witness stand, with mustard and ketchup, he demonstrated that the man had killed his wife first and then stabbed himself in an attempt to commit suicide. If you dip a knife in ketchup to a depth of four inches, representing the man's wound, and then in mustard to a depth of seven inches, representing the woman's wound, you'd have the ketchup-mustard mixture seven inches up the blade. But there was no mixture of blood types above four inches. Ergo, the wife had been stabbed first.

Lee had a hunch the man was guilty, but without forensic science couldn't have proved it; nor, without forensics, could he have proved the murder of Helle Crafts.

Lee first learned of the case on December 19, when Walter

Flanagan phoned him about the rug samples taken from Lieutenant DeJoseph. The name Helle Crafts meant nothing to Lee, on whom sensational news stories have little or no impact, his enduring interest being the abstract scientific chase across forensic fields.

Martin Ohradan asked him to come to the house on Newfield Lane, and Lee looked carefully for anything the police might have missed, including clues to where a body might have been hidden. He'd found corpses before under police noses. The mattress cover seemed to hold the most promise, because, unlike the towels and washcloths, it hadn't been washed and the stains diluted. At Meriden he performed tests, of which more than 50,000 would be made during the case. Forensic serology, the analysis of blood serums and body fluids, strongly reinforced Lee's instinct that "something happened."

Murders fail to shock or fascinate Lee. Personalities and motives don't concern him either; he says that for him the human psyche is too mysterious. But when potential evidence began to pour in from River Road, Lee was ready to drop everything else. He committed himself, his twenty-seven forensic experts, and a number of outside consultants to a round-the-clock effort that lasted two weeks. The largest investigation ever mounted at Meriden consumed, Lee estimates, fully a tenth of his annual budget. The remains were a forensic dare.

The reason is easy to understand. An adult possesses 210 bones, twelve pounds in weight for an ordinary male, ten for a female, about five quarts of blood, thirty-two teeth if all are present, 80,000 to 140,000 head hairs (Caucasians having more, Orientals fewer) if none have been lost, and fleshy mass, how much depending on gender and size. When Lee compiled what had been given him from River Road, he had seventy-five slivers of bone (sixty-nine certifiably human) weighing three-quarters of an ounce, five droplets of blood, two tooth caps, 2,660 strands of hair, three ounces of human tissue, a portion of a finger, and two human fingernails. He could literally hold the remains in one hand. Could he prove to a jury that they represented what was left of a human being of a certain sex, race, and age, that a murder had occurred?

On the mattress cover Lee could identify three different kinds of spots: spots of quarter-dollar size, a six-by-one-inch smear, and small specks in patterns that showed they had landed with medium velocity impact—the greater the velocity, the tinier the spots. Lee had measured the spots in the Craftses' bedroom and showed with a chemical test a reasonable possibility of blood. But the blood wasn't necessarily human, and the chemical change observed in the test that seemed to indicate its presence could also have been caused by vegetation.

In a forensic laboratory, method is the rule. Lee conducted more tests designed to reach the target. The first eliminated plant life, leaving reasonable scientific certainty of the presence of blood. Next, a crystal and anti-human hemoglobin test showed conclusively that the blood was human. Then antigens, developed in a rabbit, yielded the blood type O positive, that of Helle Crafts. Finally, the forensic people performed a test with a genetic marker named PGM, which remains active for thirteen weeks even in a spot of dried blood; the protein was still active.

Patient work on the chain-saw bar was done by Elaine Pagliaro, who, microscopically examining every notch, found human tissue, hair, and the same blue fiber as the major crime squad had found in the saw's housing. The serial number had been almost totally filed off but was restored by Lee's staff. It matched the number on a Stihl warrantee in the name of Richard Crafts found in the papers the Longs had given Mayo.

Every one of the 2,660 strands of hair was inspected under a microscope, and it was established in sequence that the substance was hair, human hair, human Caucasian head hair of blondish color. That the hair had been tinted might imply that the owner had been female and maybe had visited a beauty parlor. All the strands, the longest being nine inches, had suffered traumatic damage, having been cut by a heavy instrument, and the presence of roots meant they'd been chopped

227

from a skull. Mixed in with the hair was blood, which the laboratory established as human, and with one clump was a seven-inch piece of rope that had not been cut by scissors or a knife. The rope bore hairs and tested positively for blood.

The bones, too, had been destroyed by a heavy instrument. One of Lee's consultants, Albert Harper, a University of Connecticut anthropologist with an archaeological background, had never seen anything like them, though he had participated in numerous digs. Bones found in digs are often broken, but these were broken in a completely unfamiliar manner. The closest Harper could come to a comparison was cremation, which leaves fragments. That the bones were still "greasy"—that is, fatty—told him that they were no more than a few months old.

Delicate measurements and intimate understanding of the human body proved bones to be from the tibia (shin), hands, foot (big toe of the right foot), and seven from the cranial vault. The largest fragment was one and a half inches by three-quarters of an inch by one-quarter of an inch. Some, cleaned many times to eliminate contamination and made brittle by liquid nitrogen, were ground to a fine powder to allow the production of antibodies and antigens (bone is tissue). They too revealed the telltale O positive blood type.

The forensic odontologists believed beyond reasonable scientific doubt that the tooth crowns matched those in Helle's dental charts.

Blood, chain saw, hair, bone, and teeth were the core of the prosecution's forensic case. Without them, despite Crafts's incriminating behavior, he might never have been brought to trial.

Arduous as were the labors of Lee and his team, they almost paled before the intricacies of what came next: the criminal justice system.

Part IV

Trials

16

Preliminaries

Crafts was already infamous, and when Judge Patricia Geen set temporary bail at $750,000—the highest in the state's history—few doubted that the hair-raising means by which he might have disposed of his wife's body had something to do with the amount. CHOPPED TO PIECES read the headline in the New York *Daily News*. Later, bad puns emerged: Crafts must have loved her too mulch.

For the defense, Tom Farver, a thirty-two-year-old former Marine who'd practiced in the corps, asked for a delay— granted—and a few days later moved to reduce bail and have Crafts released on his own recognizance if he posted a 10 percent bond. He argued that Crafts had been given only a 2 percent chance of surviving as a result of cancer—when the cancer had been operated on, Farver should have said; the odds in fact, were now much higher—so why not let him out? Judge William Sullivan ruled against the request, reasoning that Crafts appeared in good health and might well believe he had nothing to lose by skipping bail; if indeed he was destined soon to die, he certainly had nothing to lose.

Crafts couldn't raise bail on his own. Ten percent of the $750,000 was required in cash and the rest in notes, which had to be secured by bond insurance. He might have been able to use some of his Eastern pension fund, but not enough.

His family might have helped, but the lawyers assured them and him that bail reduction would be granted. Meantime, Crafts languished in the Bridgeport correctional facility, where he stared at the walls.

The Rodgerses quickly learned how expensive a murder defense can be if handled by a top law firm. Since Sagarin was on vacation, they met with his partner, Lewis Hurwitz, who told them, "If we don't have thirty thousand dollars by the end of the week, we can't continue with this." Rodgers paid (he eventually recouped most of the sum by selling off some of Crafts's assets, using his power of attorney), but a much bigger bill lay in store. Sagarin charged $150 an hour, Farver $125, and paralegal time was charged at $40 an hour. In court Sagarin would receive $1,500 a day, Farver $1,000. Hurwitz put the cost of a normal homicide defense at $50,000 plus a roughly equal amount for forensic witnesses, private detectives, and so on.

As insurance against the legal bills, Hurwitz suggested liens against the Craftses' properties, but described the liens as largely meaningless because someone would file a wrongful death (murder) suit and attach them. (That someone proved to be Karen Rodgers, executrix of Helle's estate.) Hurwitz assured the Rodgerses that he wouldn't place the liens without notifying them, but surprised them a few days later when Crafts signed papers and two $100,000 liens were filed.

When Hurwitz visited Crafts in jail, he brought with him two secretaries for a female impression of Crafts's character. Incapable of murder, they pronounced.

Helle's friends wanted to have a memorial service, but the medical examiner hadn't released the death certificate. Father Dunn held a Eucharist service instead at Trinity Church. Forty or fifty people came. It was sad and more than a little unsettling because Helle didn't seem dead, only missing.

The war between the state's attorney's office and the Newtown police continued, with DeJoseph and Noroian pursuing
a question that would have been fruitful for the prosecution.
When had Crafts actually taken possession of—rather than
when had he rented—the chipper? Darien Rentals was not
sure. Flanagan, learning of the inquiry, sharply told DeJoseph to stay off the case.

In a publicized letter Mayo charged the department with
incompetence and worse—"What they did bordered on ob-
struction." The Newtown police commission was disturbed
and the Spartans' mood combative. DeJoseph wrote Flanagan
demanding an investigation of his department's performance,
but Flanagan, concerned about the effect of publicity on
choosing a jury, wrote a letter to the first selectman arguing
that such an investigation "might well jeopardize the criminal
proceedings. . . . I anticipate the trial should be resolved
within six months of this date."

The Newtown PD would not be put off, for, on January 27,
DeJoseph, Noroian, Tvardzik, and Stormer signed a letter to
the chairman of the police commission. "We are hereby requesting an immediate investigation into the allegations
brought against the Newtown Police Department by Mr. K.
Parker Mayo . . . cognizant of the fact that personnel from
our department investigated the case with consummate professionalism, we feel very strongly that the citizens of our
community come to realize the same fact. . . . The morale of
the entire police department hinges on your decision. . . ."

Though Newtown's honor was on the line, the commission
voted three to two against the investigation, on Flanagan's
grounds. Even private hearings couldn't be held, because they
would violate the Freedom of Information Act, town counsel
Ray Connor advised. But the commission promised an investigation when the trial was over.

The wonder was that the Newtown detectives failed to give
Pat O'Neil a shot at their grievance, which was in fact that
Flanagan had run roughshod over them when they had only
dragged their feet; they'd withheld information because they

233

thought that they could solve the case. But these were policemen, not PR people.

Furious at Flanagan, DeJoseph attacked the state police investigation, implying that Mayo had been responsible for some of its evidence. Mayo had committed a felony in the past; testified before a grand jury to save his own skin in a New Milford police theft case; entered the Crafts house to obtain a letter from Richard Crafts's mother and the return-address stickers and planted them on River Road; dropped the chain saw under the bridge—allegations for which DeJoseph would offer not a shred of proof. They were beneath his intelligence but showed how deeply Newtown had been cut.

Long after the trial, an article in *Connecticut* magazine, packed with factual errors and unsupported inferences, and quoting DeJoseph heavily, strongly suggested that Crafts had been framed. DeJoseph said afterward, "Crafts is guilty, guilty, guilty. I told the reporter that but he didn't use it. What bothers me is how some evidence got where it was. And if Walter Flanagan objects to what I've said, to hell with him. After all, he went behind our backs, he threw the first stone."

DeJoseph appeared more interested in punishing the state's attorney than in Crafts's conviction.

Courthouse action in the Crafts case at the end of January 1987 centered on defense motions to exclude the press and public from the deliberations, these being part of a broader strategy aimed at demonstrating that the case ought to be moved elsewhere because Crafts could not obtain a fair trial in the Danbury region. Pretrial hearings were set for early March.

On Monday afternoon, February 9, Crafts was brought to Family Court in Danbury in manacles and leg irons. Inside the courtroom, heart-shaped ornaments on a plastic tree blinked cheerfully, as though Yuletide was imminent; a sign in the middle of the tree read "Merry Christmas."

The Crafts children, who had been living with Sue Lausten, were present, bewildered Kristina clutching a black
teddy bear. The Rodgerses were ordered to take temporary
custody, since Karen was their aunt, and gladly complied.

Rodgers had driven to the court in Helle's Tercel, which
didn't survive for much longer. One day, when the children
were visiting their father in the Bridgeport jail, the car was
stolen and found completely wrecked.

To put an animal through the "suspect" chipper was the idea
of Wayne Carver, who chose a young pig because of its size
and skin, which is similar to human skin in thickness and has
the same amount of hair. Pigskin is sometimes used for skin
grafts. The purpose of the experiment, conducted at Meriden
in February, was to learn how quickly the carcass, drained of
blood and eviscerated, would go through the machine and
whether the bone fractures were consistent with the remnants
found at River Road.

Introduced to the chipper, the thirty-six-pound pig emerged at once as pulp. The destruction of smaller pieces such
as the tail (what emerged bore a remarkable similarity to a
River Road finger) was virtually total, with a complete loss of
soft tissue. The larger pieces, the size of chops, fell nearer to
the spout than the small ones. Carver reasoned that meat had
not been found at River Road because wildlife had eaten it.
The bone fractures were consistent.

Pretrial hearings approached, at which a judge would hear
testimony and decide if probable cause existed to prosecute
Crafts — a foregone conclusion. But the proceedings would
also give the defense advance notice of the prosecution's case
and the right to "discover" — inspect — the state's evidence.

Born in Bridgeport in 1941, J. Daniel Sagarin first studied
engineering, but gave it up for law. He attended Lehigh Uni-

versity, graduating magna cum laude, and Yale Law School. He clerked for a U.S. district judge, became a U.S. attorney, and went into private practice in 1970. In 1976 he teamed with Hurwitz.

Hawkishly handsome with curly silver hair and eyeglasses, and scrappy, articulate, quick, Sagarin is primarily a trial practitioner He'd handled many dozens of cases, including personal injuries, a fire bombing, and two previous murders, both of which he won for the defendant. He took the Crafts case, apart from the money and repute it was likely to bring him, because, he says, "You shouldn't have been in this business if you turned down a challenge like this."

Sagarin's job in a criminal matter is not to determine guilt or innocence, and he pointedly avoids asking his clients such questions. He told Rodgers, "Crafts may have done some bizarre things around that time, but that doesn't prove he's a murderer." His obligation is to provide the best possible defense. His method is to form his theory of the case within an hour of talking to the accused and after that look for any opening he can exploit.

He and Farver filed a raft of motions. One, on March 2, asked Judge Sullivan to remove himself from the case because he'd met with Flanagan in private about it and read the arrest warrant. That made him biased in favor of the prosecution, in Sagarin's view. What's your evidence for the meeting? asked the judge, and Farver answered, "We were given evidence to that fact and Your Honor would be a potential witness to that fact." The claim was unsupported and filed too late, said the judge, and if he hadn't read the arrest warrant, he wouldn't have been doing his job. Sagarin's objective was to replace Sullivan, who had denied reduction of bail, with someone who might be more lenient.

For the probable-cause hearing, which started March 10, Flanagan had planned to call twenty witnesses, but had got through to only the first seven—Dianne Andersen, Sheriff Sullivan, Darien Rentals's Richard Cenami, Trudy Horvath, Helle's mother (who stared grimly at Crafts), Marie Thomas, who testified for five hours, and on the third day, Joseph

236

Hine, who'd seen a medium-sized man with a chipper on River Road — when Sagarin called it quits. He was concerned about the adverse publicity, he said. The case could go to trial.

Just before she took the stand, Marie, waiting in the state's attorney's office, suddenly remembered something she hadn't previously mentioned. In the basement around Thanksgiving she had seen a new freezer in the place of the old one. A freezer! The idea had already occurred to the state's attorney's office, because Dalessio, an amateur chef, knew beef for carpaccio, an elegant Italian appetizer, was easier to slice thin when frozen.

They reasoned that before he cut her up, Crafts must have put Helle in the old freezer, and that was the reason he'd replaced it. Another piece of the puzzle seemed to fall into place.

Still another bail reduction hearing took place at the end of March, this one before Howard Moraghan, the administrative judge at Danbury. Sagarin charged that bail had been set too high and only because of heavy press reporting of a gruesome crime. He insisted that Crafts himself was reliable. He had flown constantly in December and traveled to Vermont in January, always returning home. He would surrender his passport and report to a probation officer.

No, Flanagan argued, bail should not be reduced. The risk was too great. An airline pilot and experienced world traveler might easily take off.

Crafts testified, telling of his CIA-Air America employment, as if to indicate he was a responsible citizen. He fought back tears when Sagarin asked him about his relationship with his children. Crafts asserted that he spoke to them every night and wrote them letters every other day. Would he abandon them if released from jail? Crafts cried and said, "I would never do that." Though he had reported losing fifteen pounds in prison and bleeding internally, five weeks had passed before he'd had a physical. Out. Please let me *out*. I didn't do it, he seemed to say.

237

Motion denied.

Agreement: Flanagan will provide Sagarin with forensic reports, relevant photos, Helle's dental X rays, chain-saw record, Caldor receipt, flight records, Southbury and Newtown police records.

Motion on Return of Property: Flanagan agrees to the guns but not the seized Crown Victoria or Toyota pickup.

Motions (eleven of them on April 24) for transfer of prosecution (denied); for suppression of statements and evidence (denied), for an extension of time (granted), for full copies of all news releases issued by the state's attorney and the police and transcripts of all press conferences (granted); for production of witness statements (granted).

And Sagarin tried a new maneuver: to tie the disappearance of Helle Crafts with that of Regina Brown.

The parallel was indeed uncanny, though the Browns were black. Both women were flight attendants with three children, lived in Newtown, were married to pilots, and were in the midst of a divorce. Regina Brown was last seen by her live-in nanny on March 26, 1987, when dropping her children at Kennedy Airport for a flight to Texas to visit their grandparents. Regina Brown's car had been found, keys in the ignition, in Harlem. The Newtown PD investigated and this time had asked the state police for help.

In May, Sagarin and Farver demanded the records on the Regina Brown investigation. The tactic, clear if farfetched, was intended to suggest that the disappearances of Helle Crafts and Regina Brown were "signature" crimes, that is, crimes marked by factors so similar that it can be assumed one individual is responsible. If that was the case, since Crafts was in jail when Regina Brown vanished, he couldn't have been the culprit. Flanagan responded that Regina Brown's being a stewardess didn't make the two occurrences similar, nor was there evidence that she was dead. But the motion raised the specter of all missing-persons cases in Fairfield County having to be reviewed to ascertain if any were signature crimes.

Judge Myron Ballard having sided with Flanagan, Crafts remained in jail, visitation rights suspended for forty-five days because contraband had been found in his cell—apparently nothing more lethal than a ballpoint pen, which in the jailors' view could be used for suicide or to pick handcuffs. ("Richard's been a bad boy," said a guard to someone who had tried to visit him.)

Though he knew the date wasn't realistic, Sagarin had demanded a trial by jury on March 26. A date for the trial, July 3, wasn't even settled until June 2. Then, because some essential person was always on vacation or otherwise occupied, the trial was put off to the fall.

David Rodgers's loyalty to the man he believed had killed his sister-in-law was so strong that he risked jail himself. Without informing his charmingly straightforward wife, who was appalled when she learned of them, he involved himself in activities that might have led to perjury. He even planned to testify he'd loaned Helle a lot of traveling money the morning she disappeared.

Crafts had asked him to find evidence of major flaws in Helle's character that could be used in his defense. Rodgers thought he understood what that meant: "I came across an unrelated man and woman in Long Island who would have sworn in court that they saw Helle with unsavory foreigners after the eighteenth of November and again at Thanksgiving at a drug party. I paid them $3,000 each as a retainer with another $7,000 each guaranteed upon court appearance. They would have been lying, of course, but they were capable of pulling it off, and they were fairly clean as far as police records go. It would have raised enough questions in the minds of enough jurors, I was sure, that a conviction would have been impossible."

Not only perjury beckoned but also fixing evidence. In prison, Crafts let Rodgers know he was concerned about some linens and burn barrels at the house and the mat missing from his Crown Victoria's trunk, which he wanted "found."

Rodgers made sure those concerns were handled. He surmised that the mat might be damaging evidence, and he was prepared to locate a matching gray mat, sprinkle it with sawdust and remains of a dead cat, and pretend to find the mat on the Currituck Road property. The defense could use it to undermine prosecution claims about waht the police had found in the trunk of the car. Moreover, being in charge of the now empty house on Newfield Lane, Rodgers purposely failed to take security precautions like an alarm system and double-bolted doors. He says he actively encouraged a break-in, which occurred, by someone who had worked for the Craftses, to provide ammunition for a defense claim that the chain saw found under Silver Bridge had been stolen from the house (for which there was no evidence).

But Rodgers got sore.

The immediate objects of his wrath were Crafts's mother, Lucretia, and Richard's other sister and brother-in-law, the Birds. Rodgers claims to have been disappointed with his in-laws for not contributing more than $15,000 to the bail and legal defense fund originally and with Malcolm Bird for entering the Newfield Lane house and his own house without permission and removing possibly incriminating objects. On Crafts's instructions Rodgers himself had destroyed items that might have been incriminating.

However, the real target of his ire was Crafts, who, operating from jail, was feeding him falsehoods and items behind his back. Rodgers, whose time had been spent on Crafts's cause to the exclusion of virtually everything else, felt betrayed. He stopped helping the defense and he eventually turned against Crafts, and began to find him sinister.

The state's attorney's office was working on the assumption that the murder of Helle Crafts and the destruction of her body took place on the snowy night of November 18-19 because that was when Joey Hine recalled he saw the chipper and the U-Haul. Yet that assumption was undermined by the U-Haul rental agency's records, which showed that Crafts had not received the truck from McLaughlin Ford until November 20. Was there another U-Haul? Try as they might, the police couldn't locate one.

Sagarin knew about Flanagan's problem with the U-Haul, since Flanagan had been forced to disclose it. Sagarin would be able to pounce on it in court, and a jury, sensing prosecutorial problems in a case that hung on circumstantial evidence, suspicious movements, and inconsistent stories, might have trouble delivering a guilty verdict.

Somebody who seemed well informed had ideas about the case, for the state's attorney's office received an anonymous letter.

Mr. Flanagan —

The Crafts detectives are still at the wrong tree. Tell 'em to try premise that blue Toyota was in garage, and body in the freezer, at 6 AM on 11/19 — then you'll find everything fits; except for plow guy (who's probably in 48-hour error), and rental guy (who's probably covering a reservation overcharge).

Blue car probably went to NY that noon. Did you know he (Crafts) owned a tow bar which he had a relative dump last spring? Along with disposal containers — materials which weren't too obviously so?

Also figure paper at scene planted by overzealous, but correct, detective.

Whoever wrote the letter — David Rodgers must have had something to do with it; no one else was so knowledgeable about certain aspects of the case — was right on one thing, at least: the plow guy, Joey Hine.

Detective James Monroe had been with the major crime squad for about a year when, on the day of Crafts's arrest, he was assigned to the investigation. In February he became case officer, yet he still had a fresh eye that summer. The others had gone stale from too much poring over evidence and interviews in the process of trying to explain discrepancies. Flanagan asked Monroe to look again at the evidence to see if he could figure out exactly when the murder was committed. He said, "The night of the snowstorm can't be right. It just can't be."

Monroe spent two weeks in the state's attorney's office in August in a methodical review of the flight schedules of Richard and Helle Crafts, phone calls to and from the Crafts residence, the testimony from the probable-cause hearings—all the relevant material. From this material he prepared a time line, which reconstructed Crafts's activities for the month of November and after. He concluded that the critical dates the prosecution had for Crafts's use of the machines simply had to be wrong.

Monroe spoke first with Hine, but even with time cards and weather reports in front of him Hine wouldn't budge from his version of events—he was adamant that he had observed the chipper on the night of November 19—except to admit that, since he'd seen it twice, the second sighting might have been on the night of November 20-21. But before dawn on November 19 Crafts had been home—his phone record showed that he'd called Rodgers at 4:44 A.M.—and it didn't seem possible that he had been on River Road with the chipper he had rented the day before. Equally puzzling, Officer Wildman of Southbury had reported spotting Crafts with the woodchipper and U-Haul on the night of November 20-21. Wildman's date, since he had taken notes, seemed firmest. Monroe was led back to Darien Rentals.

"When you talk with someone, you try to document the facts. But it's not unusual to talk with someone five times with different questions, and suddenly it clicks," says Monroe. He spoke with Louis Braun of Darien Rentals over and over. Braun's memory of the time of day Crafts had picked up the chipper was inconsistent with the recollection of others in the store, just as Richard Cenami's remembrance of the date itself didn't square with that of anyone else at Darien Rentals. All of them were influenced by the fact that Crafts had rented the chipper on November 18. In September a meeting was held with all the Darien Rentals people, and the date and time when the Brush Bandit had actually left the lot, pulled by the U-Haul, was finally settled. Everyone agreed on November 20, and the search for a second U-Haul was finally put to rest.

Monroe learned from a real estate agent that Rodgers, in cleaning out 5 Newfield Lane to rent it, had taken some items with him. Rodgers, who didn't like being questioned, let Monroe look in his garage, where he observed a new Westinghouse freezer, which Rodgers admitted had once been in the Crafts basement. Monroe traced the freezer through the serial number from manufacturer to distributor to Zemel's in Danbury, where he learned the machine had been purchased for cash and taken away by a nameless individual on November 17.

"Jesus Christ! Unbelievable!" Monroe exclaimed. Just before Monroe's discovery, Rodgers had sent the freezer to Danbury to sell on consignment—from jail Crafts had asked him to get rid of it. The machine was hurriedly returned to him when the newspapers reported that the police were looking for Crafts's freezer—by which was meant not the new one but the old one.

The new freezer was never examined by the state police.

Set for September, the pretrial proceedings finally began on Tuesday, October 20, 1987, the day after the stock market collapse.

The defendant wore gray trousers, a light shirt, a tie, and a blue blazer that seemed to get shabbier as the weeks wore on. His hair had been cut and touched up (photos had showed him graying). He appeared pale but in good spirits, smiling and chatting with his lawyers, alert to everything. His hands and jaws were never idle as he put on and removed his eyeglasses, wrote on a legal pad, and chewed gum. He had books with him, including *Connecticut Rules of Evidence 1981*, which Rodgers had bought for him. "Crafts" was penciled across the bottom of the pages.

Presiding was Judge Moraghan, a short, bulky man with a great dome of a bald head that sometimes appeared like a rising moon from behind the law books lining the bench. At the outset Moraghan imposed a gag order on all the lawyers. They were not to speak to news people for the duration of the trial, which was expected to last into the following year. "Counsel will not try the case in the press," he commanded. The order was understandable; Sagarin could be expected to do exactly that, hoping publicity would help his motion for a transfer of prosecution, on which the judge had said he'd rule in about two weeks.

Sagarin, playfully clutching his throat, objected that the gag violated the First Amendment and was unfair. Publicity had already damaged his case, and the order denied him a means of refutation in the media. The defense's answer was to subpoena local newspapers and radio stations for circulation and listenership figures and for clips and tapes. Sagarin had a dual purpose: to demonstrate that the news media had covered the story to saturation level and to show that his client had been convicted by journalism and therefore couldn't obtain a fair trial in the Danbury district.

If the media inquiries were largely a joke to the prosecution, what followed was not: Sagarin's motion to suppress evidence that came from the December 26 and January 9 search warrants from the Crafts house. He wrote to the court, "Nothing . . . remotely suggested a 'crime of violence,' let alone a murder. It simply amounts to a claim a woman was missing, a divorce was pending, the woman had expressed some undefined and amorphous fear, and the husband did not acknowledge she was missing. Nor is there anything that suggests that evidence of six weeks prior should still be expected to be there."

The prosecution worried about the suppression motion. The December 26 warrant could be said to rely on hearsay and to lack probable cause. The January 9 warrant had contained forensic material and was far stronger, but suppose Moraghan threw out both? If the state was prevented from presenting the evidence contained in either one, the case would be lost.

Sagarin roundly attacked the competence of the major

244

crime squad, proclaiming the River Road evidence was the "ill-gotten fruit of a poisoned search." The prosecution and the major crime squad denied the accusation, and Moraghan's questions seemed to indicate that he agreed with them.

Sagarin insisted Judge McDonald wouldn't have signed the search warrants had the polygraph results been included, but Flanagan shot back at him that if Crafts had failed the test, inserting the results would have been prejudicial and inadmissible; Sagarin couldn't have it both ways. In any case, McDonald had signed the papers because there had been plenty of proof.

Responding to Sagarin's endless complaints about the case's notoriety and to demands for a change of venue (transfer of the trial to another location), Moraghan wanted to know how it compared with the Arne Cheyenne Johnson "demon" trial in 1981, which hadn't been moved. Johnson had been charged with stabbing his landlord to death over an argument about his girlfriend, who claimed Johnson was possessed by a demon. A pair of demonologists claimed Johnson had participated in at least three exorcism rites on an eleven-year-old boy, prompting the Bridgeport archdiocese to dispatch an investigator. Flanagan grinned. The demon trial had taken place early in his tenure in the district. He had argued successfully to bar the devil from the courtroom, and Johnson got ten to twenty. The demon trial had been rated top story of the year by the *News-Times*, and Flanagan had been a technical consultant for the film, a stinker.

With Moraghan reserving decision on most of the motions, jury selection began on November 5, after ten tedious days of pretrial.

Sagarin did not like the jury panel, which had been selected from voting lists and telephone books. Nearly all the potential jurors were white and members of the middle class. One of the reasons Sagarin wanted a change of venue was that he wanted represented on the jury blue-collar working people, the self-employed, the poor, and nonwhites. He was concerned by the "deaf and dumb" syndrome of jurors who would not admit publicly to a bias against his client.

245

Indeed, as juror after juror was interrogated by prosecution and defense in the courtroom, an overwhelming impression of sameness emerged. Generally they worked in executive or clerical positions (or their husbands or wives did) for IBM or Pitney Bowes, were married and had never been divorced, had two or three children, owned their own home, and lived in the suburbs. They seemed to desire to be jurors for such a famous trial.

The judge could disqualify jurors and he could agree with a challenge; if he did, it didn't count as preemptive challenge. Each side had eighteen of these until Sagarin argued for double that number and Moraghan gave both sides fifteen more. Flanagan used few of his—exuding confidence, he pranced around the small area of floor, across which Sagarin managed to stride—while the defense exhausted its allotment.

Though Sagarin said he decided pro or con by instinct shaped by his courtroom experience, he had a long list of fixed principles. Understanding the presumption of innocence and having an ability to keep an open mind for the duration of the trial were musts. ("Do you reach conclusions quickly?") Those who showed too much leadership potential were out. ("This guy could turn the jury around. I can't take the chance.") Being too close to, or displaying too much deference toward, law enforcement meant rejection, as did a CIA connection. Candidates who were too familiar with a chain saw or had used a woodchipper got the ax. Sagarin refused sentimental women, people who had moral objections to divorce, and anyone who had seen a poster or T-shirt displaying the slogan DIVORCE—CONNECTICUT STYLE and a drawing of a woodchipper. In some sessions nine out of ten potential jurors would be challenged and excused.

What with late starts and days off, because Moraghan not only had administrative duties to attend to but also sat on the Willis Brown divorce and child custody case (which was also a sort of test trial of the pilot who was suspected of having done in his missing wife), December 24 arrived before twelve jurors had been selected, leaving three alternates to go. Four jury pools totaling 240 prospects had been gone through. Over one hundred had been excused by the judge in the voir dire room and eighty-six others in court. Sagarin had challenged twenty-one, Flanagan only four. The effort to assemble a complete jury would begin again in early January.

Had the individuals in the jury panel broken the rule against letting themselves be exposed to the case, they could have learned from subsequent reporting that on November 19 Karen Rodgers, executrix of Helle Crafts's estate, on behalf of Helle's children, had filed a wrongful death suit against her brother for $234,000, representing unpaid child support and half the value of the properties the couple had jointly owned. The purpose was to tie up Crafts's assets. The suit stated explicitly that Crafts had caused his wife's death. Karen had to make that claim for legal reasons, but had no doubt about its truth.

Unknown to Karen, however, Sagarin had quietly transferred the liens on the properties to Lucretia Crafts in exchange for her sending the defense lawyers $100,000 to $140,000 (the Rodgerses didn't know the exact amount) in addition to the $15,000 she'd already contributed. With the $35,000 from Crafts (the $5,000 retainer to Sagarin and the $30,000 advanced by Rodgers), plus about $10,000 more from David Rodgers, Hurwitz & Sagarin almost certainly received close to $200,000 for Crafts's defense.

The jury might also have learned that in late December a federal judge threw out Moraghan's gag order as unconstitutional. Few doubted that Moraghan wished to preside over the case, and some suspected his ego might have been bruised by being overturned—judges dislike that. Certainly he waited a long time before stepping down, though a ruling by the Connecticut supreme court bound him to at least go through the motions of determining whether a defendant could get a fair trial in Danbury. Sagarin disagreed with the Connecticut supreme court. In his view, the judge, Flanagan, and he should have been able to settle the venue issue among themselves before jury selection began.

On January 5, to the surprise and chagrin of the state's attorney's office, Moraghan — having learned, he said, that several jurors knew that Crafts was accused of having put his wife through a chipper — suddenly granted a transfer of prosecution. He agreed that a fair trial couldn't be held in Danbury. It was an honorable decision, in view of the time and effort Moraghar had put in. In March he announced the new location: New London.

17

New London

On the steps of the New London courthouse Sagarin removed his eyeglasses and scratched his gray head. "Maybe Helle had a secret nobody knew, and this is why she didn't want to go to divorce court against her husband. Nothing in divorce court is sacred, and she had a secret she'd kept so long that she was nervous. Helle vanished because she had something to hide. Or somebody killed her. And somebody planted evidence." That somebody, Sagarin strongly hinted, was Keith Mayo.

Sagarin's strategy was three-pronged: make the prosecution prove beyond reasonable doubt that somebody was dead, that the somebody had been Helle Crafts, and that Richard Crafts had killed her. The task would not be easy. The state had a powerful circumstantial case, but Sagarin had a weapon, the tremendous publicity the case attracted.

Even before it commenced in the old whaling town of New London, part-time home of Eugene O'Neill and birthplace of the nuclear submarine, the Crafts trial was well on the way to becoming the most famous in the state's recent history. It was the first to be tried without a body, a body that had been destroyed in a bizarre fashion, if the prosecution was to be believed. Spousicide had become almost a run-of-the-mill event, but a woodchipper! Truly shocking was the ingenuity displayed in the use of machinery, and some people were quietly admiring.

Connecticut's death penalty, last exercised in 1962, applied (with technical exceptions) only to cop killers and serial murderers. If convicted on a single count of homicide, Crafts faced twenty-five to sixty years in prison, sentence depending on the judge.

The judge would be Barry Schaller, fifty, Connecticut-born, graduate of Yale and Yale law, and specialist in civil litigation when in private practice. He had been appointed to the circuit court in 1974 and the superior court, the state's highest trial tribunal, in 1978. A good many judges wanted to be assigned to the Crafts case on account of its visibility and unprecedented forensic evidence. Schaller, who had presided over hundreds of trials, had been chosen because he was considered an especially adroit practitioner. A poll taken in 1986 of 1,200 lawyers, rating sixty-six judges up for reappointment on courtroom demeanor, competence, and fairness, put Schaller close to the top.

New London administrative judge Seymour Hendel, who knows Schaller, says, "Judges are as different from one another as other people. Each has his own style. Schaller tries to be unaggressive, peaceful, and polite. But judges vary in their sentencing too, from easy to tough." Schaller's reputation tended to toughness, but he bridles at the charge, believing it stems from a handful of repeated offenders in unusual cases in which long sentences have seemed to him appropriate, like the sixty years Schaller gave to one repeater convicted of armed robberies.

Schaller had sat on about ten homicide trials, sometimes as part of a judicial panel, and what with acquittals and findings of insanity, had never himself sentenced a murderer. He had looked forward to the proceedings. In the midst of the case he commented, "To match the interest and excitement of this trial will be hard."

Jury selection began on March 14, 1988, a Monday.

250

Mondays hadn't been Crafts days in Danbury, because there courts and judges had been tied up with administrative business and short motions, but Schaller, on loan from New Haven, had the murder trial as his only juridical occupation. Courteous and often quiet, Schaller, who has sandy-gray hair and a gray-white mustache, listened intently as the lawyers subjected prospective jurors to voir dire questioning, intended to winnow, in the view of either side or the court, those who should not serve. Sagarin's assertion that the case had received more publicity in Danbury than anywhere else seemed borne out. Many candidates were virginal in their knowledge of the alleged murder. Most worked for Electric Boat, which produces nuclear submarines, or Pfizer, the drug manufacturer. Sagarin had escaped the white-collar trap he'd professed to worry about; now he'd have technicians and factory workers on whom to cast his spell. He wanted "*real people*—they don't buy circumstantial evidence so easily—instead of middle management nonpeople, who don't care about anybody." Sagarin had a knack for being outrageous.

Flanagan claimed he didn't want a homogeneous jury, though he seemed to prefer homeowners, and those who read detective stories or watched "LA Law" or "any of those silly programs" were not looked upon by him with favor. In actuality, the two sides had in mind quite different specifications. Flanagan feared people whose reactions might be unpredictable, subject to fantasy or hidden concerns, too easily swayed by the defense—wild cards, loose cannons. Sagarin, whose bias against middle management people tipped his hand, was not nearly so interested in the emotional stability of jurors and wouldn't have minded a couple of wild cards.

After Sagarin had objected, unsuccessfully, to the proceedings' being televised—Crafts didn't want his children to suffer from the greater exposure television would give the case—jury selection went smoothly. A Navy civilian had told his wife a joke: "The man's innocent. He instructed his wife not to clean the machine while it's running." But he had

251

no opinion on the case and was accepted.

The thirty-third to be questioned was Warren Maskell. Maskell was forty-seven, former army staff sergeant and Vietnam vet, married, carpenter for Electric Boat, a home-owner, who liked to plant things, he said. That Maskell had in his living room a five-foot-high statue of St. Joseph, the patron saint of carpenters, was not brought out nor the fact that he had been a game warden.

Because of the great number of witnesses to be called, the Danbury district for the first time in any of its cases used two prosecutors. The second was Brian Cotter, forty-four, a graduate of Boston University Law School. Cotter had worked a year for a Danbury law firm and been eased out, according to one of its partners, for laziness. He'd become a state's attorney in 1972 and evidently shaped up, because he was Flanagan's best assistant prosecutor. On March 18, Cotter put Maskell through the voir dire, Flanagan having been up late to celebrate St. Patrick's Day. Maskell would be proud to serve on the jury, he said, and though Sagarin had said he didn't trust those who wished too much to serve, Maskell was the tenth juror chosen.

Schaller privately expressed surprise at the speed of selection. On Wednesday, March 23, the jury panel of twelve and three alternates was complete. Expected to last six to eight weeks, the trial was set for April 4.

Two serious setbacks for the prosecution forces occurred that day, but they were aware of only one.

Schaller ruled that evidence from Crafts's Crown Victoria was inadmissible because the search warrant failed to include the car once it had been removed from the Currituck Road property. This was a blow for Flanagan, since the human tissue and wood chips found in the trunk were vital links to the accused.

The second event, occurring within the mind of Warren Maskell, was even more serious. Lis Nielsen, Helle's seventy-nine-year-old mother, whom the prosecution had flown from Denmark, was the first witness. She testified through an interpreter that Helle had telephoned or written to her every two weeks without fail, as shown by postmarked letters she had brought with her, but suddenly the calls and letters had stopped. She stated that in November 1986, when Crafts had told people she was sick, she was in fact well. But for Maskell her expression outweighed her words.

Sometimes seeming on the verge of tears, Lis Nielsen gazed nervously around the courtroom and tried to smile. She glanced at Crafts and the fleeting smile may have lingered on her face but not in her heart. The man had been accused of murdering her only child, and she must have loathed him. Nonetheless—alone among the jurors—Maskell believed she had conferred a smile upon Crafts. From then on, Maskell continued to doubt that Helle Crafts was dead. In a sense, the trial had already ended.

Flanagan proceeded to draw a cohesive story from more than thirty witnesses—Helle's demand for a divorce and her fears, Mayo's surveillance, Crafts's renting and buying of equipment. With Officer Wildman's testimony, tension descended on the courtroom; surely Flanagan was about to bring on Hine, the roadworker who had testified at the pretrial hearings that he had seen the woodchipper on River Road. That would have been the next logical link in the evidence chain, leaving only the forensic evidence. But Flanagan produced Judy Kurzner.

Crafts's sometime girlfriend was a pretty brunette who had known him since 1972. She lived near Newtown. She had dropped Crafts in 1980 not because he had a wife, Flanagan established with mock astonishment, but because he had another girlfriend. In 1986, when he was on duty as a Southbury policeman, he had sirened her down for speeding.

"Did he give you a ticket?"

"No."

The relationship had been rekindled. In December he

stopped by her condo. Flanagan brought down the house with, "What was he wearing, if anything?"

"His police uniform. He came back that night. He said nothing about Helle's disappearance and I noticed nothing unusual. He left a little after six in the morning. He had to see the kids and make their breakfast."

Learning that Nancy Dodd was scheduled to visit Crafts, Flanagan had subpoenaed her at the Montville jail, avoiding the cumbersome out-of-state witness procedure. With both women at the courthouse on the same day, he kept them in separate rooms. On the stand Dodd told Flanagan she had nothing to say – she'd been good friends with Crafts since 1977; yes, she had been aware that he was married, she had known about Kurzner. Small and slender, with a silicone silhouette, Dodd was a reluctant witness but had worn a tight dress for the occasion.

Flanagan's intention was to show Crafts's callousness in blithely continuing to see two women when he should have been distraught about his wife. With Hine still on hold, the prosecutor moved on to the state police investigation, which included the divers, and reached the forensics. Following testimony by Dr. Albert Harper that the River Road bones had been completely fractured, Flanagan turned to the dental evidence, which was vital to the case. Harper had testified that the bones were human, so somebody must have died; and Flanagan had to prove that the person was Helle Crafts.

Since the Craftses' family dentist, Dr. James Fox, was not deemed by the court to be an expert forensic witness and was not permitted to testify on whether the two crowns found belonged to Helle Crafts, the state retained the services of Dr. Constantine Karazulas. A dentist, oral surgeon, and forensic odontologist, Dr. Karazulas appeared first on May 11. In practice since 1960, Karazulas had interned at Kings County Hospital in Brooklyn, which housed a prison where bite-mark analyses aroused his interest in forensics. A fellow of the American Academy of Forensic Sciences, he had been consulted by prosecution or defense in over one hundred cases. He'd participated in the forensic investigation of the crash of two 747s in the Canary Islands, in which 349 people died, many having been incinerated, and helped identify close to three hundred, the majority by X rays. He'd also identified dead sailors from the USS *Stark* in 1987.

Karazulas explained that identification of a dental cap required X-raying the cap from all five sides and comparing the results with original X rays, which inevitably have been taken from slightly different angles. He looked for patterns that were repeated in the two sets of X rays and might have to take nine hundred X rays to accomplish this. The more teeth you had to work with the better, but a single one would suffice.

Equipped with X rays taken by Dr. Fox, Karazulas had paired the first hollow cap found on River Road in an early try. The second cap, which he himself had found, had proved to be a lower left second bicuspid. The root—he had never before seen a root fracture—had been sheared in half by traumatic force. Again he'd matched his X rays with Dr. Fox's. He showed photographs of the two sets of X rays. They appeared to be identical.

"What tooth was it?" Sagarin asked heavily.

"I determined it to be a lower left second bicuspid," Karazulas answered slowly and precisely.

Sagarin's level of argumentativeness, always high, rose for his cross-examination of Karazulas, as though this was a round he needed to win. He attacked Karazulas's training and tried to show that teeth other than Helle's might have produced the same configurations.

"Is it fair to say you can take a great number of X rays of the same object and they will appear different in size and shape?"

"In size, yes," Karazulas admitted, but not shape, that being distinctive, because the five surfaces were like fingerprints. But Sagarin succeeded in rattling him, and Karazulas blurted, "Ask my wife," and "You can give me a lie detector test." Inwardly Flanagan must have groaned.

The last thing he wanted from his supposedly detached scientific witness was a temper fit.

Supporting Karazulas's position was Dr. Lowell Levine, part-time director of forensic science for the New York state police. A dental surgeon and former U.S. Navy captain, Levine had been part of the team identifying some nine thousand people buried by the Argentine military government. In 1985, using German dental records, he had helped identify the remains of Joseph Mengele, the Nazi criminal infamous for experiments on concentration camp prisoners. He worked on the MOVE and *Stark* victims, and for the U.S. Congress he established that the corpse of President John F. Kennedy was indeed Kennedy. He identified victims from the Ted Bundy mass-murder case. Fifty years old, Levine feared he looked like Buddy Hackett.

Having examined Karazulas's X rays and Fox's, Levine wasn't quite prepared to state that both teeth had been the victim's — so the experts could differ, as Sagarin noted. That a tooth was consistent with X rays was not positive identification by itself; Levine looked for unique characteristics. In the tooth encompassing a portion of root and jawbone, he had discovered one. "That tooth, that tooth, the lower left second bicuspid, belonged to Helle Crafts when she was alive," Levine stated.

With both forensic odontologists agreeing "with reasonable scientific certainty" — which meant they had no doubt whatever — that at least one capped tooth had been placed in the mouth of Helle Crafts by Dr. Fox, Sagarin's second line of defense — to make the prosecution prove that the victim was Helle Crafts and no other — had seemingly been swept away.

Sagarin accomplished what he could. He extracted from Levine his fee for the trial, $175 per hour in and out of court, including witness waiting time, plus expenses. (Levine, as part of Lee's forensic team, had worked for nothing in the early stages of the investigation.) That meant that Levine would bill the state for at least $6,000, and he testified ten to fifteen times a year in different cases Sagarin intended to show that Levine was a gun for hire. He then attacked him on scientific grounds. Sagarin tried to master the forensic fields so he could speak their language, but as an instant odontologist he was plainly in over his head. Hadn't somebody written, he asked, that in charting the human mouth two and a half billion configurations could be found? Enough to leave room for error, he seemed to suggest. The figure, from a book fifteen years old, applied to written dental records, Levine replied, not to X rays. He added, "I have absolutely no doubt that the tooth belonged to Helle Crafts." Sagarin had succeeded in changing "reasonable scientific certainty" to "absolutely no doubt."

Sagarin's third line of defense, to make the prosecution prove that Richard Crafts had killed Helle, was also threatened. The jury had heard testimony, which the defense had yet to discredit, about Crafts's possession of the woodchipper. But where was Hine? Why wasn't Flanagan having him appear?

Instead, the forensic evidence continued. Dr. Alan Reffer, a radiologist with the University of Connecticut School of Dentistry, agreed with Levine, and so did Wayne Carver, now Deputy Chief Medical Examiner, who in Sagarin's opinion would testify as he was told by the prosecution. Sagarin objected that Carver had usurped the role of the jury by having ruled the cause of death was homicide.

Dr. Lee at last, the cleanup hitter, a forensic star if there ever was one, smiling, modest, and superbly confident. Lee was careful to note that the findings of his laboratory had been sent to outside experts for verification, the hair for instance, to Dr. Harold Deadman of the FBI, the blue fibers found by the police in the chain-saw housing and elsewhere to Dr. John E. Reffner, a textile specialist, who had used infrared microspectrum photography (both of these experts had already testified). Flanagan introduced a piece of the fabric on which hair and blood had been found, and Crafts studied it intently, as he did every piece of evidence.

"Lee is about the best witness I've ever seen," says Sagarin. "He understands the courtroom and he's a man of substantial integrity." Sagarin didn't try to confront Lee, hoping instead to find grounds in his testimony for attacking other forensic witnesses for the prosecution. But one part of Lee's testimony Sagarin found weak: the prosecution's handling of the absence of a matching fingerprint.

Attached to the polished nail found at River Road was a tiny piece of flesh and on it was a section of a fingerprint. The state police had failed to dust the Crafts house for Helle's fingerprints, knowing they would inevitably be found and believing, before the nail had been found at River Road, that they would have no significance (though, as it turned out, those prints might have been important). In any case, the print from the flesh was from a section to the side of the nail. Not all organizations roll prints to cover the side of the finger. The FBI and Interpol do it, but not Pan Am, so the police, having only Pan Am prints, could not match the print from the flesh placed in evidence with Helle's known fingerprints. But the prosecution failed to establish clearly the reason for absence of a matching finger· print.

Sandwiched between Lee's appearances (he testified for three days, touching on all the major forensic evidence) on May 26, in the ninth week of the trial, was Dr. Robert Hoadley of the University of Massachusetts. Hoadley, a professor of wood sciences, was slightly deaf from using a chain saw. Sagarin complained bitterly that he should have received Hoadley's reports earlier, implying that a sort of statute of limitations existed on evidence, and Hoadley's had expired. Flanagan said, "Justice is not a perishable commodity and contains no expiration date."

Before the jury heard Hoadley, Farver argued strenuously that he should be precluded as a witness on the grounds of lack of credentials in that the professor had never taken or taught a course in toolmaking. Motion denied and the jury back, Hoadley began to describe differences in cutting marks made by various tools, explaining that irregularities in blades mirrored themselves in wood. He was inching toward the chipper when Farver broke in.

This was the first the courtroom had seen of Farver at any length. Sagarin's calculated style was to take control, if he could, impressing the jury with his authority and knowledge. He used well-practiced sonorous phrases—"rank with speculation," "opinion evidence"—and knowing stares. Farver by comparison seemed boyish, bland, and boring, but in endlessly questioning Hoadley's competence as a witness, the defense had a purpose. Memorial Day had arrived; and, rather than giving the jury too much to chew on over the three-day weekend, Farver stalled.

On Tuesday Hoadley was back. Using instruments, he had examined wood chips from the River Road site, from the U-Haul, and from the Currituck Road property. The River Road chips—sycamore, white pine, maple, beech—matched species found in the U-Haul, which contained, in addition, other woods, which were to be found on the Currituck Road land. Since the River Road chip mixture and the Currituck chip mixture did not match, the conclusion was that the chipping had been done at different times (but before Crafts had returned the U-Haul, since chips were aboard when he did).

All the samples had been chipped by the same machine, Hoadley deduced from the cut marks, but when used on the Currituck wood, the blades had been duller, which had to mean that the Currituck chipping had been done later. And the blades had been exposed to hard objects, such as rock, metal, or bone.

The chips from the Crown Victoria trunk would have vastly aided Hoadley's analysis.

Next the jury saw a videotape of the pig's destruction in the chipper, proof of what the blades could do.

Detective James Monroe, examining interviews in the prosecutor's room next to the courtroom, came across his own interview with Joe Williams the previous January. Monroe hadn't followed up the interview because Williams had been so vague on the date and time of day he'd seen the chipper on Silver Bridge that his version didn't sound feasible. On a chance, Monroe phoned Williams's Chinese girlfriend, Nonnie Lowe, and left his number. Nonnie, whose English was imperfect, didn't get the message straight Williams returned the call to the Monroe, Connecticut, police department, which advised him to call Newtown. Williams explained the situation to Harry Noroian, who, no doubt smirking, referred Williams to Detective Monroe.

The Newtown PD tipped O'Neill, who wrote a story, the publicity more or less assuring Williams's appearance in court, though Flanagan had considered Williams a loose cannon.

When Monroe interviewed Nonnie Lowe and Williams at the courthouse during the weekend before he appeared, their story was different from the one Williams had previously given, though he hadn't notified the police about his change of mind. Sagarin objected violently that he'd learned of Williams only two days before he took the stand.

Joe Williams, reinterviewed by Detective James Monroe the week before, testified that he had assumed snow had been falling when he sighted the chipper on, he thought, the early morning of November 20, and at first he had recalled being alone in his car, but Nonnie Lowe had reminded him that she'd been with him and that it had been raining.

When he nearly ran his car into the chipper he'd cursed. That meant Nonnie's children were not in the car, since he never used bad words in their presence. That told him the children had been with their father, which helped lead Williams to the conclusion that he'd actually seen the chipper on the evening of the twentieth. Williams said he had finally remembered the truck attached to the chipper was a U-Haul.

"I was going to Southbury to find a McDonald's or a Chinese restaurant to have some tea or coffee. First I heard this loud noise and I said to my girlfriend, 'What is this?' Then I nearly ran into the chipper. I had owned a chipper and that one was bigger."

The back of the U-Haul was partially open and he had

noticed plastic bags. He had also seen a man between the U-Haul and the chipper.

"Can you describe him?" Brian Cotter asked.

"Yes. I saw a picture of him on TV. He was about five foot nine, a little bigger than me. He was white, maybe about my age. I'm fifty."

Cotter said, "Is the individual you saw that night in the courtroom?"

Williams looked hard at the defendant. "I would say there are similarities, but I'm not positive because it was dark outside. He wasn't wearing any glasses." He pointed at Crafts. "But that gentleman over there, of everybody in here, he looks the most similar. But I wouldn't say yes."

In court Crafts habitually put his glasses on and off but in front of Williams he wore glasses continuously. Further to confuse Williams, Sagarin and Farver, both well over six feet tall, slumped in their chairs and Crafts sat on something that raised him so that they all appeared to be the same height.

About the sighting, Sagarin asked, "Isn't it fair to say that even last week you didn't know what day it [the sighting] was?" and Williams had to agree. But Cotter guided Williams through on the weather and the date.

Williams's testimony set the stage for the long-awaited testimony of Joey Hine.

Flanagan had waited to call him until other witnesses had given credibility to the prosecution's version of events because Hine stuck to his story even though his time cards and the weather contradicted the dates and times he claimed to have spotted the chipper—November 21 was the only night he had worked past 1:18 A.M. that week. With Hine on the stand, Flanagan carefully gave him latitude on dates.

"Were you plowing out on those roads between the nineteenth and the twenty-first?"

"Yes, I was. We were plowing."

"You plowed along the Housatonic River? Would you tell us the name of the road?"

"River Road."

"On the nineteenth did you sand or plow River Road?"

"I don't believe I plowed, but I was going up and down."

"And you were there some of those days?"

"Yes, I was."

"You were plowing all those days?"

"Yeah."

Williams having changed the date of his sighting from the morning to the evening, and now Hine sticking to the nineteenth, Sagarin jumped in. He accused the state of trying to "fit pieces of the mosaic together and the pieces just don't fit."

If Flanagan had problems convincing some of his key witnesses that their dates and/or times were wrong, Sagarin had one too. Wildman and others had encountered Crafts, the U-Haul, and the chipper on the night of November 20-21; with Sagarin insisting that Hine had witnessed the mechanical combination on November 18-19, he had to reconcile the dates, and he came up with an ingenious solution: there had been *two* trucks and *two* chippers. The first set must have been driven not by Crafts but by someone who had some sinister connection with the River Road evidence. Sagarin went on to say that the state might have commingled tiny human bone fragments of whatever origin (drowning victims? migrant farm workers?) that had already existed at the River Road site with the remains of a body brought from some other place.

Crafts had been framed, Sagarin wanted the jury to believe.

Planting evidence was a rough charge, and Flanagan said stiffly, "Aren't you concerned about ending your case on that note?"

"You knew you were in trouble when the jury said, 'Good morning, Dr. Lee!' as he returned to the courtroom," Sagarin says.

The defense had moved to have the mattress cover from

262

the Craftses' bedroom excluded because the bloodstain evidence was too speculative—the state admitted it couldn't say where and when death had occurred. Flanagan responded that the case was notable for its circumstantial nature and since prosecution was contending that the bedroom had been the last location of Helle's life and an unusual series of events had occurred there, the jury must be allowed to speculate. Schaller overruled the defense; he had broad discretion and thought the evidence admissible. Besides, he said, bloodstain evidence was less likely than before to lead juries astray, because scientific progress had brought accuracy.

With the jury present, Lee, producing a collapsible pointer, indicated stains on the mattress cover that had been made by blood. Splashing red ink, Lee demonstrated medium velocity impact on a piece of paper. He pointed to the swiping pattern on the side of the mattress that could have resulted from an effort to clean up.

Lee reviewed the entire forensic evidence and got to the dark patch on the rug of which Marie Thomas had spoken that Crafts had told her had been caused by kerosene.

Lee had tested four kinds of kerosene, including diesel, and the stains had disappeared in five minutes.

On the stand again, Marie Thomas answered to a question from Flanagan about nail polish, referring to the nail found on River Road, that Helle had used two kinds, Shisheido 25 and Revlon Raven Red, sometimes mixing them. She drew a gasp from the courtroom when testifying that Helle often wore a blue nightshirt with pockets. The blue fiber! (The jury also learned from Lee that the silky material discovered on River Road might have been fragments of panties.)

Flanagan had one more surprise. Riffling through the River Road finds at the courthouse, he had belatedly come across a crumpled paper that turned out to be a letter, postmarked November 12 in Florida, from "Mother Crafts" and deftly slipped it into evidence at the beginning of May. "Nobody could have planted *that*," he said triumphantly in the corridor. Of course, Sagarin claimed exactly that.

Few had been aware of the letter until Karen Rodgers testified the signature was indeed her mother's. The letter was nicked, and the assumption Flanagan intended the jury to make was that it had been on the person of Helle Crafts when she had been chipped.

At 11:37 on the morning of June 7, Flanagan uttered the momentous words, "The state rests."

Sagarin's talent for infighting and his assertive style gave him an advantage over the more staid prosecution in the media theater, where he constantly alluded to collusion to convict his client. But he would never say who was supposed to be plotting or how high collusion went in the planting of evidence. When asked, he would raise his eyes suggestively.

Sagarin's stated aim was to balance the attention the prosecution's case received. He wasn't encouraging the jury to heed his innuendos, he insisted, but if, in violation of the court order, some or all of the jury were following the trial in the news, directly or through their families, he wanted his version listened to. A trial created its own atmosphere, and even chance remarks overheard by jurors could have a major effect.

Outwardly, relations between prosecution and defense appeared cordially collegial, but Flanagan fumed. In his opinion, he had bent over backward to be fair to Sagarin in providing evidence when he had it, well in advance of its being presented — more so than in any of his trials — but Sagarin told reporters the prosecution held out on him. Cotter was livid about Sagarin's innuendos: "We have to stick to the letter of the law, but he says whatever he wants."

Cotter had become nervous about the outcome. Sagarin hammered away, hinting of major developments now that his turn had come.

His client dwelled in Montville jail, eight miles from New London, supposedly a country club compared to Somers,

264

where, if convicted, Crafts would be sent. Although the warden and his staff tried to be humane, one look at the crowded, noisy place would make anyone realize how fervently Crafts wished to be out of prison.

Breakfast was at 8:15—on court days, a problem because lunch is the big meal of the day in jail, and the accused takes a sandwich with him. Every time he returns from court he is subjected to a body search. Supper starts at 4:30. Lights out at eleven, though Mr. Chips or Buzz, as the inmates called him, a celebrity, could read by the light in the corridor. The other six-by-eight cells in the maximum-security unit were decorated with girly pinups, but Crafts's was monastic. Towels and socks hung above the seatless toilet. A calendar marking the children's birthdays was posted on the wall, and a box filled with papers lay on the floor.

"Dear Karen and David," Crafts wrote on April 19, 1988:

> During a discussion this morning with Mr. Sagarin, he advised me of the necessity for additional funds in order to complete the trial. He enumerated several options available in order to acquire these funds. The least bothersome method will require some modification of our present arrangement regarding civil litigation pending [Karen's wrongful-death suit to attach his assets]. . . . A little indulgence please. The time has come to put differences aside and demonstrate a family solidarity. I need some help and I'm calling on you to provide it. Thank you, Richard.

In the previous January, Flanagan had marshaled the evidence against Crafts for the Rodgerses, and Karen had put aside whatever small doubt she still possessed. Now, hating her brother for murdering his wife, her friend, she declined to accommodate him.

The homicide indictment, and for David Rodgers, Crafts's manipulation of his relatives, had torn the once close-knit Crafts clan asunder. Two issues divided Karen

265

and David Rodgers from the Florida part of the family. One was Crafts's guilt—neither Lucretia nor the Birds accepted it—and the other was the children, whom the Southern branch wanted to live with Malcolm and Suzanne in Florida. Crafts also wanted his children sent to Florida, despite the love and care they received in Westport. It seemed that he wanted to get them out of the state: two of them could at least testify they'd seen their father strike their mother, but Flanagan genteelly refused to call them to the stand.

Karen couldn't believe anyone would subject the children to another relocation.

"Dear Mother," she wrote on May 15, 1988:

> There is no point in responding to your letter item by item. It would only create more animosity. Suffice it to say that we are currently in opposing positions. I see no remedy for that at the present time. I'm sorry you had to mortgage your house and you don't sleep at night. It's a shame that events have done that to you.
>
> If you are concerned about the welfare of any of your grandchildren in my care, I suggest you catch a plane and come appraise the situation for yourself. I'll be happy to make a motel reservation for you.
>
> Sincerely,

Not friendly words! Karen prayed a guilty verdict would enable the family to reunite, but of that she hadn't much chance.

As the defense round opened, Sagarin said he now worked for nothing; Hurwitz & Sagarin, with their bookkeeper tallying court days, outside hours, and expenses, had simply run through the $200,000 or so the Crafts family had paid him.

Sagarin told reporters that the state's case was extraordinarily weak; because reasonable doubt existed, his defense would be minimal. It was, partly because he could not emulate Flanagan by producing a stream of character witnesses. He could only try to cast doubt on previous testimony.

Flanagan had previously called William Goldstein, Crafts's pilot pal, to establish that Crafts had been in Newtown on the morning of November 19, where Goldstein had seen him. Goldstein had then stated that Helle had told him, referring to Crafts's affairs, "He has his and I have mine." Now, as Sagarin's witness, Goldstein testified that he had been with his wife to the house on Newfield Lane on November 20, and to find reading material for the toilet, had entered the master bedroom; he noticed no patch on the rug, smelled no kerosene; his wife saw no tire tracks in the yard. But there was no special reason she should have looked there; and Marie Thomas had observed Goldstein and Crafts conferring seriously on the afternoon of that day. To the prosecution, at least, Goldstein lacked credibility.

So also did Michael DeJoseph, who testified that Marie Thomas had told him she'd heard Helle cough at three in the morning of November 19. Flanagan was convinced that DeJoseph was in collusion with Sagarin; both denied the allegation. Sagarin said he'd tried to talk with DeJoseph, and DeJoseph said he'd refused. They both said they had never spoken to each other. Sagarin had found a note about Marie's statement DeJoseph had scribbled in the Newtown file and had subpoenaed DeJoseph, who testified truthfully to his own note. But the state's attorney's office believed DeJoseph was helping Sagarin in the hope that the Newtown PD would be exonerated if Crafts were acquitted. Suspicion ran high.

On June 10, Sagarin presented his first forensic expert, Dr. Jeffrey Burkes, oral and facial surgeon and consulting medical examiner for New York City. Burkes, who had won awards, had credentials equal to the prosecution's forensic

267

odontologists and he knew Lowell Levine well, having studied under him Burkes threw out one of the two teeth as useless for identification purposes, and on the other he couldn't quite rule on either side. He'd compared the cap with the X rays, and "They appeared to be similar, but I couldn't say they were the same with reasonable medical certainty." But he could not exclude the possibility that the tooth had belonged in the mouth of Helle Crafts.

Cotter suddenly dropped his mild demeanor. "Dr. Burkes, where's your written report? You don't have one, huh? No? Did you consult with anyone? No? You looked at the teeth for fifteen minutes this morning? You made no photos?" But Burkes still wouldn't say with reasonable medical certainty that the tooth and the X ray matched. It was Sagarin's first coup.

Professor James Taylor, anthropologist from Lehman College in the Bronx, New York, and member of the American Academy of Forensic Sciences (using the term *gravewax* for the fatty substance present on bone remains) offered an opinion that the method of bone recovery was very important to preserving the bones' relationship with the environment. The state police method of recovery failed to please Taylor, who, evidently thinking of an archaeological dig, thought the proper technique would have been to bring a slab of earth into the medical examiner's office and excavate the bones there. That fit with Sagarin's weak theory that the River Road bones had been mixed with fragments from somewhere else. Taylor could identify some bones as human but their age was "hard to bracket."

Flanagan drew from Taylor that only as a result of fire or an explosion had he seen bones so traumatized — exactly what the prosecution's forensic bone specialist testified. Sagarin had not progressed much, if at all, past Burkes.

One of Sagarin's next moves smacked of desperation and surprised even the judge. Was Sagarin looking ahead to an appeal? Essentially, he wanted a summary of all materials Flanagan judged exculpatory, that is, freeing from blame, fault, or guilt. The attorney's argument was over the meaning of *exculpatory*. Sagarin wanted the broadest possible definition of exculpatory materials, in which he wanted to have included all prosecutorial materials and all the original notes from which police reports had been written. To Schaller this definition meant that Flanagan would have to decide at every turn what—even among his own words—might be exculpatory. Such a procedure would throw the courts into disarray. The idea was so unusual no practical formula could be found to fit it. Motion denied.

Malcolm Bird, an ex-Marine major with ramrod bearing who'd served with Crafts in Air America, spoke of how Crafts always made a determined effort to be with his mother on her birthday. When he stayed with the Birds over Christmas, Bird had asked where Helle was and Crafts had said he didn't know. He'd seemed harried, because, Bird assumed, he had sole responsibility for the three children. Richard Crafts was a devoted, caring parent.

Helle had been too, Flanagan murmured.

Suzanne Bird, a self-employed interior designer, also gave her brother rave reviews as a father. A week to ten days before he went to Florida, Suzanne had asked him whether he'd be bringing Helle. Crafts had said he didn't know. Suzanne had wondered whether Helle had gone on a trip, and Crafts had said he didn't know where she was. Suzanne wouldn't press the point with him, because "Richard is very private and I didn't want to intrude." Crafts failed to mention anything about a woodchipper and U-Haul or whether he'd been to the Newtown police and reported his wife missing.

Sagarin produced his last forensic witness. He later regretted not having had twenty more, and attributed their absence to the cost. The prosecution's claim that Sagarin's forensic experts put only a limited time into evaluating evidence, usually on the very day they appeared in court, was misleading, Sagarin pointed out. The defense could have brought them to New London earlier but would have had to compensate them for the day's work.

Here is disturbing territory. If as many experts from the forensic community can be found to testify as the money allows, what does that say about scientific objectivity and even about the value of forensic testimony itself? As freelance experts, those who are not employed by a government (and even some who are) can be hired for any case, and a single case can sometimes find one group of experts working for one side and another group of experts in the same fields working for the other side.

Dr. Peter DeForest is a microscopist with training in X rays and optics. He'd gone to China with Henry Lee and there they'd taught the forensic trade to Lee's former countrymen. DeForest's quarrel with Lee concerned the bloodstains. He believed that bloodstains don't always yield patterns that can be interpreted with reasonable scientific certainty and that medium velocity impact was not the only explanation for the spots on the mattress, which could have also come from a scratch or a pimple.

With the jury out, DeForest proceeded to unfurl a device that, with light shone from different angles and distances, could be made to produce distortions in shadows. Plato, who had likened reality to shadows in a cave, would have enjoyed the show, but not Flanagan. DeForest, he said, was being used to lay the foundation for an attack on the prosecution's forensic odontologists' proof, and the demonstration was irrelevant to the proceedings. Schaller upheld Flanagan. Without his light box, DeForest was not a forceful witness.

Hiltz and Ohradan, called by Sagarin, endured questions about whether they, because of a long-standing dispute between Marchese and the state police, had asked Mayo to leak information to the press so as to give the Newtown police a black eye. "Certainly not," Ohradan said disdainfully, and Schaller, in the closest he'd come to anger and for once not sounding benign, called Sagarin's words "argumentative, misleading, or incomplete." He wouldn't admit the testimony.

270

To testify was the defendant's right, and while defense lawyers in murder trials often discourage their clients from taking the stand, Sagarin chose otherwise. He believed Crafts would be convincing, or convincingly sincere enough to persuade at least a juror or two that he was not the sort of man who would have killed his wife. But Sagarin had never admitted that Crafts would appear.

Flanagan's visibly heavy breathing on the morning of June 16 signaled that something extraordinary was about to happen. Despite his innumerable courtroom appearances, the trial affected him on a personal level; Flanagan was deeply involved emotionally. He had been on the case almost full-time since December 1986, and he'd reviewed the evidence again and again as a theologian might study the Scriptures. His understaffed office was in tatters, one prosecutor having resigned because of overwork and Bob Brunetti having been hospitalized for diverticulitis. For Flanagan, much rode on the outcome of the trial, and he had to fear that Crafts would manage to accomplish what Sagarin hoped.

Reporters crawled over one another to reach a phone. Crowds had been building, and the courtroom was full.

In a light blue suit, blue shirt, striped tie—his clothes were brought to him in his cell—Crafts took the stand at 10:32 A.M. to answer Sagarin's questions.

On the morning of November 19, he began, Helle said, "I'm leaving now."

Rarely moving his hands, speaking clearly in a subdued voice, Crafts testified for a day and a half. The pool photographer for the newspapers in the courtroom complained Crafts blinked so much that he had trouble getting a shot.

Crafts reviewed his life and Helle's. Divorce had been brought up over the years: "I'm not certain about Helle's degree of sincerity. She'd mention divorce as a way of trying to make me change my behavior. She wouldn't specifically say divorce but 'Don't you want to be married to me?' Two,

271

three times a week she'd say that." In the fall of 1986 Helle had sincerely wanted a divorce—"My continuous playing around was a sore point"—and he'd tried to placate her. "I couldn't get her to change her mind."

Crafts said that after their fight on the Friday before Helle left for Germany he had tried to be "lovey-dovey" with her. Flanagan leaped to his feet, grabbed a photo of Crafts and Nancy Dodd embracing and showed it to him before Sagarin could object. With a pugnacious smile, Flanagan snapped, "Is this what you mean by lovey-dovey?"

Crafts's version of November 18 and the morning after was utterly banal. He had been home when Helle returned. After they had put the children to bed they had watched TV in the family room. She had asked if he'd received the divorce papers from the sheriff. "I put her off a little bit. 'Maybe we could talk about it at a later time.'" When she left, early in the morning of the nineteenth, he assumed she'd gone to Westport.

"There has been," Sagarin said, "some discussion about two freezers."

Crafts testified that he and Helle had decided to buy a new freezer because the Wheat Berry co-op, of which Helle was treasurer, bought frozen foods in large quantities. He'd left it crated until after Thanksgiving. At some point he'd removed the door from the old freezer (as was required by law) with difficulty and put it in the Newtown landfill.

In response to Sagarin's questions, he said he'd rented the chipper to clear brush on the Currituck Road property. Familiar with Darien, where he had grown up, he'd seen the Brush Bandit in the Darien Rentals parking lot. He'd gotten the U-Haul in the early afternoon of the twentieth, picked up the chipper, and driven to Newtown for the class that had been canceled. He had his police uniform with him. Then he'd driven to Southbury on Route 84, which he'd left by exit 14, and traveled down Main Street to the PD.

When Sagarin asked him the four criminal questions that

had been asked in the Meriden lie detector test, he calmly repeated what he'd told the polygraphist.

Crafts had had three interviews, one with the Newtown PD and two with the state police (including the lie detector test). He'd signed Miranda waivers. "You had a right to remain silent," Sagarin said to him, "to have an attorney present or an attorney appointed for you. Why didn't you assert your constitutional rights?"

He didn't think that necessary, Crafts replied. He had no idea Helle was anything but alive.

Sagarin invited Crafts to explain the dark patch on the rug. He had two kerosene heaters, he said. When the electricity failed during the storm, he'd placed one in the family room and the larger one in the master bedroom. On Saturday morning, while refilling the heater, he had allowed the kerosene to overflow and it had left a spot on the carpet. He'd accidentally knocked off the cap, which left a soot mark.

Asked to explain what he intended when he told Marie Thomas "Helle called" the day after Helle disappeared, Crafts said that he had meant Helle's Danish friend, Helle Meyendorf.

Speaking clearly, Crafts told the court, "I never raised a finger in anger at Helle in my life. I didn't use a chain saw or a woodchipper in any way to dispose of her body. I believe she's alive. I certainly hope she is. I hope she's coming home soon. I believe it to be true."

On June 17, no mention of the CIA having been made by Crafts, Flanagan questioned him about his service with Air America. To Crafts, it seemed, Air America was a wholly owned subsidiary of the Pacific Corporation of Delaware. If he had worked for the CIA, he had been unaware of it. He had received no CIA training. Faced with a blank wall, Flanagan tried to bring out his propensity for violence with questions about courses he had taken at the Lethal Force Institute, which had taught him how to kill.

Did Crafts know that places where woodchippers could be rented existed nearer to Newtown than Darien? No, nor had he been looking for one with a twelve-inch capacity (the largest opening), nor had he had a discussion with Richard Cenami over whether the Toyota pickup was too small to haul the Brush Bandit, nor had he talked Cenami into holding the machine for him—all statements in complete contradiction of testimony previously offered to the jury.

Flanagan's close grilling—his technique was to stand across the room from the witness so as to make Crafts look at him, not at the jury, and so seem evasive, while Sagarin stood near the jury box to make Crafts look at the jurors—established Crafts's complete preoccupation with the U-Haul and chipper during November 19 and 20.

Gaps appeared between the times Crafts stated he had been in one place or another. By noon that day Crafts had offered "I don't recall" thirty-four times, which, though Sagarin minimized the importance, was a large number.

When Crafts had finished, for all the journalists who'd followed the trial from the start, except for one, a woman, the verdict was unanimous: guilty. An experienced criminal lawyer who dropped in pronounced, "Crafts is evasive and very cold. The jury doesn't like him."

One of Flanagan's basic goals had been to show the jury Crafts's personality. Crafts came across as detached, flat, remote from the very experience he was then undergoing. Never once did he say with emotional authority, "I did not kill my wife!"

When Mayo had testified for the prosecution on April 6, Sagarin subpoenaed him to appear on April 25, which provides a good idea of how seriously the defense underestimated the length of Flanagan's case. A Connecticut subpoena is good for sixty days, and by the time Sagarin called Mayo, the subpoena had expired. The defense had neglected to serve another, and, without one, Mayo refused to appear in court.

Sagarin sent a sheriff with a new subpoena, but Mayo avoided service. After several tries, the sheriff chased Mayo at high speed into Millerton, New York, where he threw the paper at his car, which wasn't good enough.

Sagarin had cross-examined Mayo on April 6, planting seeds he planned to harvest later. Facing him, Mayo had been nervous; he had taken a sip of water twenty-two times in twenty minutes, once holding a cup in either hand.

There wasn't any question what line Sagarin had intended to pursue in June — he'd made it apparent he wanted to present Mayo as a man with the opportunity to frame Crafts and reap the reward in publicity and cash. He would claim Mayo had access to the Crafts house and could have taken potential evidence, such as the self-address stickers discovered on River Road and the chain saw found beneath Silver Bridge, and put them in those places.

He would wonder aloud whether Mayo had been responsible for Helle's death — if she was indeed dead — or at least had contributed to his client's plight. It was the same line peddled by DeJoseph.

Sagarin probably could have rattled the water-sipping Mayo, and the jury would have noted that. But Mayo refused to expose himself and holed up in Vermont. "Hiltz knows where I am," he told O'Neil.

The prosecution breathed easier with Mayo out of the way.

Instead, Sagarin subpoenaed Mayo's wife, who wished only to pursue her training as a nurse. She knew nothing about her husband's case file.

Sagarin, who had read Mayo's file on the case, said that Mayo had misrepresented to him that it was complete. He asked for a bench warrant for Mayo's arrest within or outside of Connecticut, which Schaller refused. Sagarin took strong issue with that but after the trial he claimed he had been secretly pleased. The jury had been given the impression that Mayo had dark secrets to keep, whereas on the stand he would have denied everything Sagarin suggested or the judge would have ruled the questions out of order.

Flanagan had stayed away from the question of former acts of violence by Crafts against his wife, but Crafts's statement, "I never raised a finger in anger at Helle in my life" was a fabrication and gave Flanagan an opening. With the jury out of the courtroom, he called Floortje Smith, who in her own home had seen Crafts slug Helle. Sagarin objected, the event having taken place years before; the testimony wouldn't have been admitted even in a divorce case. Cotter argued that the basic issue, credibility, is never secondary. Schaller sustained Sagarin on the ground that the event had occurred too long ago. There were those who wondered if, convinced the prosecution had prevailed by a wide margin, Schaller hadn't leaned over backward for the defense, anticipating an appeal.

The fact was that two aspects of Crafts's character — violence and preoccupation with firearms — had not been illuminated. Sagarin later said that his bitter and successful fight to keep the word *guns* out of the trial caused more trouble than it was worth. The terminology used instead — objects that cause harm — was even more prejudicial.

John Roma, who had been on the rug hunt, said that Mayo had not been in his office, where Roma now worked, to receive the subpoena, and on this flat note Sagarin ended his case. Flanagan called a few rebuttal witnesses. One was a Japanese-American flight attendant. Sagarin had introduced a letter Helle mailed to her mother from Japan and, citing the postmark — 7.2.86 — claimed the letter had been mailed in July. Helle's flight schedule put her in Japan only in February but if she had been in Japan in July she might well have gone there again, in late November, say. The stewardess testified that Japanese postmarks place the day first, the months second. The letter had been written on February 7. "I goofed," Sagarin said outside.

Another was Helle Meyendorf. Crafts had testified a few

276

days earlier that when he told Marie Thomas on November 20 that "Helle called" he meant Helle Meyendorf, and now she testified she had *not* phoned the Crafts house until December 2.

At 3:00 P.M. on June 21 evidence concluded. "We were heavy underdogs but we've shortened the odds considerably," said Sagarin, who had called thirty-three witnesses, six of whom had also been Flanagan's. Prosecution witnesses numbered eighty-six, who, with repeats, had appeared 107 times. The prosecution had introduced more than 650 exhibits. The trial was the stuff of courtroom legend.

Usually in a murder trial both sides are allowed an hour for summing up, but Schaller let Sagarin and Flanagan opt for two hours each. Between them, the attorneys decided that Flanagan would speak first and Sagarin second, and then Flanagan would speak again.

Flanagan told the jury he'd endeavored to prove the death of Helle Crafts. Would she have left her children? Would she have told her mother to send her a pair of slacks if she intended to disappear? Paid Dianne Andersen a $2,500 retainer? She wanted a divorce, not escape.

The forensic evidence also supported the conclusion that Helle Crafts was dead. Nor should the body parts be regarded in isolation. The nicked papers and stickers found at River Road were also important.

That Helle had died naturally and somebody had decided to bury her with a woodchipper appeared most unlikely. Was Richard Crafts responsible for his wife's death? He had motive and opportunity, he had a chain saw, a U-Haul, and a chipper. River Road was close to his residence and work; he had familiarity with the area as a Southbury policeman. And he'd made false statements to the police and to the jury.

In the first part of his summing up, Flanagan used only half an hour of his time, but he let the jury know he had much more to offer later.

Sagarin displayed more fervor. He appealed to the jurors as being the kind of people who respected the Constitution.

277

He intimated that their patriotism could be judged by their faith in the concept that the accused must be considered innocent unless and until proved guilty. If the evidence was consistent with two interpretations, guilt and innocence, he told them, the jury had to choose innocence.

In an entirely circumstantial case, Sagarin continued, every single fact had to be proved beyond reasonable doubt. If Helle Crafts was a good mother, Richard Crafts was a wonderful father, and, especially in view of his shortened life expectancy, would he orphan his children? Could a man be jailed on the basis of two-thirds of an ounce of bone and five cubic centimeters of blood?

The prosecution had been guilty of asking leading questions, leaving evidence hanging, and working with witnesses for days to get their stories straight. No single witness had not given inconsistent statements at a prior time, Sagarin asserted. In a widely publicized case such as this, suggestions were taken as fact. Dates and times had been changed. Witnesses (Hine and Williams) had been instructed not to talk to the defense because parts of their testimony did not fit the prosecution's case — and what kind of justice was that?

Now he sought to persuade the jury that Helle had been no saint. Hadn't she contacted John Parrott, the United Airlines pilot? Bringing up the testimony of Goldstein, Crafts's friend, who had said Helle had looked older and, when he had seen her last, glassy-eyed, Sagarin seemed to be suggesting that Helle had been on drugs. Crafts had served his country in Southeast Asia, yet the prosecution made something sinister of the CIA and the USA. The Craftses had not spent much time together, but that did not mean that their marriage was a bad one.

Sagarin was a rhetorical gatling gun, firing in all directions in hopes a round would hit. Did the jury remember how Crafts had taken Cub Scouts on an outing? Was that the act of a hardened killer? Could they believe Hine, who knew Crafts but failed to recognize him on River Road, or Williams, who could not have seen anything with fog inside his car? Was Marie Thomas, who'd appeared in court in a pink jumpsuit and white shoes, the kind of person to trust? She was nice, but none too smart.

He repeated his accusation that evidence including the chain saw had been planted by the state police, perhaps with an accomplice, Mayo. As for the key piece of forensic evidence, the cap for the lower left second bicuspid, wasn't there reasonable doubt? "I am certain that in the Middle Ages many scientific experts would have told you that the world was flat, that the universe revolves around the earth, to eat red meat and eggs. . . . These are the Middle Ages of the science of odontology."

Maybe the police really had a print for the side of Helle's finger; maybe it didn't match the print section they possessed.

Sagarin reverted to Mayo. Would he profit from Crafts's conviction? Had he been following Crafts or bugging his phone? Had Mayo rented a woodchipper? Could he be tied to Joey Hine?

Sagarin returned to his client, whom he portrayed as a victim, and a brave one at that. Crafts had too much pride to admit that Helle had just walked out on him. Sagarin added, for good measure, "Maybe she didn't want anyone to know either."

No motive existed, nor evidence of homicide by Crafts, who had told the state police, "She's got to come home."

Too much doubt existed to convict Richard Crafts.

Flanagan, back, said that Crafts had cried before the state police for only twenty seconds—that was the sole emotion he ever displayed, and he couldn't have been sincere. "You've observed his lack of emotion as he handled damaging evidence."

Flanagan refused to let Sagarin use Mayo as a scapegoat. To cast Mayo as a villain was "rank speculation." Since Newtown had not been up to handling the investigation— "the sloppiest police work I have ever seen"—Flanagan admitted that "the state shamefully enough concedes that without Mayo as catalyst the Crafts case might never have gone to trial." But to blame Mayo for Crafts's arrest was a perversion of logic.

The jury had no choice but to acquit Crafts if it believed the state police or Mayo or both had planted evidence. Neither had rented a U-Haul and chipper, but Crafts had, and why should he have asked Darien Rentals to hold the chipper for him if his only aim was to remove brush? Why the urgency? Sagarin could claim the chain saw had been planted, but how could he explain the fact that the bar had been found two-thirds covered with sand? It must have lain in the same place for a considerable period of time. Seizing the chain-saw bar from the table, Flanagan dropped it on the floor with a startling clatter.

Raising his voice, Flanagan said, "What kind of person would have committed an atrocity like this?" He paced the floor to impart motion to his words. Murders, he said, are committed every day, but they're usually done on the spur of the moment. This murder had been calculated by a man capable of killing his wife, the mother of his children. What had the neighbors said about him? Aloof. What had he felt? "He hopes she's alive, but he brings his kids to his girlfriend's house in New Jersey." His sister Karen had been asked if he'd showed concern at Thanksgiving or Christmas, and she'd said no.

Crafts, Flanagan said, had intended to commit a perfect crime, and he had succeeded to within three-quarters of an ounce of bone. Nobody would ever have known what had happened to Helle Crafts, who would still be unaccounted for, "except for an accident of God and fate, a snowstorm that brought Joey Hine."

The jury liked the tricky Sagarin, whose job was to get Crafts off, but Flanagan, austere and deeply judgmental behind his cutting wit, had established murder by psychology, motive, and deed.

* * *

Schaller's instructions to the jury, which required a dozen hours to write, were filled with the phrases "presumption of innocence" and "reasonable doubt." He pointed out, however, that the state was not required to remove doubt to the point of mathematical certainty, and told them, "If all the evidence produces an abiding belief in guilt, you must find him guilty." Near certitude, he said, was enough for a verdict of "Guilty." On June 23, the jury retired.

With the overwhelming nature of Flanagan's case and Sagarin's failure to punch sizable holes in it, the betting in the corridor was that a verdict would come quickly, but the jury, respecting the reasonable doubt instructions, reviewed the entire testimony, using both sides of two, then three blackboards.

Each day votes were tallied, and though the jury had started about evenly divided between those convinced of Crafts's guilt and those either undecided or believing in his innocence, the balance shifted toward guilt, and tempers and tension rose.

Warren Maskell banged his head against one wall and angrily punched another. ("Stupid of me," he said. "I hurt my hand.") On July 1, driving home in his pickup in the clear, hot afternoon, Maskell crashed into a utility pole, landing in the hospital with a fractured skull and two broken ribs. Some jurors were aware by then that Maskell suffered from petit mal epilepsy. That might not have had any bearing, but some surmised he had had a seizure, seizures also being the cause, in their opinion, of Maskell's inability to remember portions of the trial.

The jury had been scheduled to meet on Saturday, but with Maskell out, the session was canceled. Flanagan was willing to proceed without him; Sagarin wanted to wait before he consented. One juror, visiting Maskell in the hospital, gave him a copy of Scott Turow's *Presumed Innocent*, which he later regretted having done; the novel is about a man who narrowly escapes conviction for a murder he has not committed. Another juror encouraged Maskell to return, and on Tuesday, following the July 4 break, Maskell came back. After that, the relationship between Maskell and the rest of the jury began to deteriorate.

For one thing, the others were irked because Maskell violated the judge's instructions, though they failed to inform Schaller. Maskell read newspapers, he told them; other members of the jury heard him discussing the case with his wife; he arrived at the deliberations with notes he couldn't always decipher. Jurors worked hard to convince Maskell about the validity of this or that piece of evidence and believed they had succeeded, but in the morning Maskell would have returned to his original stand. Some jurors thought Maskell's wife made up his mind for him.

Maskell firmly believed Crafts's testimony to be true and seemed to identify with him. Like Crafts, he had served in Southeast Asia, he told the jurors, and escaping capture, he'd killed someone in Vietnam. His own mother-in-law would have raged against him on the witness stand had he killed her daughter, but Mrs. Nielsen had smiled at Crafts. (In vain did other jurors argue that she hadn't smiled at Crafts.) He could not be convinced that Helle Crafts was a Danish national and not an immigrant. He insisted that as an immigrant Helle would have been fingerprinted, just as his own German wife had been, and so the prosecution should have been able to match Helle's print.

Maskell was not the only juror who had problems with the fingerprint and other parts of the prosecution case, notably Karazulas's and Williams's testimony and the absence of Mayo, but as the votes progressed—no less than twenty were taken—the number of dissenters dwindled. After lunch on Saturday, July 9, Maskell said he was ready to vote for conviction, but if he had to wait until Monday he might waver. But another juror announced he'd like the weekend to think. The foreman, Ken Messier, later regretted letting the vote be put off. By Monday Maskell had again become adamant against conviction.

The rest of that week was a jury nightmare. Maskell was

the only one who wouldn't vote to convict. They gave him an entire day to present the reasons for his position. Maskell was constantly forgetting evidence and testimony and constantly demanding replays of testimony and Schaller's instructions, all of which had been recorded. On Friday, at the jury's — that is, Maskell's — request, Schaller delivered in person a ten-minute charge to help the jury clarify "reasonable doubt," and that turned out to be more difficult than one would have supposed: a "precise" definition is not possible; based on reason and not on the mere possibility of innocence; something for which a valid reason can be assigned; not a "conjecture or a fanciful doubt." What Schaller tried to explain, repeating his original instructions in different words, was that little in life is 100 percent certain. The emphasis in "reasonable doubt" was on "reasonable."

By then the deliberations had surpassed the previous Connecticut record of fifty-six hours, and the corridors heard talk of Chip Smith. The Chip Smith charge, dating from an 1881 ruling and upheld by the Connecticut supreme court in numerous cases, meant that the judge could instruct the minority in a deadlocked jury to examine the majority's opinion closely in order to try to reach a unanimous verdict. But the New London jury had not reported an impasse until on Friday, July 15, at 5:06 P.M.; it sought guidance. With Sagarin objecting, Schaller read them the Chip Smith charge, and the jury reconvened. At 5:30, Messier asked, "Okay, anyone want to change their mind?" No one did. Messier said, "We're going to be here awhile," and started taking dinner orders. With that Maskell left the room. Overheard by Schaller, he told a sheriff, "I'm out of there and I'm not going back in." He sat down on the floor at the end of the corridor. The judge told the sheriff to place Maskell in a separate room.

"He just got up and left. No one said anything to him. We didn't know what was happening," Messier said afterward. Twice Schaller asked Maskell to continue, but when he summoned the jury again, Maskell could not be found.

There was fruitless talk of meeting the following morning, but at 9:11 P.M., after Maskell had suddenly entered the room, to groans from the other jurors, Schaller announced, "This court will declare a mistrial."

At 9:27 P.M., the judge dismissed the jury.

Who could have rated the outcome satisfactory?

Not Schaller, sorry that the effort and care invested in the trial had been for naught. The vulnerability of a system that requires unanimous consent of the jury concerns him, but not so much that he wants it changed (though he did tell the Crafts jurors Connecticut considered a change to an eleven to-one or ten-to-two verdict). People on a jury disagree. The attorneys had perhaps not found out as much as they should have about the prospective jurors, but Schaller refused to criticize—he thought the lawyers on both sides had done a good job.

At the end of 1988 Schaller ruled against bail reduction. A poll for the defense, taken to show Crafts could not obtain a fair trial anywhere in Connecticut, failed to prove the point, and when Farver dropped his motion to free Crafts on that basis, Schaller moved the case to Norwalk-Stamford. It was no longer Schaller's responsibility. Judge Martin Nigro, a highly respected man with many years of experience who had also served as a prosecutor, was assigned the new trial.

Flanagan had failed to obtain a guilty verdict and would have to endure another trial with the same evidence and witnesses as before. His enemy in the next go-round would be boredom

Sagarin's client had not been found innocent, and fourteen jurors (eleven jurors and three alternates) found Crafts guilty when Flanagan polled them after the trial. Sagarin would not be present at the next encounter. He asked to be relieved for financial reasons. He claimed his firm had gone $65,000 in the hole defending the case.

Schaller replaced Sagarin with a public defender and Farver, who would receive $25 an hour in court and $20 an hour out of it while working on the case. Sagarin believed Farver's time on the Crafts case would cost Hurwitz & Sagarin $120,000. Nonetheless, Farver and his firm professed to be pleased he would participate.

The other jurors, bitterly angry, asked whether legal action could be taken against Maskell. Maskell was furious with Flanagan for calling him a coward. ("Twelve people took an oath to administer justice and one of them, in the end, lacked the courage to do it.") Maskel sued Flanagan for defamation of character—seemingly the first case on record in which a juror had sued a state's attorney.

In a rambling interview with Patrick O'Neil, Maskell attacked the prosecutor, the judge, the other jurors. "I'm not nervous about what I did," he said. "In fact, I'm proud of what I did." He received, he said, hundreds of crank calls and letters in the following weeks and he blacked out his name on the mailbox so curiosity seekers couldn't discover where he lived.

Which left Richard Crafts eating prison food. Sagarin reported him as saying, "I didn't kill her. I'll stay here until I die rather than say I did." He taught geography on a computer to other inmates, earning $25 a week. The nearest he came to women, aside from guards, was when Nancy Dodd came to visit, and when his sister Karen brought the children, who were intimidated by the prison and reluctant to go there. In 1989 the children refused to visit Crafts or to talk with him on the phone because by then even the youngest believed that he had killed their mother.

The Rodgerses and their new brood got on fine—David had fallen in love with the Crafts children—and the one serious cloud over them was Richard Crafts. The Rodgerses didn't want him released until the youngest, Kristina, had reached eighteen at least, and Karen hoped that her brother would confess.

On July 22, after the mistrial, Karen wrote him:

> . . . All three Crafts children have been seeing the

psychologists (a team of two) since the end of June, when I thought a verdict was imminent. They will continue to go indefinitely. Do you begin to comprehend the heavy load you have dumped on these children? All their lives they'll be trying to work through this tragedy in their minds, and it was all so preventable. There is still an opportunity to improve the situation if you would plug into reality. You told so many obvious lies when you testified; people are not as dumb as you think they are. Did McFarlane [Richard's Air America buddy] get to Maskell or is Maskell really a total idiot?

Sometimes I think of how our lives were years ago. We were close, we had fun, and it was all a farce because you were lying to everybody about so many things. Your whole life is a lie. I'm glad Daddy is dead. He wouldn't be as blind and stupid as Mother and he would be ashamed.

Crafts was silent.

18

The Second Trial

Richard Crafts spent over a year in jail waiting for the second trial because it took almost that long for the massive transcript of the previous one to be completed for review by defense. The work of a pool of typists working sporadically during that time, the entire document was 10,000 pages long and riddled with technical jargon from the forensic testimony. Flanagan offered to proceed without it, but the defense required it done before the trial could start.

The jury was selected during the summer, however, and the trial commenced on September 7, 1989, in Norwalk. The lead prosecution witness was Helle's mother, Elizabeth Nielsen, flown in from Denmark by the state once again. At the first trial, in New London, juror Warren Maskell believed to have detected a smile on Mrs. Nielsen's lips when she identified the defendant, convincing him, he said, that she held no grudge against Crafts and therefore he could not be guilty. No amount of evidence or jury deliberation could shake Maskell's fixed idea. This time, however, Mrs. Nielsen's feelings were abundantly apparent: she shed tears on the witness stand, and her expression was somber as she looked at Crafts.

For trial two, the state's attorney's script generally followed the previous occasion, although there were new details. Marie Thomas added that on the morning Helle disappeared, Richard told her that his wife had left the house because she had a cold and wanted to go somewhere warm. That was ironic for students of the case who believed that Crafts had placed her in a freezer. Marie, who called Crafts a "sweet guy," also wept, but that was because she had to testify again.

In trial one, Dr. James Fox hadn't been permitted to testify concerning the ownership of the two crowns admitted into evidence, but Judge Martin Nigro let him at the next trial, over Tom Farver's violent objections. "This is a root of a tooth with a crown attached. I believe it is Helle Crafts's," Fox said. *Is, was* — nobody seemed quite sure what tense to use. Of the second tooth he testified, "It appears to be a crown I inserted in Helle Crafts's mouth."

At New London, Dan Sagarin had stubbornly hinted, both in and out of the courtroom, that the state police had planted evidence on River Road, where the teeth, bone shards, and envelopes were found. While Crafts's second trial defenders were less strident, they hinted that the envelope containing self-address labels had been altered. The prosecution produced a direct-mail expert, who had not appeared at the first trial. Among his customers was the American Cancer Society, and he testified that the envelope had indeed been mailed to Helle L. Crafts.

Another newcomer for the state was woodchipper designer Michael Morey, who gave the jury a portrait of the Brush Bandit rented by Crafts. Morey noted that paper he had put through the machine had emerged almost unscathed. Schaller had refused to admit the results of a similar experiment conducted by a state policeman on the grounds that the trooper wasn't an expert; nor was the test relevant, Schaller said. Nigro ruled that Morey's experience entitled him to present his opinions, and Morey also offered one on why human debris had not been found in the chipper. "The blades spin so fast that the interior is left free of wood chips and other shredded material. It's a self-cleansing machine," Morey testified.

As before, Professor Robert Hoadley, the wood man, matched chips from River Road, from the U-Haul, and from the Currituck Road property, showing that all had similar markings and had therefore been cut by the same blade. The forensic experts paraded along, among them the irrepressible Dr. Henry Lee, who shook hands with the judge and the defendant. Lee cleared up a minor matter, where Helle's fingerprints had come from. They had been rolled, and poorly, by the U.S. Department of Immigration.

Court watchers had wondered for weeks whether Crafts would take the stand again, but Flanagan decided for him. He would introduce the pilot's two-day testimony from the previous trial. Crafts's other public defender, Gerard Smyth, argued that allowing in the tape would deprive his client of proper legal counsel and, in effect, force him to testify. "It undermines my ability," Smyth said. "It deprives Mr. Crafts of a fair trial." Nigro, whose knowledge of the law is considered among the best of any judge in the state, ruled that the taped testimony was no different from other statements made outside of that courtroom, and Crafts had testified of his own volition. The judge would cause to be deleted, as had Schaller, any reference to Crafts's arsenal in either the tape or the sixty-two page transcript of Crafts's statement to the state police, as prejudicial to the defense.

The result was a little eerie—the rigidly controlled and rehearsed voice seemingly detached from the impassive man who listened to it as the jury watched him.

The big surprise of trial two was David Rodgers, Crafts's sister's husband, who, on the stand, described Crafts as the "nearest thing I ever had to a brother." But, Rodgers and his wife were flat-out for a conviction. Rodgers repeated remarks made by Crafts about how police divers wouldn't find Helle's body because "it's gone," and even the discovery of the chipper would prove to be a "dead end." These statements, indicating that without a body the police would be stalemated, were extremely damaging to the defense.

Asked why he hadn't come forward with them at the first trial, Rodgers replied that he feared revenge on his family and himself if Crafts was acquitted, and that Sagarin preferred him not to talk to investigators and, if forced, not to volunteer information. (Rodgers might have added that he feared becoming an accessory after the fact.)

Rodgers being the last, the state called eighty-six witnesses, the same number as in the first trial, though not always the same ones or for such long periods. Flanagan had aimed at streamlining his case, and he clipped a week from the nine he had taken in New London.

When the prosecution rested, Smyth predictably argued — even before his motion Nigro ordered the jurors to report to court the next day — that the case should be dismissed for lack of evidence that Crafts had planned and committed his wife's murder. The judge disagreed.

Marie Thomas's character was attacked by a Connecticut woman who hired her after she stopped working for Richard Crafts. Marie, the woman said, talked about the case continually, driving the family crazy, and frequently gave conflicting accounts about what had happened. Marie's driving had become an issue, and the woman stated that the nanny had had an accident with the family car and gave contradictory versions as to how.

That had relevance for the defense, which tried to show that Crafts had bought the used VW Rabbit not because his wife's Tercel was at Kennedy and he'd had to provide transportation for Marie, but because Marie put nicks in cars.

The prosecution appeared content, or afraid of rocking its boat, for of the seven defense witnesses called that day it chose to cross-examine only five and the questions were perfunctory.

Defense forensic experts broke no more new ground than they had in the first trial, and, as before, one seemed mostly in agreement with Dr. Lee, except for quibbles. On the stand for the third time, William Goldstein claimed he witnessed Crafts fixing dents in the bumper from his Toyota pickup that Crafts avowed Marie Thomas had put there. The bumper, which had been removed by Crafts, was dragged into the courtroom by the prosecution. No nicks were visible, and Goldstein's credibility had been dented.

The last witness the defense called was Dan Sagarin, who challenged the assertion by David Rodgers that he'd suggested that Rodgers withhold information from the police. "I told him to answer the questions put to him, said Crafts's former attorney. "I told him to tell the truth."

The defense rested. It had called, over a period of two weeks, twenty-seven witnesses, the same as in the first trial. A California forensic dentist had testified that he didn't believe one tooth had belonged to Helle Craft but, even so, courtroom observers felt that Crafts would surely be convicted unless another Warren Maskell lurked among the jurors.

Tom Farver appealed to him or her in the closing arguments. Given the paucity of human remains and at least some dispute among the forensic experts on whether they could be positively identified as belonging to Helle Crafts, "Is that reliable evidence that you would be willing to be tried on yourself?" he asked. (His performance since trial one had measurably improved.) His partner, Smyth, concentrated on the question of intent, which Flanagan had claimed "doesn't take more than a second to form."

Intent was crucial for what Smyth had in mind.

He argued that only four events before November 19 could be presented by the state to suggest that Crafts had had a plan: the used car he'd bought, the reservation of a woodchipper, the buying of a dump truck to pull the chipper, and the purchase of a freezer. He explained them as happenstancical, and, he averred, had Crafts concocted a murder in advance, he would not have made so many mistakes, such as telling conflicting stories as to Helle's whereabouts.

Although he didn't concede that, Smyth proceeded to a dangerous deduction for his client. Suppose Crafts *had* killed his wife? The evidence showed that the deed had been done under the stress of a failing marriage, not planned in advance. If so, Crafts could be convicted on the lesser charge of first-degree manslaughter, a choice not presented in the previous trial.

The Rodgerses were startled and dismayed at the door Smyth opened, because Nigro went through it. He offered the jury that possibility. If they returned with a manslaughter verdict, Crafts could be on the street in a matter of a few years.

291

The individual the jurors chose as foreman (whom Dan Sa·
garin, with his distrust of leaders, almost certainly would have
rejected from the panel) was a vice-president at Bristol-Myers
who, in the jury room, stressed teamwork. The jury gave
careful consideration to the lesser charge, but decided that
Crafts had not killed his wife under "extreme emotional dis·
tress," in the judge's words. After eight hours of debate at day,
plus many hours reviewing the tapes — for one of them, Hoad·
ley, the wood man, was decisive — they voted after four days
for guilty of murder in the first degree.

The minimum penalty allowed by the state on that charge is
twenty-five years, and Crafts had already been in jail for
three. Under a formula that awards extra credit for time
served before conviction, an extra day for every three, plus
time off for good behavior, Crafts might have been released in
eleven or twelve years. The maximum is sixty years, called life
imprisonment.

At his sentencing, on January 8, 1990, both extremes were
heard from. The Rodgerses had written letters to the judge
urging the harshest penalty, and Walter Flanagan concurred.
In court he rehashed his case, speaking of "the heinous enor·
mity of the crime" and the most extensive police investigation
in Connecticut history. He asked Nigro to sentence Crafts on
the basis of four underlying principles. One, the possibility of
rehabilitation; there wasn't any because Crafts had planned
the murder and had not demonstrated remorse. Two, the de·
terrence of others by proving that crime doesn't pay. That,
Flanagan said (in contradiction of much thinking on the sub·
ject) was important. Three, the convicted man must be sepa·
rated from society for as long as the law allows. Perhaps Helle
Crafts, mercifully, had suffered the least. The secondary vic·
tims, the children, would suffer for the rest of their lives. Four,
retribution. Helle Crafts deserved to live, and Crafts, to prove
the justice system works, should never again be free.

On the stand, Karen Rodgers agreed while her sister, Su·
zanne Bird, pleaded for leniency.

Smyth, sad-faced as if he bore the world's woes on his shoul·
ders, battled the retributive tide. His client had adapted well

to prison; during the trial he'd swept floors at midnight; he had been a model inmate; he had been rehabilitated. If he ever saw his kids again they'd be grown up. Couldn't Crafts be granted the hope that someday he would be out? Anything more than the minimum sentence condemned him to life, with the specter of recurrent cancer never far away. Mercy was called for.

Crafts spoke, looking older, smaller, frailer than he had in the previous trial. His mouth was bunched like a chipmunk's. His lack of emotion hadn't been fully covered, he said woodenly. "I have feelings just like everybody else. Anger, fear . . . I have them all. I failed to express them because I spent six years in Southeast Asia, being shot at almost every day. You get used to holding back, more immune to the outside. I never thought that was a defect in my personality."

Karen Rodgers had a financial inducement to have him put away for life. He had done "lots of things" with his kids, and they had no reason to fear him. "I love my children, and I want them to know I love them. Though our relationship has been physically interrupted, it won't be interrupted in spirit."

Judge Nigro said he had solemnly weighed the pros and cons—Crafts's age, his impeccable military record including an honorable discharge, his long service as a pilot, as against the seriousness of the crime. Nigro had given the jury the chance to find for extreme emotional disturbance and thus a manslaughter verdict, but they had not, and the "horrendous," premeditated destruction of the body indicated otherwise. Expecting to get away with it, Crafts had not only killed his wife but murdered the childhood of his children.

"I sentence you to fifty years." A gasp could be heard in the courtroom.

With the various time-credits allowed by the state, plus early releases occasioned by prison overcrowding, Crafts could reasonably expect to serve a minimum of twenty years and very likely more. He filed a handwritten appeal in federal court without the knowledge of his lawyers. Crafts wrote, "On the basis of the irreparable prejudicial publicity generated by the state violation of wire tap statute in the second ground (a

293

reference to a recent scandal in which it had been disclosed that the state police barracks routinely taped phone calls including those between lawyers and their imprisoned clients) and the failure to abide by the requirement for continuing disclosure in the first ground, the petitioner would respectfully request that the verdict be set aside, the petitioner released from custody, and the state be directed to enter a nolle prosequi in the case."

Motion denied.

In a year or so, when the new transcript was ready, Crafts's lawyers would also appeal, on, among others, the ground that Nigro had refused to dismiss jurors familiar with details of the case. But any prospective juror claiming he had known nothing about it either lied or was too stupid to serve.

When Crafts was brought to Somers, Connecticut's maximum security prison, a chant went up: "Chip, chip, chip!" And for years to come, whenever many people see a woodchipper in operation, disgorging a plume of debris, they will think of Richard Crafts, who demolished the dreams of many, among them his own.

He continued to appeal, and until that process was exhausted the Newtown Spartans would be unable to obtain a hearing on Walter Flanagan's sharp attack on their competence.

On February 1, 1990, a man named Michael Fiori who had been released on probation from Somers, was arrested in Agawam, Massachusetts, not far away, for assault and battery against a police officer during a burglary. Fiori had on his person a communication that seemed to be from Richard Crafts, and concerned the Rodgers's house in Westport. It had a hand-drawn diagram of the place, where the front door could be found and an "X" marking the location of Crafts's gun cabinets which the police had removed from Newtown Lane and eventually returned to the Rodgers. A note said: "All gone Presidents week." It was true that the Rodgers habitually went skiing between Lincoln and Washington's birthdays. It con-

294

tinued, ". . . you take care of my split, I'll split it with you, you know what I want, so take of it for me. This is a perfect job, I don't see how anybody could blotch it up."

Attached was a typewritten list of sixty-four revolvers, semi-automatic pisstols, rifles, shotgun, some exotic fire-arms — plus a Barnett crossbow. Fiori was evidently meant lift the cache and sell it, splitting the proceeds with Crafts. And right *there* was the soul of this murderer, tricky, preoccupied with plots, dreaming of lethal gadgets, infantile down deep.

Index

300

301

303

state police and, 173
trial testimony of, 263, 267, 279
Turow, Scott, 281
Tvardzik, Robert, 66, 105, 129, 143-45, 149, 153-54, 172, 233

United Airlines, 62, 276
U.S. Agency of International Development, 85
U.S. Army intelligence, 132, 158
U.S. Naval Air Training Station, 84
USS *Stark*, 255, 256

Vietnam war, 85, 86

Warchol, Chris, 98, 169
Watley, Fred, 47
Watson, John, 174, 201
Western District Major Crime Squad, 75, 79, 135, 149, 157, 158, 160-70, 172-74, 181, 245
Crafts interviewed by, 195-99
divers and, 185-87
Ford seized by, 180
Karen Rodgers and, 192
search of Crafts house by, 175-80
and woodchipper evidence, 181-85, 187-188
White, James, 177
Wildman, Richard, 122-23, 181, 220, 242, 253, 262
Williams, Joe. 121, 219, 260-62, 278, 282
Worrell, William, 63

Yaworski, Jerry, 71-72, 80

Zemel's T.V. Appliances, 116-17, 209, 243

THE BESTSELLING NOVELS
BEHIND THE BLOCKBUSTER MOVIES –
ZEBRA'S MOVIE MYSTERY GREATS!

HIGH SIERRA   (2059, $3.50)
by W.R. Burnett
A dangerous criminal on the lam is trapped in a terrifying web of
circumstance. The tension-packed novel that inspired the 1955
film classic starring Humphrey Bogart and directed by John
Houston.

MR. ARKADIN   (2145, $3.50)
by Orson Welles
A playboy's search to uncover the secrets of financier Gregory
Arkadin's hidden past exposes a worldwide intrigue of big money,
corruption--and murder. Orson Welles's only novel, and the basis
for the acclaimed film written by, directed by, and starring himself.

NOBODY LIVES FOREVER   (2217, $3.50)
by W.R. Burnett
Jim Farrar's con game backfires when his beautiful victim lures
him into a dangerous deception that could only end in death. A
1946 cinema classic starring John Garfield and Geraldine
Fitzgerald.

BUILD MY GALLOWS HIGH   (2341, $3.50)
by Geoffrey Homes
When Red Bailey's former lover Mumsie McGonigle lured him
from the Nevada hills back to the deadly hustle of New York
City, the last thing the ex-detective expected was to be set up as a
patsy and framed for a murder he didn't commit. The novel that
inspired the screen gem OUT OF THE PAST, starring Robert
Mitchum and Kirk Douglas.

*Available wherever paperbacks are sold, or order direct from the
Publisher. Send cover price plus 50¢ per copy for mailing and
handling to Zebra Books, Dept. 3113, 475 Park Avenue South,
New York, N.Y. 10016. Residents of New York, New Jersey and
Pennsylvania must include sales tax. DO NOT SEND CASH.*

MYSTERIES TO KEEP YOU GUESSING
by John Dickson Carr

CASTLE SKULL   (1974, $3.50)
The hand may be quicker than the eye, but ghost stories didn't hoodwink Henri Bencolin. A very real murderer was afoot in Castle Skull — a murderer who must be found before he strikes again.

IT WALKS BY NIGHT   (1931, $3.50)
The police burst in and found the Duc's severed head staring at them from the center of the room. Both the doors had been guarded, yet the murderer had gone in and out *without having been seen!*

THE EIGHT OF SWORDS   (1881, $3.50)
The evidence showed that while waiting to kill Mr. Depping, the murderer had calmly eaten his victim's dinner. But before famed crime-solver Dr. Gideon Fell could serve up the killer to Scotland Yard, there would be another course of murder.

THE MAN WHO COULD NOT SHUDDER (1703, $3.50)
Three guests at Martin Clarke's weekend party swore they saw the pistol lifted from the wall, levelled, and shot. *Yet no hand held it.* It couldn't have happened — but there was a dead body on the floor to prove that it had.

Printed in the United States
16354LVS00007B/13